THE PROPHETIC PULPIT

Clergy, Churches, and Communities in American Politics

PAUL A. DJUPE and CHRISTOPHER P. GILBERT

ROWMAN & LITTLEFIELD PUBLISHERS, INC.
Lanham • Boulder • New York • Oxford

ROWMAN & LITTLEFIELD PUBLISHERS, INC.

Published in the United States of America
by Rowman & Littlefield Publishers, Inc.
A Member of the Rowman & Littlefield Publishing Group
4501 Forbes Boulevard, Suite 200, Lanham, Maryland 20706
www.rowmanlittlefield.com

PO Box 317
Oxford
OX2 9RU, UK

British Library Cataloging in Publication Information Available

Library of Congress Cataloging-in-Publication Data
Djupe, Paul A.
    The prophetic pulpit : clergy, churches, and communities in American
politics / Paul A. Djupe and Christopher P. Gilbert.
        p. cm.
    Includes bibliographical references and index.
    ISBN 0-7425-1192-8 (alk. paper)—ISBN 0-7425-1193-6 (pbk. : alk.
paper)
    1. Clergy—United States—Political activity. 2. Evangelical Lutheran
Church in America—Clergy—Political activity. 3. Episcopal
Church—Clergy—Political activity. 4. Christianity and
politics—United States. I. Gilbert, Christopher P. II. Title.
    BV4327 .D58 2003
    261.7'0973—dc21

                                                          2003000333

Printed in the United States of America

∞™ The paper used in this publication meets the minimum requirements of
American National Standard for Information Sciences—Permanence of Paper for
Printed Library Materials, ANSI/NISO Z39.48-1992.

CONTENTS

TABLES AND FIGURES

TABLES

v

FIGURES

ACKNOWLEDGMENTS

Like so many academic books, this volume is the product of a sabbatical leave, albeit not in the traditional fashion. Chris Gilbert received a year-long sabbatical from Gustavus Adolphus College for the 1997–1998 academic year to prepare another book manuscript. By coincidence, Paul Djupe had just completed his Ph.D. and agreed to return to his alma mater to replace Gilbert for the year. Neither of us had contemplated writing a book about clergy politics before. But in the midst of our teaching and writing, and with numerous Chicago Bulls victories being broadcast in the background, we came to see an opportunity to propose a unique study, through which we could probe some long-standing questions about the interrelationships among clergy, congregation members, and American political behavior.

The result of our evening collaborations in the winter of 1997–1998 was a National Science Foundation grant (SBR-9809536) to Gustavus Adolphus College to conduct a two-year, two-stage study of the political beliefs and actions of clergy and congregants in two U.S. denominations—the Episcopal Church and the Evangelical Lutheran Church in America (ELCA). We were also awarded a small research grant from the American Political Science Association to support our study. Any opinions, findings, conclusions, or recommendations expressed in this book are ours alone, and do not necessarily reflect the views of the National Science Foundation or the American Political Science Association.

The first phase of our study required a national sample of clergy from both denominations. After six months of mailing, receiving, and entering data from 2,400 respondents, we spent almost eighteen months surveying congregation members in sixty selected churches whose clergy had responded to our initial survey. While the congregation surveys were in the field, we began to explore and write about the political beliefs and behavior of our clergy sample. This book is the culmination of four years of conference papers, e-mail debates, and textual revisions focused on what members of our sample clergy were trying to tell us about their political and religious lives.

We cannot express strongly enough our gratitude to over 2,400 busy professionals in the ELCA and Episcopal Church, who pondered twelve dense pages of questions about their own lives and vocations, as well as the beliefs and actions of their congregations. We have endeavored to report their responses faithfully and interpret their attitudes and behavior in ways that remain faithful to the work they do. Some of our responding clergy objected to our inquiries, questioned our motives, or expressed their frustration at the length of the survey. A greater number encouraged us, thanked us for the opportunity to participate, or revealed that the survey had helped them understand at least one aspect of their professional work in a deeper way. Both types of input proved useful to us in the course of our work.

Throughout this project we have benefited from the advice and support of numerous professional colleagues and friends. In the initial stages, two people proved invaluable. Bob Weisenfeld, director of Corporation, Foundation, and Government Relations at Gustavus Adolphus College, took our rough ideas and (in three days) turned them into a successful grant proposal; we join numerous Gustavus colleagues in recognizing with pleasure Bob's tireless efforts to advance the intellectual work of the college and its faculty. James Guth of Furman University sent us copies of the clergy questionnaires he and his colleagues have used with great success for over twenty years, which proved invaluable as we drafted our own survey instrument. As this book neared completion, Laura Olson (Clemson University) and Ted Jelen (University of Nevada-Las Vegas) read the entire manuscript and offered excellent ideas about framing the discussion and exploring other literatures to which our work pertained. Laura, Ted, and many other colleagues have read conference papers along the way, pushing us to sharpen our focus and helping shape the final product. We note especially the advice of Geoffrey Layman (Vanderbilt University), who encouraged our emphasis on questions of representation, and David Leege (University of Notre Dame), who pointed us toward the ethnic and denominational roots of the behavior patterns we encountered among our ELCA clergy. Tim Johnson, Dan Hofrenning, Dave Peterson, Jim Pletcher, and David Anderson also read chapters and provided helpful critiques and insights.

Our NSF grant was awarded through the Research in Undergraduate Institutions (RUI) program, which funds projects that include significant participation by undergraduate students. Gustavus has a strong tradition of faculty-student research collaboration, and thirteen Gustavus students (plus two from the University of St. Thomas and Denison University) contributed to every facet of this project— mailing and collecting surveys, entering data, organizing the congregation survey phase, analyzing results, and coauthoring several conference papers with one or both of us. We could not have completed this project successfully without their expert and tireless assistance, beginning in the summer of 1998 and continuing through the spring of 2002. Gustavus student research participants included full-time summer and semester research, data collection, and paper coauthors—Devin Colvin, Robert DeHaven, Martin Kaduc, Julie Moberg, Jaclynn Moen; data entry and mailing assistance over two academic years—Steve Biljan, Heather Boyd, Erin Holloway, Jonathan Keske, Theo Mbatha, Alissa Manske, Michael Ryan, Tobias Stalter. Participants at St. Thomas (Djupe's employer, 1998–1999) and Denison (Djupe's current home) included James Hanneman and Marie Zimmerman.

In addition to the direct financial assistance of the NSF and the APSA, we were supported by our employers in numerous ways. Faculty travel funds provided by Gustavus, St. Thomas, and Denison supplemented our budget and allowed us to attend even more academic conferences, often with our student researchers. Library staff at all three institutions offered their usual excellent assistance tracking down familiar and obscure sources. Finally, the Gustavus post office and director Naomi Quiram worked very efficiently to get the mail out on time, roughly 20,000 surveys in all.

The staff at Rowman & Littlefield, particularly our editor Mary Carpenter, have been efficient and supportive for almost two years; we appreciate their confidence in our research and their efforts to get this book into print.

Of course, the most important contributors to this project have been our life companions, Megan Webster and Julie Gilbert. They have abided our mutual habit of phoning just as the other sits down to dinner, they have listened with endless patience to endless monologues about the project, and they have read more of this book than we had any right to expect. We thank them for all these gifts.

Chapter 5 is a revision of our article "The Political Voice of Clergy," which appeared in *The Journal of Politics* (vol. 64, no. 2, May 2002, pages 596–609). Thanks to Blackwell Publishers for granting us permission to reprint this article.

1

CLERGY, CHURCHES, AND COMMUNITIES

THE RELIGIOUS RESPONSE TO SEPTEMBER 11

In the wake of the September 11, 2001, terrorist attacks on New York City and Washington, D.C., the religious character of American public life came to the forefront. Observers around the nation noted increased church attendance for weeks after September 11, as U.S. houses of worship strove to help members and the general public understand the horrible events and to discern God's purposes (Briggs 2001). Memorial services, candlelight vigils, and regular worship events all served to ease Americans' sense of loss and despair. In keeping with the president's unique role as national prophet within American civil religion (Bellah 1975), George W. Bush was both visible at religious events and consistent in using religious language and imagery to frame and justify the U.S. response to the attacks (Dart 2001, 11).

Clergy were also quite active, both in the stricken locations and in communities around the nation, serving to comfort the afflicted and to attempt to make sense of the events. As the *Christian Century* noted in an October 10, 2001, editorial, the question "where is God in these events?" is both a natural and a practical inquiry for Americans, and religious leaders and institutions have met and continue to meet the challenge of answering this difficult question in worship and other venues.

St. Paul's Chapel, an Episcopal church located two blocks from the World Trade Center site, emerged as a critical presence for relief workers in the aftermath of the towers' collapse. Led by its clergy staff and Episcopal officials from New York City, the chapel immediately set up food service and logistical support for the thousands of workers clearing the rubble from the WTC site. Volunteers from Episcopal churches and other denominations across the United States came to St. Paul's to assist in these efforts. The head verger of nearby Trinity Church, which administers St. Paul's Chapel, summed up the nature of the parish's response: "Trinity has never been more relevant to this neighborhood. We didn't have to invent what to do; we just had to be who we are" (Donovan 2001).

THE SOCIAL AND POLITICAL ROLES OF CLERGY

While U.S. church attendance returned to normal levels by the end of 2001, the burst of visible, public religious activity in the aftermath of September 11 points to an important truth about religion's role in U.S. public life: despite decades of hypothesizing to the contrary, the United States remains a deeply religious nation, and U.S. religious professionals—clergy—occupy a prominent role in shaping the activities churches undertake and the attitudes congregation members hold. In fact, clergy are *always* present to guide, reassure, and interpret local, national, and global events. September 11 may have been an extraordinary event, and Trinity Church and St. Paul's Chapel may have gone to extraordinary lengths to respond, but the religious responses observed across the nation are in fact *typical* occurrences in U.S. public life. Here are more examples of congregational civic and political activities from across the United States, nearly all of which are organized by clergy.

Responding to Community Crisis

Shortly after Thanksgiving 2001, the Houston-based Enron Corporation laid off over 4,000 workers as part of its collapse. The rector of Palmer Memorial Church, an Episcopal congregation in Houston, immediately organized a lunch and prayer session for laid-off employees who belonged to his parish. The rector soon created a web page where former Enron employees could post their résumés and be matched with other parishioners whose businesses had job openings. The parish also offers a morning coffee hour for unemployed members, and some former Enron workers have become involved in lay ministry activities (Blanton 2002).

Meeting Contemporary Urban Challenges

St. Aaron's Evangelical Lutheran Church,[1] a large congregation located in a medium-sized midwestern city, recently opened a food shelf to complement its numerous social service programs, which have been operating for over a decade. With three clergy, two lay professionals, and 2,000 members, St. Aaron's is actively engaged in the life of its neighborhood and city. Each Sunday adult education hour focuses on a political or social issue, with speakers from inside and outside the congregation. The parish also runs a substance abuse ministry, assisting members caught in the grips of alcohol or drug abuse. The new food shelf represents a renewed commitment to helping the homeless, whom the church already assists by operating a shelter and participating in a local affordable housing advocacy group. The clergy staff is actively engaged in all these pursuits.

Reaching Across Denominational Lines to Fight Racism

Trinity Episcopal Church, located in a large mid-Atlantic city, works closely with neighboring Protestant and Catholic churches to combat racism in several forms. The parish sponsors tutoring and youth mentoring programs, serves meals every weeknight, offers counseling and rent assistance to those in need, and provides grants to neighborhood organizations working with at-risk children. A clergy staff of two priests and three deacons manages these programs as well as adult discussion groups, book clubs, support groups for the unemployed, singles ministries, outreach to new mothers, and yoga classes. The parish also founded a local organization that highlights perceived racist practices in housing, employment, and competition for city contracts.

Providing Services in a Small-Town Setting

Transfiguration Lutheran Church, located in a midwestern town of 1,200, offers its 125 members several opportunities for local civic involvement. For two decades the church has sponsored an all-night party following the high school senior prom. The pastor's wife founded the local chapter of Mothers Against Drunk Driving and works with the prom party committee to educate students about the dangers of underage drinking. The pastor is head of the town clergy council, which meets every other week to discuss Scripture and share information about events and ministry opportunities. The adult education hour frequently invites faculty from a nearby college to speak on state and national current events; one by-product of these sessions is a new outreach ministry to Somali immigrants who recently settled in town. Although the pastor and congregation would never consider taking partisan political stands on local or state issues, the congregation has a strong reputation for being actively involved in town politics through attendance at city council and school board meetings. The pastor also writes a column for the weekly town newspaper, connecting Lutheran theology with pressing issues of the day.

TOWARD A THEORY OF CLERGY
POLITICAL ACTIVITY AND INFLUENCE

These brief accounts offer a multifaceted depiction of the roles clergy and congregations play in U.S. political and civic life, and they demonstrate how clergy set the tone for congregational action—serving in formal decision-making roles, leading protests and vigils, conducting worship services for members and nonmembers, and facilitating links between citizens and government authorities. Clergy also perform many other tasks related to politics and civic life that are not visible to the public eye, and a small number of clergy do nothing at all in this regard.

These examples paint a far different picture of why clergy take political action than has been proposed in previous studies. Typical studies of American political behavior tend to focus on individual citizens in isolation. Research in the field of religion and political behavior usually embraces this strategy, despite the fact that the bulk of religious experience in America occurs in a group setting—a congregation in a distinct local community with a particular constellation of concerns. Clergy have a mission to minister not only to their own congregations but to the communities in which they work and live. Clergy thus stand at the intersection of three different, perhaps competing forces that attract their attention and impinge on their decision making: *the congregation, the denomination, and the community.* To study and understand clergy political behavior one must take into account all of these factors, as well as the individual motivations that lead clergy to become politically active.

In recent years political scientists have devoted more attention to what clergy say and do politically, and what effect such words and actions have on members of the congregation (Guth 2001; Jelen 2001). With the publication of *The Bully Pulpit* (Guth et al. 1997), a study of clergy attitudes and activism in eight U.S. Protestant denominations, political scientists (and others interested in the political life of clergy across denominations and faith traditions) now have an extensive knowledge base from which to explore further (see also Crawford and Olson 2001; Olson 2000).

Our book adds to this body of research through a detailed study of clergy political activity in two large Protestant denominations—the Evangelical Lutheran Church in America (ELCA) and the Episcopal Church. Using a 1998 national survey adapted from the instruments utilized by the *Bully Pulpit* research team, we have collected information from ELCA and Episcopal clergy on a wide range of political issues, past political history, aspects of congregations, perceptions of congregation viewpoints, personal characteristics, theological orientations, and information sources. As the examples in this chapter indicate, ELCA and Episcopal clergy are highly engaged in the lives of their congregations and communities. Being active in civic and political life is an integral part of life for many ELCA and Episcopal clergy, and investigating the sources and consequences of their political activity requires a more complete understanding of the forces that affect clergy choices and the impact of clergy activities. In this chapter we will briefly describe these forces and how we interpret their relationship to the political activities and opinions of ELCA and Episcopal clergy; we will also explain our unique survey methods and outline the analysis that will follow in subsequent chapters.

CONGREGATIONS, COMMUNITIES, AND DENOMINATIONS

Throughout this book we posit that clergy roles in politics and civic life result from the intersection of their personal beliefs and interests, the specific needs of their congregation and community, and socialization and ongoing influences emanating from their denomination. This perspective on the motivations for clergy political and civic activity helps address the critical question of what roles organized religion and religious leaders play in U.S. political and civic life. Research on clergy roles has always incorporated a public affairs dimension (e.g., Blizzard 1956). While many clergy in the United States do not see political activity as a legitimate part of their ministry, most clergy—especially those in the sample that forms the basis for this book—do see politics as a meaningful part of their lives and an essential component of their ministries.

Previous research has delineated two primary and interrelated roles of clergy in politics: as *cue givers* (Guth et al. 1997; Verba, Schlozman, and Brady 1995; Welch et al. 1993) and as *opinion leaders* (Beatty and Walter 1989; Morris 1984). In both roles, clergy are perceived to have considerable power to mold the political attitudes of their congregation.

Cue giving refers to activities by clergy that suggest courses of action for members to follow. For example, clergy provide a weekly message to members through sermons that interpret biblical texts (often in conjunction with contemporary events), prodding listeners to further reflection and perhaps action. Clergy may also make public statements outside of church. Significant numbers of our sample clergy regularly write letters to the editor or newspaper columns, for example. Sermons and other formal and informal church venues (announcements, newsletters, bulletin boards, church meetings) as well as public statements by clergy can have significant effects on parishioners, mainly through the respect and high stature accorded clergy in certain denominations (including the two we have chosen to study). Through these verbal and behavioral cues clergy can exercise a significant *agenda-setting* power within their congregation. Clergy are also often political and social activists themselves (Guth et al. 1997), and they have the means to actively recruit congregation members to protest unfair housing practices or local abortion providers, write elected representatives, form study groups on various political subjects, or conduct voter registration drives.

It is not as easy for clergy to change members' minds about specific political issues, but a significant reason that clergy undertake most activities that send cues to members is to do just that—to shape members' opinions. Sermons can and sometimes do achieve more than simply indicating what members should be considering when entering a voting booth or watching candidate debates. Clergy and their denominations work deliberately to make congregants believe specific precepts and see the world in unique ways. It is easy to see why clergy would wish their members to reason through the political (and other) implications of their religious beliefs. This reasoning does not take place in a vacuum; clergy are powerful moral leaders, well positioned to lead members to opinions that are consonant with church teachings and that intimate political preferences as well (Lenski 1961; Wald, Owen, and Hill 1988).

Against the argument that clergy typically lead opinions and set the political agendas for their congregations, it should also be noted that clergy may adapt to the prevailing sentiments of the congregation, especially in churches where members have substantial control over the clergyperson's job status (as is usually the case in the ELCA and Episcopal Church). These contrasting perspectives help explain why research investigating the power of clergy to affect public opinion has produced ambivalent results; some researchers have shown significant effects (Beatty and Walter 1989), some report only anecdotal effects (Morris 1984), and others have found no effects (Huckfeldt and Sprague 1995). Inadequate or incomplete data account for some of these results, but the theoretical assumption that influence is essen tially a one-way street—clergy politics affect congregation member politics, rather than vice versa—is also an incomplete depiction of how clergy engage in political activity.

We need additional distinctions to discern the full meaning of clergy political activity and the intertwining of personal orientations with pressures from congregations, communities, and denominations. Several pertinent questions arise: Do clergy engage in political activity for themselves personally, and if so should we account for their voice as one among many? Are clergy politically active in order to further the beliefs of their denomination or faith tradition, and if so should we consider their voices as distinctive and representative of that denomination or faith tradition? Are clergy active in order to promote and protect the interests of their congregation, and if so should we treat them as representatives of a constituency? If some combination of these roles constitutes the most appropriate frame of reference for clergy political activities, how can we sort out the intensity of and interrelationships among the varying roles clergy play?

We do not intend through our inquiries to suggest that any one of these possible clergy roles is more or less correct or proper, nor do we take a position on whether it is desirable for clergy to take part in politics and civic life. We simply assert the bald fact that clergy across the U.S. religious spectrum *are* active participants in local, state, national, and international politics; indeed, clergy have engaged in such activities since the founding of the United States (Ahlstrom 1972; Fowler, Hertzke, and Olson 1999; Noll 1990). Our task in this book is to develop and test a coherent theory that explains the range of clergy political activities, the motivations that underlie clergy political efforts, and the significance of clergy political activity. Clergy political activity *for whom and for what* is the heart of the matter we seek to investigate.

A REPRESENTATIVE ORIENTATION

Some familiar political analogies are useful in mapping out the possible bounds of clergy political roles. In many ways the *representative-constituent* relationship resembles the bond between a clergyperson and her congregation. Schneier and Gross (1993) offer this description of the dilemmas inherent in the representative-constituent relationship:

> People's attitudes toward representation are paradoxical. On the one hand, they admire politicians, like those described in John F. Kennedy's

Profiles in Courage, who damn the consequences to vote for what they think is right. On the other hand, they want [members of Congress] who will represent them, who will follow the will of the majority. (1993, 97)

The same might be written about clergy. The life and work of Jesus Christ can be perceived as offering revolutionary ideas and challenging societal norms, and many Christian clergy view their task as translating and broadcasting such countercultural claims to congregation members and the larger society. At the same time, members want a spiritual guide, comforting in good times as well as in periods of grief and hardship; clergy who fill this role also convey core messages of their faith traditions. Some congregation members see the problems of society as properly existing outside the church's walls and range of vision, while others believe their faith calls them and their church to act in the world. How do clergy navigate the potential conflicts inherent in these differing visions?

To address this conflict in the political arena, political scientists posit two basic roles of representatives: the *delegate* and the *trustee*. Delegates are sent to the legislature or some other political gathering to follow the will of the people, often explicitly. For example, delegates to a party convention are typically bound to express formally the will of some prior convention or a state's primary election voters. In the first century of the U.S. republic, some states prohibited their U.S. senators (who were then elected by the state legislature) from voting their conscience (Schneier and Gross 1993).

Trustees, on the other hand, are exemplified by Theodore Roosevelt's self-described role as "steward of the people": "it was not only [a representative's] right but his duty to do anything that the needs of the nation demanded unless such action was prohibited by the Constitution or by the laws" (Thomas and Pika 1997, 28). Edmund Burke's 1774 speech to his Bristol constituency is the classic statement of the trustee model—not "to mirror Bristol's wants, but to express its higher virtues through the application of his own intelligence" (Schneier and Gross 1993, 98).

A more contemporary metaphor to describe the tension in this form of relationship comes from the philosopher and theologian Cornel West, who characterizes public officials as having to be *thermometers* or *thermostats*. Corresponding to the delegate model, a thermometer presents the temperature of its location—representatives or clergy simply reflect what they see in their surroundings, seeking not to change conditions or opinions but only to report them whenever and wherever called upon to do so. By contrast, thermostats—akin to trustees—not only read the temperature but also react to it. Unlike Roosevelt's trustee, who is explicitly given free rein to do whatever she wishes, the thermostat takes into account the prevailing mood and acts accordingly—perhaps to temper the situation when things get too hot or stir up action when things cool down.

West's metaphor captures the interrelationship of representatives/clergy and constituents/congregations more subtly than the usual delegate-trustee model. Moreover, West also points us to consideration of *temperature*—what congregation members are thinking and how societal norms and prevailing attitudes affect clergy decisions about political and civic activities. In many respects, clergy cannot help but fulfill the thermometer role—they cannot afford to be oblivious to what their members think, especially if members hold the power to hire and fire them. But clergy also serve important *prophetic* roles—to remind or sometimes tell members what the denomination teaches about a particular issue, strengthen the shared identity that binds people to a particular congregation or denomination, or simply be present with the congregation in times of intense struggle and unrest.

REPRESENTATIVE ROLES IN CONTEXT

How do clergy reconcile the dictates of their theology and conscience with the needs and desires of their constituencies? With care. Stories abound from the 1960s and 1970s of mainline Protestant church boards firing clergy or reducing their salaries because of unwanted activism in civil rights and other causes. In other cases, church membership would drop or clergy would face a backlash of sentiment and deteriorating relations with members over political differences. Many analysts attribute the declining membership of most mainline Protestant denominations to some extent to the unpopular and out-of-step political activities and opinions of mainline clergy beginning in the 1960s (Hadden 1969; Quinley 1974; Roof and McKinney 1987; Wuthnow 1988).

Most of these stories apply to controversial public activities, such as protesting and civil disobedience. The idea of the "gathering storm in the churches" driving members away also assumes that most clergy hold views that differ radically from their members', that clergy focus primarily or solely on controversial social issues, and that clergy act mainly to further their own policy goals. Other venues of clergy activity do not receive the same public scrutiny, such as internal congregational issues, where the clergy's pastoral guidance is critical. Furthermore, clergy do *not* always hold opinions and values opposite those of their members, nor do clergy choose only to engage issues where they disagree with their members.

For instance, Moore (1986) illustrates the role of churches in promoting the interests of minorities in the United States. Initially outsiders, religious groups can use their resources to develop institutions that turn a minority group, united by its status and relationship to society, into a political force. McGreevy (1996) details the alternative set of social institutions, from unions to schools, created by U.S. Catholics in the face of often hostile Protestant majorities. African American churches and the Latter Day Saints (Mormons) also offer numerous examples of using the church as the basis for organizing a community for political and social purposes. Clergy in such situations become engaged in public life, perhaps through electoral politics (still very common in African American communities) or in myriad other ways—serving on local boards, testifying to government bodies, participating in civic events, marching in the streets. *When the church is a more salient institution to its members and its community, clergy are more likely to represent the church in various ways.*

In this type of environment, where clergy are encouraged to be representatives to the broader community, they are most likely to be delegates (or thermometers) for two reasons. First, the congregation is mobilized and attentive to the political issues engaged by the clergyperson. Clergy are more likely to know what their members think, and clergy and members may well have participated together in public meetings or other events. Second, if clergy take on a formal decision-making role, such as service on a task force or local board, members have more opportunity to see or to hear about clergy actions. In activities that are less public, under conditions where the church is not a significant base of support, clergy are likely to have a freer hand in politics and are less apt to merely register the temperature of their members.

But who is represented by the representative? Members of Congress have not one but many constituencies, and district voters are not always the most important one; nomination constituencies, party and other national constituencies, and other attentive publics play significant roles in a representative's decision making. Moreover, understanding legislative behavior requires ascertaining what constituencies matter on different issues, and why. Scholars of Congress and other legislative bodies find little congruence among representative votes in different policy domains.

For clergy, the question remains: Do they represent their denomination or faith tradition, themselves, their congregation, or some combination of these? Which set of interests dominates and on what issues? We argue throughout this book that most clergy place themselves closer to Burke's trustee or West's thermostat role—their public actions and political activism should express the core theological beliefs and mission of the congregation and denomination. Most clergy are acutely aware of just how far their vision and presentation of these core beliefs and mission can differ from the congregation's without causing serious repercussions.

Clergy may also have a distinctive role to play in a democracy, especially when few other respected mediating institutions exist to represent the needs and beliefs of a constituency in and to government. The heightened secularism of American public life since World War II contributes to this sense that the clergy's perspective is all the more necessary and unique. Robert Putnam's *Bowling Alone* (2000) demonstrates that organized religion has been a significant source of what he and others term social capital, both historically and today. With Putnam and others, we suggest that clergy are a major resource shaping how religious group norms are translated and communicated to public policy makers, and that clergy significantly affect how religious social networks are mobilized to engage in political and civic activity. Just as interest groups link citizens to governments, clergy too may be considered a mainspring of democratic governance, though usually to a lesser degree.

Thomas Jefferson suggested that true leadership exists "to inform people's minds, and to follow their will" (Genovese 2001, 194). Political scientist Bruce Miroff offers a twist on this idea that would resonate with many clergy: leadership "not only serves people's interests but furthers their democratic dignity as well" (Genovese 2001, 194). These two conceptions of leadership characterize well the roles of clergy, especially mainline Protestant clergy, who have a clear sense (no doubt stemming from a relatively privileged and dominant role in U.S. public and religious life for nearly two centuries) of how religion can relate appropriately to public life. Few clergy approve of direct involvement in electoral politics by religious institutions (on theological as well as constitutional and legal grounds), but many more clergy approve of and justify actions that are more civic in orientation. As we will see, these clergy place heavy, though not exclusive, emphasis on discussion of issues and activities that informs constituents of all kinds.

Moreover, *clergy at times see themselves as working in the interests of their congregations.* This is generally what Blizzard (1958) referred to as an integrative role. However, previous studies of clergy political action have largely missed this aspect, assuming that political activity is issue based rather than interest based. For example, Nelsen et al. (1973) conceive clergy action as motivated by self-determined roles—a psychological basis. Viewed from an interest-based perspective, a black minister protests racial discrimination in part because of strong civil rights convictions, but also as a way to advocate for the interests of the congregation in ending discrimination.

A substantial portion of clergy action may encompass this dual character. Testifying at a school board meeting about prayers and moments of silence, textbook choices, or curricular issues (e.g., sex education and teaching evolution) may be driven by the clergy's moral values and theology, but it also performs the function of representing and protecting the interests of the congregation. Tocqueville's classic description of the primary American political mind-set as pursuing "self interest, properly understood" would seem to fit contemporary clergy well.

Clergy can slip in and out of representing their congregation as the need arises. Further, the types of action with which clergy represent the congregation are distinctive. Clergy would contribute money to political campaigns—a private act—to further their own personal political agendas, whereas serving on a local board or council would more likely benefit or represent the congregation. We will explore this distinction and its implications in the course of our analysis.

These ideas constitute a comprehensive perspective on the political activities of clergy, one which posits the congregation as a key inspiration and sometimes as a mobilizing force for clergy political and civic activity. Such a perspective forces us to consider how clergy relate not only to their congregational members but also to their communities, their denominations, other civic and local groups, and other external factors that could impinge on their political decisions and actions. *In order to understand the political activities of clergy—how much, how public, how expressed, how effective—we must consider the environment in which clergy live their public and private lives.*

HOW DO WE FIND OUT?
RESEARCH DESIGN AND METHODS

The data necessary to address the ideas we wish to explore come from a random national sample of 1,500 ELCA pastors and 930 Episcopal priests and deacons who responded to an extensive mail survey in the summer and fall of 1998.[2] This extensive survey (with over 350 individual questions) captures essential information about clergy, their congregations, and aspects of the local community. As noted above, we asked our sample clergy a broad range of questions about their personal backgrounds, their theological orientations, the frequency and means by which they present political messages and take political actions within and beyond their congregations, and their personal political attitudes and actions. Our sample clergy also gave us information about how their congregations compare with others in the local community and in the denomination, and how often and in what ways clergy interact with their community and denominational clergy colleagues. Finally, clergy offered their views on denominational organizations and issues, and they told us what political and religious information sources they use on a regular basis.

The primary question type in our survey involves asking for clergy *perceptions* about their members' viewpoints, their local community's attributes, and the attitudes of their ministerial discussion partners. Perceptions are a theoretically sound and an economical way to gather information about the contexts in which clergy live and work (Huckfeldt and Sprague 1995; Thomas and Thomas 1928). The self-reports of clergy about their own political behavior and perceptions of their congregations provide significant information that will allow us to assess the organizational, religious, and political factors that impede or encourage political activity among clergy.[3]

To explore the full range of contextual influences on clergy political and civic behavior, we gathered several other types of information in addition to the rich survey data. For each responding clergyperson, we recorded publicly available county-level statistics on poverty (U.S. Census Bureau), voter turnout and presidential election results *(World Almanac),* and 1990 levels of church membership (Bradley et al. 1992). We also incorporated information on 1998 state ballot initiatives (Initiative and Referenda Institute), yet another aspect of contemporary politics that clergy might discuss with members.

Taken together, our data offer a comprehensive portrait of the political, social, and religious environments in which clergy and congregations are situated. The advantages to this approach should be obvious; through careful statistical and substantive analysis, we can fully address the complex questions we have posed, and we can offer the best possible test of competing explanations for clergy political activity.

One important feature of our sample should be noted as well. Not surprisingly, it appears to have a high concentration of politically active ELCA and Episcopal clergy. Given the length of the survey, those clergy who engage in minimal political and civic activity would have been less interested in responding (although for obvious reasons, we strongly encouraged all chosen clergy to respond, in order to generate the most representative sample). Beyond political activity levels, we have no reason to believe the sample is not representative of the clergy of these two denominations. Nevertheless, we will be careful throughout the book to refer to our *sample ELCA and Episcopal clergy* as the group being studied, rather than ELCA and Episcopal clergy in general. Even if the sample clergy do not constitute a representative subgroup

of all clergy in the two denominations, the patterns of activity and the differences between politically active and politically inactive clergy can be clearly
discerned through the methods we employ, particularly since our total sample size of 2,450 is much larger than the ones in previous studies of clergy political activity.

WHY CHOOSE THESE
TWO DENOMINATIONS FOR THIS STUDY?

There are several sound and practical reasons for selecting the ELCA and
Episcopal Church for our study. First, recent politically oriented surveys of
U.S. Protestant clergy have not included these two denominations (Guth et
al. 1997). Thus at the most basic level, responses to many of our clergy questions can be compared to these other survey findings about major Protestant denominations.[4]

The ELCA is a good choice for several other reasons. It is the fourth
largest Protestant denomination in the United States, with over 5 million
members (*2001 World Almanac*, 689–90). Further, most ELCA parishioners
grew up Lutheran and remain Lutheran throughout their lives (Djupe
1997); this high level of what is generally termed *brand loyalty* suggests that
few outside influences have penetrated the denomination, which helps isolate the factors involved in processes of clergy-congregation influence. The
denomination still encompasses a considerable diversity of congregations,
however, in one important sense: the merger of three bodies to form the
ELCA in 1988 has not completely obscured the old loyalties based primarily on ethnic identity. This form of solidarity may also be expected to affect the salience of the congregation in shaping clergy political activity, and
our survey included questions about prior congregational affiliations to sift
out these effects.

The Episcopal Church has generally been more politically engaged
than the ELCA, and Lutherans generally, are thought to be. Episcopalians
have been and remain overrepresented in the U.S. Congress and other government institutions, relative to their share of the population. Episcopalians
nationwide continue to be the most wealthy and best educated of all Protestants (Kosmin and Lachman 1993; Roof and McKinney 1987). In terms of
sheer numbers, Episcopalians now have less than half as many members (just
over 2 million) as the ELCA (*2001 World Almanac*, 689). These differences
suggest the existence of somewhat different social mechanisms operating
within Episcopal churches, the more politically oriented Episcopalians seem

to be more comfortable with politics, while ELCA Lutherans are often thought to be more wary of political activism.

The two denominations have some important connections as well. Their doctrines and organizational structures (at local, regional, and national levels) are similar in many respects. Both denominations give local congregations substantial authority to hire and remove clergy, and both have a strong tradition of congregational layperson leadership to augment the work of ordained staff. Both place heavy emphasis on congregations coming together in corporate worship, which employs set liturgies, stresses music as an important component of worship, and centers on the celebration of the Eucharist (communion). Even allowing for the unique qualities of each denomination and the idiosyncrasies of local practices, it is probably safe to say that the typical ELCA Lutheran adherent would feel fairly comfortable in an Episcopal worship setting, and vice versa.

Since January 2001, the ELCA and Episcopal Church have officially entered into a cooperative agreement with each other. This agreement, contained in the document *Called to Common Mission* (CCM) and usually referred to simply as full communion, remains a contentious issue within the ELCA, as we will explain further in chapter 9. We have included questions about this issue in our surveys in order to see whether the same influences that affect clergy political activities might influence clergy speech and action on denominational matters.

Finally, the broad geographic distribution of ELCA and Episcopal congregations offers the opportunity to test our hypotheses about clergy political activity in a wide range of communities. Our sample includes clergy all over the United States, serving in very small towns and in the nation's largest cities, with significant numbers ministering in suburban communities. The diversity of the sample clergy means that we can isolate particular characteristics of communities that may impede or heighten the propensity of clergy to engage in political activity. Not all U.S. denominations and faith traditions possess this type of diversity (geographical and type of community). Hence the patterns we observe are not just ELCA or Episcopal patterns; to the extent that location and type of community matter, what we observe in these two denominations is readily generalizable to U.S. churches as a whole.

PLAN OF THE BOOK

This book focuses on the political activity of clergy. Before we can explain the patterns of political activity among Episcopal and ELCA clergy, we need to discuss the effects of key factors on their political activities and beliefs. Chapter 2 explores the personal attributes of clergy that might affect their political behavior and provides a brief history and overview of the Episcopal Church and the ELCA. Chapters 3–4 investigate how the congregation, the denomination, and the community can affect clergy political choices and actions in myriad ways. This first section of the book thus builds a theoretical framework leading to testable hypotheses about clergy activities in later chapters, while also providing a thorough portrait of the social, professional, and political environments in which ELCA and Episcopal clergy live and work.

Beginning with chapter 5, we move on to a substantive investigation of significant political activities that clergy choose to pursue. Chapter 5 presents a complete five-part typology of explanatory factors, pulling together information in the opening chapters to provide a comprehensive framework for explaining clergy political behavior. The first of these behaviors to be analyzed using our five-part typology is public speech, the primary mechanism through which clergy influence opinions, set agendas, mobilize, and empower congregation members. Chapter 5 explores the types, amounts, and motivations for clergy public speech. We find significant and intriguing effects from clergy's communities of concern—the congregation as well as the secular community at large.

The most widely noted and analyzed connection between religion and politics in the United States concerns the political involvement of clergy in electoral politics, which we explore in chapter 6. Clergy participate directly in political campaigns through a variety of roles, although perhaps their most important and prominent influence occurs indirectly through mobilizing, setting the agendas, and influencing the opinions of congregation members. We explore who participates as well as the types, amounts, determinants, and potential impact of clergy electoral participation.

Despite the historical importance of clergy political activity within local communities, such activity has been largely ignored by scholars. In chapter 7, we examine local forms of civic and political activity, which are among the most common outlets for ELCA and Episcopal clergy participation in community civic and political life. We find that clergy involvement in both civic and partisan community organizations depends in part on how their congregation differs from others in the local community, whether in terms of beliefs, activity levels, or sheer numbers.

In chapter 8, we examine the amounts of and compare the motivations to perform activities intended to send a message to government. This includes common activities like letter writing and calling government officials, as well as actions that can be highly controversial and provocative, such as protest marching and civil disobedience. We compare the factors that motivate unconventional activities with those that motivate conventional activities, finding unique elements that determine the choices clergy make.

Chapter 9 deals with an issue of great concern within the ELCA and the Episcopal Church—their new relationship known as full communion, which is not a merger but rather an agreement about basic theological beliefs and engagement in closer organizational cooperation across a broad range of activities. We explore the politics of this denominational issue, investigating clergy attitudes and actions, and we also link these findings to our earlier analysis of clergy political activities to find common sources motivating clergy to speak and act.

In the concluding chapter, we review the evidence presented and offer a refined theory of clergy political behavior that sees clergy as important links to the public realm for their members, both representing their congregations and mobilizing them to take part in the political process. We also assess the generalizability of our findings beyond the ELCA and Episcopal Church, setting our results in the context of fifty years of research on clergy political behavior.

NOTES

1. To preserve the anonymity of our survey respondents, we have changed the names of this church and subsequent churches described in this section.

2. Approximately 3,000 clergy in each denomination were chosen to receive the survey; random selection was used to generate the initial sample, and all clergy included in the denominations' 1998 active rosters had an equal chance of being selected. A second wave was sent two months after the first survey; second-wave respondents did not differ in significant ways from first-wave respondents. The overall response rate is 48 percent for ELCA pastors and 31 percent for Episcopal priests and deacons. Given the length of our survey (11 dense pages of questions), it is not surprising that the response rate is lower than what would be expected for surveys of highly educated populations. The authors' personal affiliation with an ELCA-affiliated college (which was disclosed to survey recipients on the survey's cover page) almost certainly accounts for the considerably higher response rate from ELCA pastors.

3. The second portion of our study involves sixty congregations (38 ELCA, 22 Episcopal) whose clergy answered our initial survey. Members of these congregations received surveys throughout 1999 and early 2000. In future publications, we will address the relationships between clergy and church member perceptions of

political activity within congregations, focusing on how the political attitudes and actions of church members are affected by clergy political messages.

4. The authors of *The Bully Pulpit* examined eight Protestant denominations: the Southern Baptist Convention, Assemblies of God, United Methodists, Presbyterian Church (USA), Christian Reformed Church, Reformed Church of America, Evangelical Covenant Church, and the Disciples of Christ.

2

AN OVERVIEW
OF ELCA AND EPISCOPAL CLERGY

In this chapter we address several topics essential to understanding clergy in the two denominations we have chosen for study. We begin with a brief history and organizational review of each denomination, then proceed through an overview of our sample clergy's personal attributes, theological precepts, and political attitudes. Through this overview we will develop further our expectations about the multiple factors that affect the types and degrees of political activity among ELCA and Episcopal clergy. The initial explorations in this chapter set the stage for more detailed empirical analysis in succeeding chapters.

THE EVANGELICAL LUTHERAN CHURCH IN AMERICA

Lutheranism has its roots in the protest movement sparked by Martin Luther in early sixteenth-century Germany. German and Scandinavian Lutherans began emigrating to the American colonies soon after they were established, and the Lutheran churches in America have remained organized principally along ethnic lines through the present day (Ahlstrom 1972; Mead and Hill 1992). This ethnic heritage endures, especially in the upper Midwest, where Lutherans occupy a central place in the religious, social, and political culture of Minnesota and surrounding states.

Since the early twentieth century, U.S. Lutheran bodies have moved steadily toward unity through a series of mergers. Yet there are still numerous distinct denominations within the U.S. Lutheran church family—ten branches of Lutheranism claim at least 5,000 members (*2001 World Almanac*, 689). The ELCA is the largest of these, with 5.1 million members. The next

two largest are the Lutheran Church-Missouri Synod (LCMS), a more theologically conservative group with 2.6 million adherents, and the Wisconsin Evangelical Lutheran Synod (WELS), which has 400,000 members and
is considered even more theologically orthodox than the LCMS (Mead and
Hill 1992, 146–48; *2001 World Almanac*, 689).

The ELCA was formed in 1988 through the merger of three entities:

- the American Lutheran Church (ALC), itself formed through a
  merger in 1960, which was based in Minneapolis and had 2.3
  million members, primarily of German, Norwegian, and Danish
  heritage
- the Association of Evangelical Lutheran Churches (AELC), with
  100,000 members, which was formed in 1976 by congregations
  splitting from the LCMS
- the Lutheran Church in America (LCA), also the product of an earlier merger (1962), which was the largest U.S. Lutheran branch at 2.9
  million members, with a strong Scandinavian (especially Swedish)
  flavor (Mead and Hill 1992, 143–45)

The ELCA has headquarters in Chicago and lobbying offices in the District of Columbia (the Lutheran Office for Governmental Affairs) and
eighteen states. The denomination is divided into nine regions and sixty-
five synods (including some Caribbean islands), holding annual synod
meetings and a biennial Churchwide Assembly. Various denominational
offices coordinate global programs in concert with Lutheran bodies
around the world, as well as social outreach programs in the United
States.

The ELCA has over 10,000 local congregations throughout the
United States, although the largest concentrations are in the upper Midwest.
As with most U.S. denominations, the typical congregation is quite small
(Chaves et al. 1999). The median congregation size for our ELCA sample
clergy is 350; however, factoring in clergy self-reports of active members,
the median ELCA congregation served by sample clergy has between 80
and 125 active adult members. Congregational activities, including control
of budgets and employment matters, usually lie in the hands of a church
council; annual meetings and special gatherings allow all members to have
a voice in church governance. The congregation chooses its own pastor, and
large churches have multiple clergy on staff to handle pastoral duties and
share in leading worship services.

EPISCOPAL CHURCH, USA

The worldwide Anglican Church dates its origins to King Henry VIII of England, who split with the Roman Catholic Church in 1534 and declared himself head of the Church of England. Anglican priests and missionaries constituted a strong presence in the American colonies, especially in southern states (where several colonial government officially established the Church of England) and northeastern cities. At the onset of the American Revolution, the Church of England was the second largest denomination in the colonies, and it had the most widely dispersed membership (Holmes 1993, 19–38).

The Revolution harmed the Church of England, since it was directly connected to Great Britain. Southern states disestablished the church, and its affiliated Methodist societies broke away in 1784 to become a separate denomination (Holmes 1993, 47). Nearly half of Anglican clergy and over half of Anglican lay members supported the American side in the Revolutionary War, and the prominence of Anglicans in the new nation's government (more than half of the signers of the Declaration of Independence were Anglican) helped the denomination weather the difficulties related to its roots (Holmes 1993, 49–50). By 1800, the American branch of Anglicanism had acquired a new name—the Protestant Episcopal Church, usually shortened (and officially so in 1967) to the Episcopal Church.

Episcopal Church governance follows closely the federal structure of the U.S. government. The overall head of the U.S. church is the presiding bishop, who resides in Washington, D.C. Each congregation (termed a parish, although we use congregation throughout the book) belongs to one of over one hundred dioceses in eight U.S. provinces (Central American nations compose a ninth province). Each diocese is governed by a bishop elected at diocesan conventions. At these annual gatherings lay delegates and all diocesan priests decide policy and debate other matters. The decentralized diocesan system allows each local region to chart its own course to some extent; for example, three U.S. dioceses do not ordain women as priests, which the national church first approved in 1976 (Mead and Hill 1992, 103–6). At the denomination's triennial General Convention, a two-house system (one composed only of bishops, the other of elected ordained and lay delegates) must approve all policy matters. The Episcopal Church, USA participates in regular meetings of the worldwide Anglican Communion, and it has been extremely active in public policy advocacy and social outreach ministries.

At the local level, each parish is responsible for selecting an ordained person to lead the congregation. This person can hold one of several different titles—rector, vicar, and priest-in-charge are common. Priests and bishops are typically the only ones who can preside and administer sacraments (such as Holy Eucharist). Deacons are also ordained. They assist with sacramental duties and can lead non-Eucharist worship; they preach occasionally and often engage in numerous ministry tasks such as visiting the parish's sick and shut-in members.[1] Each parish also has a vestry, the equivalent of ELCA church councils, to decide policy matters and administer budgets and programs. Episcopal parishes also tend to be rather small—the median Episcopal parish in our sample has two hundred adult members and sixty to one hundred active members.

ELCA AND EPISCOPAL CLERGY:
A DEMOGRAPHIC OVERVIEW

Figure 2.1 presents basic demographic information about our sample clergy. One distinctive characteristic of ELCA and Episcopal ministers is nearly uniform advanced education—a master's degree (usually a Master of Divinity, or M.Div.) is now required for ordination in both denominations, and nearly all our sample clergy have at least the M.Div. About one-quarter have a doctorate in ministry (D.Min.), a degree typically pursued by persons having experience in the parish setting. Clergy with doctorates are slightly more politically active than clergy with M.Div. degrees. Figure 2.1 also shows that women compose about 20 percent of the sample—one of every six sample ELCA pastors and one in four Episcopal priests or deacons. Women clergy participated in slightly more political activities than men in 1998, with ELCA women pastors engaging in the most political activities. Figure 2.1 also shows our sample clergy having extensive service and experience in their jobs—serving an average of nineteen years in the ministry and nearly a decade at their present posts.

Theological Characteristics

Ministers from the ELCA and Episcopal Church tend to fall on the modernist side of the "orthodox-modernist" divide in U.S. Protestantism (Guth et al. 1997; Hadden 1969; Hunter 1991, Quinley 1974; Wuthnow

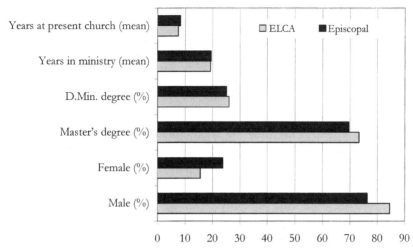

Figure 2.1.   A Demographic Description of ELCA and Episcopal Sample Clergy
Source: 1998 ELCA/Episcopal Church Clergy Study.

1988). Guth and colleagues describe the basic tenets of the modernist perspective arising out of liberal Protestant theology:

> Rather than regarding the Bible as divine, produced directly by God, liberals were naturalistic, explaining the text and the events it recounted in human terms. And rather than emphasizing God's particular revelation in Jesus Christ, liberals sought a general revelation in nature and history, a "natural theology." Finally, instead of emphasizing God's transcendence and supernatural aspects of the faith, liberals stressed God's immanence, a divine presence in the mundane world. (1997, 9–10)

This perspective, especially the final point, leads to a social theology emphasizing the church's role in addressing social and political concerns in its community and the world (Guth et al. 1997, 10). We will show aspects of this worldview when we examine the personal theology and social theology of our sample clergy.

Personal Theology and the "Two-Party System" of U.S. Protestantism

To demonstrate the nature of the political stances taken by ELCA and Episcopal clergy, the logical starting point is to examine their theological beliefs. The authors of *The Bully Pulpit* asked questions about adherence to Christian orthodoxy, eschatology, and religious terminology to assess the theological stance of ministers from their eight chosen denominations. Not surprisingly, they found more evangelical denominations Assemblies of God, Southern Baptist Convention, the Evangelical Covenant Church, and two reformed churches—leaning heavily or predominantly toward the orthodox camp, while the United Methodist Church, the Presbyterian Church (USA), and the Disciples of Christ were slanted to the modernist end (Guth et al. 1997, 45).

Our survey presented ELCA and Episcopal clergy with theological statements similar to those used in the *Bully Pulpit* surveys. For most statements, ELCA and Episcopal clergy views correspond closely with each other and with the modernist perspective, as seen in table 2.1. Large majorities of sample clergy in both denominations support the ordination of women and reject biblical inerrancy—two stances associated with the modernist camp. Responses differ on two items. Seventy-three percent of ELCA clergy agreed that "there is no other way to salvation but justification by faith in Christ," while only 45 percent of Episcopal clergy concurred with this essentially Lutheran formulation. A similar split appears on the question of whether Jesus will return bodily to earth: 71 percent of ELCA pastors but only 53 percent of Episcopal priests and deacons agree.

Figure 2.2 examines the applicability of common theological terms to ELCA and Episcopal clergy worldviews. Clergy in both denominations reject the term "fundamentalist" (only 1 percent in each say that it fits "very well"). Both are more accepting of the terms "liberal" and "evangelical," with Episcopal clergy preferring the former and ELCA clergy preferring the latter. Majorities of both sets of clergy label themselves "ecumenical," with ELCA clergy somewhat more likely to do so. Episcopal clergy are

Table 2.1. Theological Beliefs of ELCA and Episcopal Church Clergy

	ELCA		Episcopal Church	
Question	Percent Agree	Percent Disagree	Percent Agree	Percent Disagree
The Bible is the inerrant word of God, both in matters of faith . . . and other matters.	19.3	75.6	18.3	75.5
There is no other way to salvation but justification by faith in Christ.	73.3	17.6	44.8	43.4
The Bible is the norm for faith and life.	88.9	9.8	81.6	9.4
Women should be ordained as ministers.	94.2	2.1	89.0	6.1
Jesus will return bodily to earth one day.	71.0	12.0	52.7	17.4

Source: 1998 ELCA/Episcopal Church Clergy Study. Number of cases varies.
Note: The categories "strongly agree/disagree" and "agree/disagree" were combined for each question in this table.

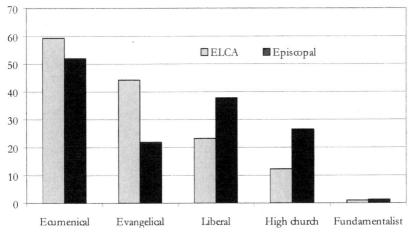

Figure 2.2.   Applicability of Theological Terms to ELCA and Episcopal Clergy
Source: 1998 ELCA/Episcopal Church Clergy Study.
Note: The bars represent the percent of clergy responding that the particular term fits them "very well."

twice as likely to label themselves "high church," reflecting the Episcopal emphasis on traditional liturgies. Taken together, table 2.1 and figure 2.2 confirm the classification of ELCA and Episcopal clergy as theologically modernist.

Social Theologies: The Public Church

The basic distinction within social theology is between competing themes of individualism and communitarianism. Evangelical Protestant denominations are typically classified with the individualist perspective, while mainline denominations exhibit much stronger support for communitarian perspectives (Guth et al. 1997, 59). Our surveys ask fewer questions on these themes than the surveys administered by Guth and colleagues; the results are presented in table 2.2 and offer mixed signals about the social theologies of ELCA and Episcopal clergy.

The first statement concerning church involvement is phrased from an individualist perspective, and responses seem to show that neither set of clergy supports this perspective strongly (less than 33 percent agreement). The next two statements concern churches transforming the social order and defining social justice as the essence of the gospel—both are phrased more along communitarian lines. Here we find stronger communitarian leanings among Episcopal clergy regarding the meaning of the gospel (53 percent agree that social justice is its essence), but stronger ELCA communitarian views on churches transforming the

Table 2.3.   Social Theological Beliefs of ELCA and Episcopal Church Clergy

Question	ELCA		Episcopal Church	
	Percent Agree	*Percent Disagree*	*Percent Agree*	*Percent Disagree*
If enough people were involved in the church, social ills would take care of themselves.	28.3	59.1	32.6	49.2
Churches should emphasize transforming the social order rather than individual salvation.	57.5	25.8	45.1	36.8
Social justice is the essence of the gospel.	35.1	49.7	53.0	32.6
Christians of different denominations need to cooperate more in politics.	59.7	21.8	59.4	18.6

Source: 1998 ELCA/Episcopal Church Clergy Study. Number of cases varies.
Note: The categories "strongly agree/disagree" and "agree/disagree" were combined for each question in this table.

social order (58 percent agree). Finally, both sets of clergy are strongly supportive of ecumenical political activity, reflecting again their commitment to ecumenism and recognition of its potential benefits for collective action.

The political implications of these stances become more clear with additional data from our survey. Both ELCA and Episcopal clergy reject association with Christian Right political organizations such as the Christian Coalition or the American Family Association; in fact, almost no clergy reported any affinity for a Christian Right group. Another clear indicator is the question of whether the denomination should be more or less involved with social and political issues. There is a clear preference among Episcopal clergy for greater involvement of their denomination, while ELCA clergy are more reluctant to see their denomination engage more with social and political issues (see table 2.5 for details and further analysis).

These tables show that ELCA and Episcopal clergy fit comfortably into the modernist theological camp. The question to be explored in the ensuing empirical analysis is *to what extent theology dictates political interest, activity, and beliefs*, compared with other salient factors. The theological stances identified in this section already suggest liberal political stances on the part of sample clergy. Before examining political ideology in detail, we turn to a summary description and analysis of political interest and activity levels among ELCA and Episcopal clergy.

CLERGY POLITICAL ACTIVITY: EFFECTS OF TIME,
INTEREST, AND THE CONGREGATION

Table 2.3 gives an overview of how the political activity of clergy relates to their overall interest in politics. The first set of numbers in table 2.3 offers two ways to characterize overall clergy political activity: a self-report of how actively involved our sample clergy consider themselves and a corresponding count of how many political activities our sample clergy report engaging in during 1998. For example, 3.3 percent of sample clergy report "a great deal" of public affairs involvement; clergy in this group engaged in an average of 8.7 political activities (out of a possible 19) during 1998 (the full list of activities can be found in appendix A and table 2.6). The second set of numbers relates 1998 mean clergy election activity levels (7 possible activities) to self-reported interest in 1998 campaign news.

Clergy who have more interest in public affairs and pay more attention to campaign news are much more politically active than clergy with little interest in either. About 20 percent of sample clergy report being involved in public affairs "a great deal" or "quite a bit," and this subgroup engages in far more political activity than the rest of the sample—seven or more political activities in 1998 on average, versus five or fewer activities for less involved clergy. This engaged subgroup has more Episcopal clergy (21.6 percent involved "quite a bit" or more) than ELCA clergy (15.6 percent), a pattern we will see repeated throughout our analysis. Table 2.3 also shows that 63 percent of sample clergy paid quite a bit or a great deal of attention to 1998 election news; these clergy engaged in more electoral activities on

Table 2.3.   Attention to Campaign News, Public Affairs Involvement, and Clergy Political Activity

	Great Deal	Quite a Bit	Some	Very Little	None
Percent actively involved in public affairs	3.3	14.9	44.5	32.8	4.5
1998 mean number of clergy political activities[a]	8.7	6.9	5.0	3.6	2.6
Percent paying attention to 1998 campaign news	19.6	43.5	30.9	5.9	0.1
1998 mean number of clergy electoral activities[b]	1.6	1.3	1.0	0.8	0.3

Source: 1998 ELCA/Episcopal Church Clergy Study.
[a]Out of nineteen possible political activities.
[b]Out of seven possible electoral activities.

average than clergy who paid less attention to the 1998 elections. The high degree of engagement with politics, electoral and not, follows from the extremely high rates of news consumption among sample clergy. Nearly all read a newspaper daily, many noted watching network news, many wrote in that they were tuned to public radio, and a significant number used the Internet for their news.

At the other end of the spectrum, clergy with little to no interest in public affairs or 1998 campaign news engage in very few political activities. About 40 percent of sample clergy report very little or no engagement in public affairs, although these clergy still have mild interest in campaign news and engage in some activities that we term political.

Table 2.4 reveals the degree to which sample clergy believe they can achieve political goals. Clergy from both denominations are in rough agreement that "it is difficult for ministers to know the proper political channel to use to accomplish some goal" (53 percent ELCA agree; 47 percent Episcopal agree). Affirmative answers to this question reflect a lack of awareness about the political process as well as recognition of the significant barriers to political change.

Table 2.4 also reveals a contrast between ELCA and Episcopal clergy on how much clergy can influence their congregations. Nearly twice as many Episcopal priests and deacons agree strongly (8.4 percent versus 4.6 percent); Episcopal clergy are also less likely to disagree (only 23 percent versus 31 percent of ELCA pastors). With just under half the sample agreeing to some degree that "ministers have great capacity to influence the po-

Table 2.4.   Clergy Political Efficacy Attitudes by Denomination

Variable	Percent Strongly Agree	Percent Agree	Percent Neutral	Percent Disagree	Percent Strongly Disagree
It is difficult for ministers to know the proper political channel to use to accomplish some goal.					
Total sample	4.7	45.9	20.3	26.8	2.3
ELCA	4.4	48.2	19.2	26.5	1.7
Episcopal Church	5.1	42.3	22.0	27.4	3.2
Ministers have great capacity to influence the political and social views of their congregation.					
Total sample	6.2	43.2	22.8	25.5	2.4
ELCA	4.6	42.4	21.9	28.2	2.8
Episcopal Church	8.4	44.2	24.1	21.3	1.8

Source: 1998 ELCA/Episcopal Church Clergy Study. Number of cases varies.

litical and social views of their congregation" and 28 percent disagreeing, obviously our sample clergy understand the potential influence they hold, even as they exercise it on political and social issues.

Do our sample clergy want to be more or less involved with social and political issues, or are they content with present levels of activity? Table 2.5 shows clergy feelings about their current personal involvement and their opinion on whether the denomination should be more or less involved with political and social issues. A majority of sample clergy (53 percent overall) wish they could engage in more political activity; only 2 percent desire to do less. Interestingly, clergy who desire to do more are already doing more than other clergy—performing on average more than five political activities in 1998, compared with 4.5 or fewer activities among sample clergy who wish to do the same or less political activity.

Table 2.5 also shows that a sizable percentage of sample clergy want their denomination to do more with political and social issues, with Episcopal clergy more desirous (46 percent) than ELCA clergy (34 percent). The final line in table 2.5 connects this question to clergy political ideologies. Using a five-point ideology scale (1 = most liberal, 5 = most conservative; see table 2.9 for a full summary), we find that clergy desiring more

Table 2.5. Clergy Desired Personal and Denominational Involvement with Social and Political Issues with Connections to Clergy Political Activity and Political Ideology

Variable	Percent Much Less	Percent Less	Percent Same	Percent More	Percent Much More
If it were possible, would you like to be more or less involved with social and political issues?					
ELCA	0.7	1.3	43.2	47.4	7.4
Episcopal	0.8	1.2	47.1	42.1	8.8
1998 mean number of clergy political activities[a]	2.1	4.5	4.3	5.4	6.6
Does the ELCA/Episcopal Church, as a denomination, need to be more or less involved with social and political issues?					
ELCA	6.4	14.4	45.3	27.2	6.8
Episcopal	7.0	13.7	33.4	30.8	15.0
Mean clergy political ideology[b]	3.6	3.3	2.7	2.3	2.0

Source: 1998 ELCA/Episcopal Church Clergy Study. Number of cases varies.
[a]Out of nineteen possible political activities.
[b]Measured on five-point scale: 1 = most liberal, 2 = liberal, 3 = moderate, 4 = conservative, 5 = most conservative.

denominational involvement on social and political issues are undoubtedly more politically liberal, while more politically conservative clergy favor less denominational involvement with political and social issues. *The more liberal an ELCA or Episcopal clergyperson is, the more active she is in public affairs and the more she desires additional activity for herself and from her denomination.*

We asked clergy several questions about nineteen different political activities—whether they performed each activity in 1998, how often they did so, and whether they generally approved or disapproved of clergy performing the activity (not asked for all 19 items). Table 2.6 presents the results, ranked by the percentage of clergy who performed the act in 1998 (first column). The table shows a reluctance on the part of ELCA and Episcopal clergy to engage in too many public, partisan political activities. Approval of candidate endorsements is very low (7.1 percent approval of endorsing while preaching, 26 percent approval of endorsing in some other public venue), as is approval of active campaigning (35 percent). These same activities are among the least frequently performed by our sample clergy in 1998. Note the clear contrast between activities that might bring *public dis-*

Table 2.6.   Clergy Frequency and Approval of Political Activities in 1998

Variable	Percent Performing Act in 1998	Frequency of Performing Act in 1998	Percent Clergy Approval of Act
Publicly offer prayer on an issue	55.8	2.9	80.9
Publicly take a stand on an issue	51.4	2.7	81.4
Take a stand on an issue while preaching	48.9	2.6	63.6
Urge church to register and vote	46.3	2.9	87.2
Serve on a local clergy council	44.6	2.9	–
Contact public officials	39.7	2.7	89.0
Active on a local board or council	30.9	2.5	–
Contribute money to party, PAC, candidate	25.7	2.2	64.8
Join a local political/community group	25.7	2.3	–
Organize an action group in church	23.7	2.3	57.0
Publicly offer prayer for candidates	20.4	1.9	39.1
Write an op-ed or a letter to the editor	16.6	2.0	–
Organize a study group in church	13.6	1.9	77.9
Join a national group	12.3	1.8	60.3
Publicly endorse candidates	11.4	1.7	25.9
Participate in a protest march	7.8	1.9	68.8
Actively campaign	6.1	1.7	35.5
Engage in civil disobedience	1.7	1.5	49.5
Endorse candidates while preaching	1.4	1.2	7.1

Source: 1998 ELCA/Episcopal Church Clergy Study. Number of cases varies.

approval (or legal action, in the case of endorsing candidates in church) versus activities that could be deemed *informational*. Over three-fourths of sample clergy approve of ministers organizing a study group in church on some political or social issue; the fact that only 13.6 percent did so in 1998 is a function of limited time and less interest in a midterm federal election year.

Clergy feel much less constrained in commenting on issues—over 80 percent believe it is acceptable to take a stand publicly or include an issue in prayer, and over half did so in 1998. Slightly smaller percentages approve of taking an issue stance while preaching. Such activities get to the heart of clergy influences on the political stances and actions of their congregations. Preaching to the assembled congregation allows clergy to show how the tenets of Christian faith relate to daily life. In commenting on the meaning of the day's assigned Scriptures, ELCA and Episcopal clergy have ample opportunity to tie old words to new challenges.

Table 2.6 also shows the important roles of clergy as civic leaders and active citizens. Clergy approve of urging their congregation to register and vote (87 percent) and of contacting public officials (89 percent); they also did these things in high percentages in 1998 (46 percent urged registration or voting, 40 percent contacted a public official). A striking 25.7 percent contributed money to a candidate, party, or political action committee (PAC) in 1998; in fact clergy were *four times more likely to do so* than the average U.S. citizen (1996 National Election Study).

Table 2.6 shows clergy to be active citizens—they join groups, give time and money (despite having considerable work-related time demands and relatively low pay), and speak out in public. Their official roles constrain some of these political activities but appear to encourage more civic-minded actions—an Episcopal priest commented, "I do not think it is correct for me to endorse one view publicly; rather, I want people to think and to get involved."

Political Activity throughout the Career

As the remainder of this book will detail, not all ELCA and Episcopal clergy engage in political activity, and among clergy who do, the amounts and types differ markedly. One factor that affects levels of clergy political activity is time. As has been documented thoroughly elsewhere, the 1960s and 1970s saw great upheaval in mainline Protestant churches. Some of today's ELCA and Episcopal clergy were active in the ministry thirty years ago or more, and we might expect to find their levels of political activity to differ from those of clergy who came to the ministry in the 1980s and 1990s.

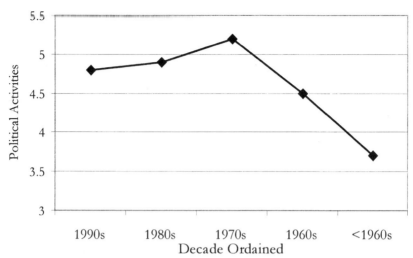

Figure 2.3.   Political Activity by Decade of Ordination
Source: 1998 ELCA/Episcopal Church Clergy Study.
Note: Political activity is the mean number of clergy political acts performed in 1998 (nineteen possible
activities).

Figure 2.3 shows average political activity levels based on the decade in which our sample clergy were ordained. Ordering by decade of ordination does not substitute perfectly for age; in fact today the average age at ordination is in the mid-forties for clergy in both denominations (Wheeler 2001). Figure 2.3 hints at the socialization effects of seminary and personal experience that lead to differing levels of political activity among sample clergy across the decades. Clergy ordained before 1960 do far less political activity on average. Clergy ordained in the 1960s are more active, and the 1970s, 1980s, and 1990s cohorts show even greater average political activity. Figure 2.3 indicates that more recently ordained clergy are going to be more politically active—*high levels of political activity are now the norm among ELCA and Episcopal clergy*, which would not have been the case forty years ago.

THE CONTENT OF CLERGY POLITICS: TWO AGENDAS

With half our sample clergy commenting in some public way on public affairs issues, the content of their comments is important to assess as well. Table 2.7 shows how often clergy addressed sixteen social and political issues in 1998. These issues can be divided into two groups—a *moral reform agenda* and a *social justice agenda*. These two groupings have been utilized by other researchers to delineate the spheres of activity in which politically active clergy might engage (Beatty and Walter 1989; Guth et al. 1997, 82–102; Hofrenning 1995). We derive these agendas from an exploratory factor analysis (detailed in chapter 6 and appendix B) instead of simply assigning issues to one agenda or the other. Although some issues may reside on both agendas depending on a clergyperson's opinion (some clergy may see support for abortion rights as a social justice issue, while pro-life clergy would more likely label it a moral concern), the factor analysis objectively establishes two logically coherent sets of issues. The placement of two issue statements related to sexual orientation helps show the utility of this approach. Our factor analysis indicates that speaking in public about homosexuality is a moral reform agenda item—comment about the morality of essentially private behaviors—while speaking about gay rights belongs to the social justice agenda, since clergy are commenting on the public policy dimensions of sexual orientation.

Table 2.7.   Clergy Frequency of Addressing Public Policy Issues in 1998

	ELCA		Episcopal Church	
Variable	Percent Addressing Issue	Frequency of Addressing Issue[a]	Percent Addressing Issue	Frequency of Addressing Issue
Social Justice Issues				
Hunger and poverty	88.6	3.8	91.6	3.9
Environment	77.6	3.2	74.2	3.2
Education	77.6	3.3	75.7	3.3
Civil rights	74.6	3.2	80.4	3.4
Women's issues	73.8	3.1	71.0	3.1
Unemployment, economy	66.0	2.9	67.5	3.0
Gay rights	45.3	2.5	60.1	2.8
Government spending, deficits	36.5	2.2	34.2	2.1
Moral Reform Issues				
Family problems	86.4	3.6	79.0	3.4
Gambling laws	51.5	2.5	32.0	2.0
Homosexuality	51.3	2.6	64.3	2.9
Current political scandals	48.9	2.5	42.1	2.3
Capital punishment	48.9	2.4	50.1	2.5
Abortion	48.2	2.4	46.0	2.4
Prayer in public schools	42.1	2.4	43.0	2.1
National defense	38.5	2.2	32.2	2.0

Source: 1998 ELCA/Episcopal Church Clergy Study. Number of cases varies.
[a]Mean score on five-point scale: 1 = never, 2 = rarely, 3 = seldom, 4 = often, 5 = very often.

Table 2.7 indicates that social justice concerns are more likely top-ics of discussion among ELCA and Episcopal sample clergy, although moral reform topics are also frequently discussed. Six of the seven most frequently addressed issues are social justice agenda items, with two-thirds or more of sample ELCA and Episcopal clergy addressing these issues in 1998. The order of the items differs slightly between the two sets of clergy; Episcopal clergy are more likely to discuss homosexuality and gay rights, and ELCA clergy are more likely to discuss current political scan-dals (mainly the Clinton impeachment proceedings in 1998), national de-fense, and gambling laws. This last item reflects the upper midwestern lo-cation of many of our ELCA sample clergy. Living in states with numerous Native American–run casinos gives these ELCA clergy a greater opportunity to perceive and thus to discuss the morality and so-cial consequences of gambling.

Table 2.7 fits with the patterns observed in the *Bully Pulpit* study of clergy public speech. Guth and colleagues found that more liberal, main-line Protestant ministers were more likely to speak on social justice top-ics, while Evangelical Protestant ministers focused on moral concerns (1997, 82–86). ELCA and Episcopal clergy fit with their mainline col-leagues in terms of the agendas they prefer to discuss in and out of church.

Table 2.8 describes differences in the agendas of male and female sam-ple clergy when commenting publicly on social and political issues. The table shows a definite tendency for female clergy to be more vocal about

Table 2.8.   Gender Differences in Clergy Addressing Public Policy Issues in 1998

	Social Justice Agenda Issues	Moral Reform Agenda Issues
Issues female clergy are more likely to address	Women's issues Gay rights Hunger and poverty Civil rights	Homosexuality
Issues male clergy are more likely to address	Budget deficits, government spending	Gambling laws Prayer in public schools Current political scandals Abortion National defense Capital punishment

Source: 1998 ELCA/Episcopal Church Clergy Study.
Note: All issues reported have statistical significance (*t*-tests), with $p < .10$.

social justice agenda items, while male clergy are more likely to speak on moral reform agenda items. These findings agree with recent research showing women clergy as more likely to pursue social justice issues in and out of their church roles (Crawford, Deckman, and Braun 2001; Olson, Crawford, and Guth 2000).

POLITICAL IDEOLOGY AND BEHAVIOR

Through decades of research beginning right after World War II, political scientists have developed reliable indicators of U.S. party identification and liberal–conservative tendencies, as well as measures of political participation and voting behavior (Campbell et al. 1960; Miller and Shanks 1996). Having shown the strong social justice interests and desire for more political involvement by most ELCA and Episcopal sample clergy, we expect such beliefs to equate with political opinions and behaviors that support Democratic Party positions more than Republican ones. Tables 2.9–2.11 and figures 2.4–2.6 explore indicators of partisan and ideological thinking among our sample clergy.

Table 2.9 shows that sample ELCA and Episcopal clergy are moderate to liberal in their basic political orientations. Episcopal clergy are more likely to place themselves at the ends of the five-point ideology scale, whereas ELCA clergy cluster more in the middle. Episcopal clergy are also shifted somewhat to the liberal end—51 percent liberal or very liberal, compared with 43 percent of ELCA pastors. Table 2.9 also reconfirms (see table 2.5) that liberal clergy in both denominations engage in more political activities than politically moderate or conservative clergy.

Table 2.9. Clergy Political Ideology with Connections to 1998 Clergy Political Activity

	% Most Liberal	% Liberal	% Moderate	% Conservative	% Most Conservative
ELCA	7.1	35.4	42.3	13.8	1.4
1998 mean number of clergy political activities	7.5	5.2	4.3	4.4	4.4
Episcopal	12.5	38.6	30.0	13.6	5.2
1998 mean number of clergy political activities	6.7	5.3	4.0	3.7	3.7

Source: 1998 ELCA/Episcopal Church Clergy Study. Number of cases varies.

Table 2.10.   Clergy Partisan Identification with Connections to 1998 Clergy Political Activity

	% Strong Dem.	% Weak Dem.	% Leaning Dem.	% Independent	% Leaning GOP	% Weak GOP	% Strong GOP
ELCA	33.3	19.1	16.1	5.8	5.8	9.6	10.3
1998 mean number of clergy political activities	5.9	4.5	4.3	3.7	4.7	4.4	4.2
Episcopal	40.4	16.7	11.2	4.4	5.5	11.3	10.6
1998 mean number of clergy political activities	5.3	5.0	4.9	4.5	4.0	3.7	4.0

Source: 1998 ELCA/Episcopal Church Clergy Study. Number of cases varies.

The ideological patterns found in table 2.9 correspond to the Democratic-leaning party identification patterns found in table 2.10. Two in five Episcopal clergy and one in three ELCA clergy classify themselves as strong Democrats, while just over one-quarter of ELCA and Episcopal clergy are Republicans. Overall, our sample clergy are about two-thirds Democratic or leaning Democratic, with very few self-identified political independents. Table 2.10 shows again that political activity levels correlate with partisanship, in general, *the more Democratic an ELCA or Episcopal clergyperson is, the more she engages in political activity.*

Over two-thirds of sample clergy voted for President Clinton in the 1996 presidential election, as shown in figure 2.4, and roughly the same percentage voted or planned to vote for Democratic U.S. House candidates in 1998. Sample clergy were far less likely to vote for an independent or third-party candidate (5 percent or less did so for president in 1996 or U.S. House in 1998), which mirrors the prevailing finding that third candidates receive more votes from secular Americans (Gilbert et al. 1999). Nearly all responding clergy voted or planned to vote in these elections.

The Clergy–Congregation Political Divide

How do these ideology, partisanship, and voting patterns relate to the views and actions of ELCA and Episcopal congregation members? Existing research has shown that Episcopalians nationwide tend to vote Republican

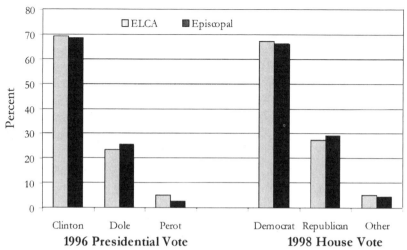

1996 Presidential Vote   **1998 House Vote**

Figure 2.4.   1996 Clergy Presidential Voting and 1998 U.S. House Voting
Source: 1998 ELCA/Episcopal Church Clergy Study.

and ELCA Lutherans tend to lean Republican, though less so in the upper Midwest (Wald 1997). The clergy who responded to our survey obviously do not fit the patterns demonstrated by their congregants.

Figure 2.5 shows the political divide between clergy and congregation in the ELCA and Episcopal Church. We asked clergy to estimate how a

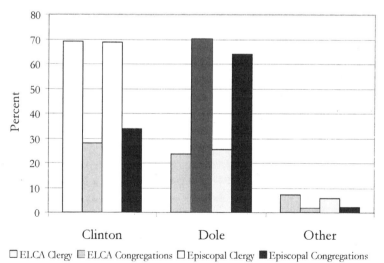

□ ELCA Clergy ▨ ELCA Congregations □ Episcopal Clergy ■ Episcopal Congregations

Figure 2.5.   Clergy and Clergy Perceptions of the Congregation Majority Vote in the 1996 Presidential Contest
Source: 1998 ELCA/Episcopal Church Clergy Study.

majority of their congregation voted for president in 1996. A majority of con-gregation members in over two-thirds of sample clergy congregations voted Republican for president in 1996. ELCA congregations were slightly more Republican in both elections than Episcopal congregations.

Figure 2.6 further explores this political divide. Clergy were asked to compare their political views with those of their members. Sixty percent of Episcopal clergy and 68 percent of ELCA pastors believed their own political views to be more liberal than the views of their congregants. Over 30 percent of Episcopal clergy and twenty-five percent of ELCA clergy felt their political views matched the congregation's, while less than 10 percent saw themselves as more politically conservative than their congregations.

These findings reveal something important about the congregational contexts in which our sample clergy work. *Most ELCA and Episcopal clergy can expect most of their members to disagree with their political stance.* In such a situation, would a clergyperson be more or less likely to discuss her opinions in worship or some other public setting? At first glance, the answer would appear to be less likely—a concern for keeping one's job could mute the clergyperson's willingness to say what she thinks. But job security is not the only consideration clergy have. Indeed, it is both likely and typical that the *religious or theological interpretations* presented by clergy to parishioners are meant to challenge parishioner beliefs and comfort levels. Mainline Protes-

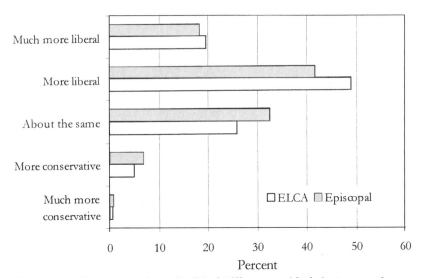

Figure 2.6.   Clergy Perceptions of Political Differences with Their Congregations
Source: 1998 ELCA/Episcopal Church Clergy Study.

tant preaching has the potential to be profoundly countercultural, especially when gospel lessons about the dilemmas of wealth are preached to relatively affluent audiences, or when Jesus' pacifism is held up as a model in times of war. In other words, clergy may feel more compelled to present their political views if those views conflict with members' beliefs, and especially so if clergy discern their political views to be in small or large degrees derived from their theological convictions. This compulsion to exercise a prophetic voice has its limits; as we will see in future chapters, the political divide seems to lead ELCA and Episcopal clergy to prefer civic mobilization and issue advocacy rather than partisan politics within their congregations.

These ideas are worthy of further exploration. In the empirical chapters (chapters 3–9), we will examine how perceived congregational approval of political actions affects clergy actions, in concert with other factors that lead to more or less clergy political activity.

Opinions on Public Policy Issues

In addition to questions about political ideology and behavior, we asked clergy opinions about several public policy issues. The issues chosen correspond closely to the topics that clergy reported speaking publicly about in 1998. Respondents could agree, disagree, or choose a neutral position on each issue, and the strength of agreement or disagreement was also ascertained.

Table 2.11 displays the percentage of ELCA and Episcopal clergy who *agree* with each statement (strongly or not strongly categories are combined). Agreement levels and rankings for ELCA and Episcopal clergy are nearly identical. The results show that our sample clergy again lean toward the liberal or Democratic end of the U.S. political spectrum. Large percentages of clergy agree with equal rights regardless of sexual orientation, gun control, environmental protection, and government action to solve social problems. Majorities of our sample clergy also favor national health insurance, the abolition of capital punishment, and special government help for African Americans and other minorities. At the bottom end of table 2.11, most sample clergy are opposed to more conservative or Republican positions on public school prayer, increased spending for national defense, greater privatization of government services, and using the federal budget surplus for tax cuts. Sample clergy are also strongly opposed to prohibiting abortion except to save the life of the mother. Overall, the percentages in table 2.11 show consistency with moderate to liberal views on most political and social issues among sample ELCA and Episcopal clergy.

Table 2.11.   The Political Opinions of ELCA and Episcopal Church Clergy

Variable	ELCA % Agree	Episcopal % Agree
Homosexuals should have all the same rights and privileges as other American citizens.	82.8	86.6
Public policy should discourage ownership and use of handguns.	72.7	73.9
More environmental protection is needed, even if it raises prices or cuts jobs.	71.2	74.2
The federal government should do more to solve social problems such as unemployment and poverty.	64.6	68.6
We need government-sponsored national health insurance so that everyone can get adequate medical care.	64.0	70.3
Capital punishment should be abolished.	59.7	68.2
Recent welfare reform laws are too harsh and hurt children.	52.6	60.7
Blacks and other minorities need special government help to achieve an equal place in America.	51.1	56.4
We need the ERA to protect women's rights.	42.5	48.0
The government should give tax credits for tuition paid by parents of students in private and parochial schools.	35.1	35.5
We need a federal law or amendment to prohibit all abortion unless necessary to save the life of the mother.	25.6	20.7
The impending budget surplus should be used to give citizens a tax cut.	21.5	21.5
Government is providing too many services which should be left to private enterprise.	21.2	21.4
We need a federal law or amendment to permit prayer as a regular exercise in schools.	10.1	16.3
The U.S. should spend more on the military and defense.	8.0	12.3

Source: 1998 ELCA/Episcopal Church Clergy Study. Number of cases varies.

Connections between Political Views and Political Activity

We also wished to see whether specific forms of political activity are related to clergy attitudes on public policy issues discussed above. To do so, we tested statistically whether the average political activity levels of the "agree" and "disagree" groups differ on the fifteen policy issues listed in table 2.11—whether clergy are motivated to more (or less) political action based on their public policy stances. Our nineteen possible political activities are divided into six different categories—public speech, church-based organizing of discussion or action groups, local political participation, electoral activities, contacting public officials, and unconventional activities such as marching or protesting (appendix A specifies the activities included in each category).

The results can be summarized in two ways. First, we can assess for which activity types issue-based motivations are most pronounced. The results show clearly that public speech is motivated by disagreement on nearly every issue (13 of 15); church-based organizing and local participation are motivated by disagreements on twelve of the fifteen issues presented. In each case, clergy on the liberal side of the issues participate more frequently. Election activities are least affected by issue stances; this indicates that clergy electoral activity does not depend only on the importance of the issue to clergy and that there are fewer differences in electoral activity levels between liberal and conservative clergy—topics we take up in detail in chapter 6.

Second, we can assess what issues appear to have the greatest separation in activity levels across activities. The results show that issue stances on equal rights for women, welfare reform, tax credits for private school tuition, government assistance to African Americans, and national health insurance all motivate each of the six forms of political activity. *For all of these issues, politically liberal clergy engage in more political activities than conservative clergy.* On all other issues, save defense spending and the question of equal rights for gays and lesbians, we find significant relationships between specific forms of political activity and the issue stances of clergy. Objections to defense spending lead to more public speech by liberal clergy, but attitudes on equal rights for gays and lesbians do not relate to any specific political activity type.

These findings demonstrate that ELCA and Episcopal clergy have the capacity to match their political views with appropriate and potentially effective forms of political activity. Clergy will talk about almost any public policy issue of interest; they will work within their churches and communities to build awareness (and possibly to change minds) on many issues of interest; they are willing to contact public officials to discuss numerous public policy ideas; and in many cases they view marching, protesting, or committing acts of civil disobedience as appropriate ways to make their point on hot-button issues. Electoral politics emerges as the least desirable outlet, and the outlet least likely to distinguish politically liberal from politically conservative clergy. Electoral politics also happens to be the place where a clergyperson's status inside and outside the church matters least in terms of personal influence, or where this status carries the most professional and personal risks when connected to a candidate or partisan position.

CONCLUSION

This broad overview of ELCA and Episcopal clergy politics has suggested several fruitful avenues for further exploration. We will say more about these types of relationships in the chapters to follow. Emerging from this chapter's overview of clergy political beliefs and behaviors, first and foremost, is that ELCA and Episcopal clergy are interested and active in political affairs, and many wish they could be even more active. Our sample clergy also desire more action by their denominations on social and political issues. Today's ELCA and Episcopal clergy are more politically active than clergy ordained before the 1960s; our evidence suggests that political engagement, rather than detachment, is now the norm for clergy in these two churches.

The political interest and activity levels of sample ELCA and Episcopal clergy have a definite liberal inclination. Our sample clergy are solidly Democratic in their voting patterns and socially and theologically liberal in outlook. This leads to an emphasis on social justice issues in public speech, and a broad willingness to assert personal viewpoints—grounded in scripture as well as personal beliefs—in sermons and other public venues. Most important, clergy express these liberal, Democratic political tendencies in congregational environments that likely oppose such views, and we have evidence to show that clergy in such environments are *more* likely to express their views and to be politically active.

Finally, the evidence presented in chapter 2 shows our sample clergy are very likely to engage in civic political activities—urging registration and voting, organizing groups to learn and study social and political issues, sparking conversation on topics that are significant to the congregation and local community. Clergy recognize the potential they have to influence their membership, but they use this tool carefully in light of the risks involved.

The question of how the congregation and local environment affect the political choices clergy make must now be considered in detail. Chapter 3 will examine how congregations assist or impede clergy political activity, and Chapter 4 will explore how characteristics of the local community relate to clergy choices about political engagement. The findings from these chapters will then inform a deeper analysis of clergy politics and political activity in the remainder of the book.

NOTE

1. Our survey was sent to Episcopal priests and deacons; no bishops were included because they tend not to have regular duties in one parish. As readers will have noted by now, we use the general term *clergy* to refer to all ordained people in this study—Episcopal priests and deacons, as well as ELCA pastors.

3

CONGREGATIONAL RESOURCES FOR CLERGY POLITICAL ACTION

As already noted, since the 1950s studies of clergy political behavior have primarily emphasized its theological roots (Guth et al. 1997; Hadden 1969; Jelen 1993; Lenski 1961; Stark et al. 1971). The role of the congregation has not been ignored, but it has also not occupied a central theoretical role in shaping social scientific theories of clergy political action. Stark et al. (1971), for instance, do not even mention the effects of the congregation; instead, they develop an understanding of the "wayward clergy" by resorting to claims about their otherworldliness.

One significant exception does exist, however, and stands in sharp contrast to the theological thrust of other researchers. Campbell and Pettigrew (1959), investigating the political activism of Little Rock clergy during the height of integration tensions in the late 1950s, concluded that congregational support was the most significant influence on whether clergy chose to speak out and take political action. This focus on congregation-based factors affecting clergy political behavior has reemerged in recent years, principally through the work of Laura Olson and colleagues. Studying the effects of urban contexts (Olson 2000) as well as neighborhood and congregational contexts (Crawford and Olson 2001b; Olson 2000), this contemporary research has demonstrated that aspects of clergy's social context—the environment in which clergy live and work, inside and outside the church—are significant indicators of and motivators for political activity (see also Djupe 1997; Huckfeldt and Sprague 1995; Gilbert 1993; Jelen 1992; Wald, Owen, and Hill 1988, 1990).

In this chapter, we explore in depth the congregation's role in shaping clergy political action by analyzing the *resources, inspirations, and constraints* that the congregation provides for clergy. The results we found restore and clarify the fundamental role that clergy–congregation relationships play in structuring if, how, and why clergy engage in the political process. Previous researchers did not dwell on the effect of the congregation because it was typically conceived as a hindrance to clergy making their views known. Drawing on the long-standing finding that mainline Protestant clergy are often more liberal than their congregations, a lack of political sermons, for instance, could be explained simply as the result of member opposition. Therefore, congregational approval of clergy activity has often been treated merely as a control variable and not given much extended consideration.

Although the ideological divide between clergy and congregation is often significant, the relationship between clergy and congregation is not always antagonistic when it comes to politics and, under certain conditions, *congregation–clergy ideological differences may drive greater clergy political activity.* The congregation sometimes opposes, sometimes demands, and sometimes is unaware of clergy political action. At times the needs and beliefs of the congregation can dominate the agenda and political activism of clergy. Olson (2000) convincingly demonstrates how clergy in churches with members of high socioeconomic status become more politically active to address the material needs of their congregants and communities.

In chapter 3 we seek to enrich the present understanding of the clergy–congregation relationship. Congregational approval is not a constant, negative influence on clergy and should not be treated as such. We investigate the systematic variations in congregational approval and the diverse ways in which the congregation can shape the political participation of clergy. Our sample of ELCA and Episcopal Church clergy offers a diverse range of clergy attitudes and political activity levels, as well as sample clergy work in a broad variety of congregational settings. These clergy and their congregations thus constitute a good test group to investigate the claims we make about how congregational resources shape clergy political activity.

In the following sections, we examine the primary ways in which the political behavior of clergy is affected by various facets of the clergy-congregation relationship. We test for the salience of numerous congregational characteristics in four areas: *church structural components* (including church size, involvement of members in church groups, denominational affiliation, the brand loyalty of the membership), *clergy–congregation political relations* (approval of clergy political action, agreement on politics), *clergy personal attributes* (gender, education, years in the ministry, tenure at present church), and *congregational factors* (internal political unity, type of community, status in the community). In focusing on the effects of the congregation, we are most interested in explaining how congregational factors affect clergy political activity. Thus we will structure the discussion around how clergy consider possible political activities and how the congregation affects what political activity clergy choose to engage in.

A VIEW FROM THE PULPIT

We begin by asking clergy what factors motivate their political activity. We presented sample clergy with eight possible factors and asked whether each encourages or discourages their political activity. Table 3.1 summarizes these results. The key factors motivating clergy political activity are overwhelmingly personal—over 80 percent of sample clergy report that their personal theological and political beliefs encourage their political activity, and less than 5 percent are discouraged by such beliefs. Although personal motivators are not the primary factors of interest in this chapter, as we saw in chapter 2, these results demonstrate that *the vast majority of our sample ELCA and Episcopal clergy see political activity as something they want to do.*

How do influences from the congregation pull or push clergy to or away from political activity? Three such items appear in table 3.1: the duties of the clergy position, attitudes of the congregation, and reactions of potential members (boldface items in the table). Clergy rank the duties of their position as the third most encouraging factor (42.6 percent) but also as the most discouraging factor (28.5 percent). Duties—those actions a clergyperson must carry out as part of her job—affect clergy political activity personally and through the congregation. The latter aspect—what the congregation expects of the clergyperson as part of her official duties—may

Table 3.1.   Clergy Self-Estimates of What Motivates Their Political Activity

Variable	% Encourage	% Neutral	% Discourage
My own theological beliefs	85.7	9.2	5.0
My own political beliefs	81.9	13.7	4.2
Duties of my position	**42.6**	**28.8**	**28.5**
Norms/culture of my denomination	41.7	43.8	14.5
Attitudes of denominational leaders	33.5	57.3	9.2
Attitudes of other clergy	29.3	61.9	8.7
Attitudes of my congregation	**22.4**	**54.3**	**23.2**
Reactions of potential members	**11.2**	**71.6**	**17.2**

Source: 1998 ELCA/Episcopal Church Clergy Study. Number of cases varies.
Note: **Bold type** indicates a congregational influence.

include political activity, an idea we take up in succeeding chapters. The high negative rating reflects a more personal reaction by our respondents; after planning and leading services, supervising a staff, and visiting parishioners, many ELCA and Episcopal clergy simply perceive little time for "extra" activities related to politics.

We find similar patterns with the two other congregational factors in table 3.1. Attitudes of the congregation and reactions of potential members are the two least encouraging and the second and third most discouraging factors motivating clergy political activity. While the percentages in each category are relatively low, table 3.1 provides some evidence for the traditional research conclusion that congregational attitudes restrain clergy political activity. However, seven in ten sample clergy give a neutral rating to reactions of potential members, and just over half are neutral on how attitudes of the congregation influence their political activity. On the whole, then, *far more factors encourage than discourage clergy political activity*, and congregational factors have mixed effects that on balance tilt toward encouraging clergy political activity.

Table 3.1 makes clear that while our sample clergy are predisposed to some involvement in politics, their congregations and surrounding communities are not sold on the idea, though they are not always discouraging. If a predisposition or interest in politics is not enough to result in political activity, which has been shown to require some external stimulus (Verba, Schlozman, and Brady 1995), then the rather quiescent context in which these clergy live and work can be significant. Only a few clergy suggested that congregational members encouraged them to preach more about topical issues such as gambling or commitment. Certainly denominations that are more politically charged demand more political activity by clergy. Therefore we need to examine the needs for, barriers against, and demands for clergy action within these denominations.

First, we analyze how the encouragement or discouragement clergy perceive from their congregations and church duties (from table 3.1) relate to actual clergy political activity. Table 3.2 shows how often sample clergy participated in nineteen different political activities in 1998 (previously presented in table 2.6), and it displays the *increase in frequency* for each activity when clergy perceive *attitudes encouraging their political activity* from their congregation and from the duties of their position. The table shows that every political activity is performed more often when clergy believe their duties encourage clergy political activity in general, and when clergy believe the attitudes of their congregation encourage political activity in general.

The specific patterns of political activities encouraged by the congregation's attitudes differ from the duties of the clergy position. *Encouraging*

Table 3.2.   The Effect of Encouraging Congregational Attitudes and Congregational Duties on Clergy Political Activity

Political Activities	Percent Increase in Activity Related to Encouraging Congregational Attitudes	Percent Increase in Activity Related to Encouraging Congregational Duties
Publicly take a stand on an issue	16.9	8.2
Contact public official	12.6	11.3
Urge congregation to register and vote	10.7	6.6
Organize a church social action group	9.8	8.3
Active in a community group	9.8	11.1
Organize a church political discussion group	9.7	5.0
Publicly endorse a candidate	9.3	7.4
Write a letter to the editor	9.2	8.9
Take an issue stand while preaching	8.8	4.3
Contribute to party, PAC, candidate	7.5	8.5
Active in a national political group	6.8	7.3
Actively campaign	6.2	4.7
Active on a local board or council	4.1	5.5
Publicly pray for candidates	3.6	6.5
Endorse a candidate while preaching	2.5	1.3
Participate in a protest march	2.5	5.3
Engage in civil disobedience	1.9	1.2
Serve on a local clergy council	1.1	2.6
Publicly offer prayer on an issue	1.0	6.9
Overall Mean =	7.1	6.4

Source: 1998 ELCA/Episcopal Church Clergy Study. Number of cases varies.

congregational attitudes bring more public political engagement by the clergy. Six of the nine activities with the highest percentage increase due to congregational encouragement (middle column) are public activities—taking a public stand on a policy issue, urging members to register and vote, organizing social action and political discussion groups in the congregation, publicly endorsing a candidate, and taking an issue stance while preaching. The other three activities with high percentage increases—contacting public officials, being active in a community group, and contributing money to a candidate or party—are generally private acts, although the first two may well involve acknowledgment of or attention to the clergyperson's occupation and church affiliation.

Encouragement based on the duties of the clergyperson's position, on the other hand, leads to increases in political activity that clergy often perform alone or in private: contacting a public official, being active in a community group, writing a letter to the editor, and making a campaign contribution. Note that encouragement from job duties does *not* lead clergy to far higher rates of urging registration and voting, or of organizing a church-based political discussion group. Most of the activities encouraged by the clergyperson's job duties are done *outside* the church walls but are closely tied to the civic skills and resources clergy develop as part of their work. Encouragement from the duties of the clergyperson's position—which may include time, money, and a mission to engage social issues—allows clergy to explore and engage their own political preferences.

The evidence from the first two tables in this chapter suggests that the pattern of political activities clergy undertake when supported by encouraging congregational attitudes fits with a *representative* role for clergy. With a receptive congregation, clergy can organize within the church, express their political views publicly, and take their activism into the public square. When clergy feel encouraged by their job duties, they tend to exercise their professionally developed civic skills—contacting, letter writing, organizing, leading, and speaking out in public on political matters.

Instead of understanding clergy goals as distinct from or opposed to the congregation's preferences, therefore, we must reorient our thinking to reflect an understanding of clergy as *organizational actors*. While clergy function in politics like ordinary citizens with their own viewpoints, the political activity of clergy is generated and channeled by the nature of their job and the support they receive from members of the congregation. One Episcopal priest expressed how this relationship relates to political action: "As my parish moves out of a major transition and becomes more healthy, the issue of involvement in politics and social action grows in importance." At times, clergy are also expected to act on behalf of the church as an institution and as a group of citizens with its own distinctive needs. This understanding helps us to see that under certain conditions, and beyond political agreement, clergy can mobilize congregants to participate in politics and community affairs, as well as to represent the church directly to government.

THE NATURE AND EFFECTS OF CHURCH–CLERGY IDEOLOGICAL DIFFERENCES

The decline in membership in mainline Protestant churches since the late 1960s is usually linked in some way to the political divide between clergy and their churches (Hadden 1969; Quinley 1974; Reichley 1985; Roof and McKinney 1987; Wuthnow 1988). Members often disagree with clergy's political views or feel that politics detracts from the pastoral duties clergy are paid to provide (Djupe and Gilbert 2002). Since this relationship has been so important to comprehending the political activism of clergy, especially mainline Protestant clergy, we will probe the nature of ideological differences further. To do so we must specify how clergy and their congregations differ on the major political issues facing the United States and how these differences affect clergy political engagement.

Table 3.3 displays the positions of ELCA and Episcopal sample clergy on several public policy issues. Clergy views tend to be clear; on twelve of the fifteen issues, over 60 percent of clergy opinions lie on one side or the other. More than 70 percent of sample clergy support equal rights for gays and lesbians, gun control policies, and environmental protection; less than 30 percent support prohibiting abortion, privatizing more government services, using the federal budget surplus for tax cuts, spending more on national defense, and instituting prayer in public schools. No strong consensus exists on three issues—whether the 1996 welfare reforms are too harsh, whether blacks and other minorities need special government help, and whether the Equal Rights Amendment is needed.[1]

The second and third columns of table 3.3 show sample clergy perceptions of how a majority of their congregation feels about these issue statements, displaying percentages of perceived congregational agreement and neutrality. On only two of the issues do a majority of clergy perceive majority agreement from their congregations—using the federal budget surplus for tax cuts and favoring greater privatization of government services. On many issues, large numbers of clergy perceive a majority of their congregation as neutral; this could mean that congregations are divided on the issue or that clergy do not know enough about their congregation's opinions to judge. In exploring this point further, we found that more politically interested clergy are just as likely to say their churches are "neutral" on issues than less politically interested clergy. This suggests lack of clergy political awareness does not lead to perceptions of congregational neutrality. We also discovered that clergy who report having a politically divided church are not more likely to perceive congregational neutrality, which suggests that a neutral rating by clergy does not necessarily indicate a divided congregation. Neutral ratings thus appear to stem from infrequent discussion of the issue in question, lack of strong congregational opinion, and/or not enough information for clergy to render a judgment about the congregation's views.

We investigate the relationship between clergy and perceived congregation majority opinions on these issues in table 3.4, which reports the mean difference between the clergy and the perceived congregation majority on each

Table 3.3. Agreement of Clergy and Perceived Congregational Agreement with Public Policy Issue Positions

Variable	Clergy: % Agree	Congregation: % Agree	Congregation: % Neutral
Homosexuals should have all the same rights and privileges as other American citizens.	84.4	42.0	28.2
Public policy should discourage ownership and use of handguns.	72.9	26.2	32.2
More environmental protection is needed, even if it raises prices or cuts jobs.	72.5	20.4	40.8
The federal government should do more to solve social problems such as unemployment and poverty.	66.6	30.0	32.8
We need government-sponsored national health insurance so that everyone can get adequate medical care	66.5	24.2	39.5
Capital punishment should be abolished.	63.1	14.9	33.8
Recent welfare reform laws are too harsh and hurt children.	55.7	21.2	44.5
Blacks and other minorities need special government help to achieve an equal place in America.	53.2	13.2	32.9
We need the ERA to protect women's rights.	44.7	19.3	46.1
The government should give tax credits for tuition paid by parents of students in private and parochial schools.	35.3	26.4	42.5
We need a federal law or amendment to prohibit all abortion unless necessary to save the life of the mother.	24.0	27.3	33.6
Government is providing too many services which should be left to private enterprise.	21.6	47.6	32.0
The impending budget surplus should be used to give citizens a tax cut.	21.5	51.5	36.8
We need a federal law or amendment to permit prayer as a regular exercise in schools.	12.7	35.0	30.4
The U.S. should spend more on the military and defense.	9.8	31.3	43.7

Source: 1998 ELCA/Episcopal Church Clergy Study. Number of cases varies.
Note: "Percent Agree" represents the combined scores of those who "strongly agree" and "agree" with the statement.

Table 3.4. Average Difference, Spread, and Correlation of Clergy and Congregation Political Opinions

Variable	Mean Difference in Clergy–Church Opinions	Standard Deviation of Difference	Correlation of Clergy and Congregation Opinions
Capital punishment should be abolished.	1.14	1.37	0.28
Homosexuals should have all the same rights and privileges as other American citizens.	1.08	1.12	0.44
More environmental protection is needed, even if it raises prices or cuts jobs.	1.06	1.73	0.14
Public policy should discourage ownership and use of handguns.	1.04	1.34	0.33
The impending budget surplus should be used to give citizens a tax cut.	0.98	1.17	0.35
We need a federal law or amendment to permit prayer as a regular exercise in schools.	0.97	1.18	0.40
The U.S. should spend more on the military and defense.	0.91	1.63	0.24
We need government-sponsored national health insurance so that everyone can get adequate medical care.	0.85	1.36	0.41
Blacks and other minorities need special government help to achieve an equal place in America.	0.81	1.29	0.36
Government is providing too many services which should be left to private enterprise.	0.75	1.21	0.27
The federal government should do more to solve social problems such as unemployment and poverty.	0.73	1.22	0.36
Recent welfare reform laws are too harsh and hurt children.	0.65	1.03	0.46
We need a federal law or amendment to prohibit all abortion unless necessary to save the life of the mother.	0.53	1.17	0.54
We need the ERA to protect women's rights.	0.44	1.06	0.53
The government should give tax credits for tuition paid by parents of students in private and parochial schools.	0.14	1.12	0.51

Source: 1998 ELCA/Episcopal Church Clergy Study. Number of cases varies.
Note: Some variables have been recoded so that a positive mean indicates the clergy are more liberal than their congregations. All correlations are significant at the $p < 0.01$ level.

issue. This difference is at least one-half point (on a five-point scale) for thirteen of the fifteen issues; the difference is one point or more for six issues. *Clergy hold more liberal views than their congregations on every issue.* The standard deviations (middle column), which measure the average spread of opinions, indicate that two-thirds of sample clergy are somewhere between having the same opinion as their congregational majority and being over two points more liberal. On only two issues do clergy and their congregations essentially agree—equal rights for women (support) and tax credits for private school tuition (mix of mild support and opposition).

Table 3.4 also presents the correlations between clergy opinions and perceived congregational majority opinions on each issue (right column). The correlations show primarily strong correspondence between clergy opinions and perceived congregational issue positions (see appendix B for a full discussion of how to interpret correlations). These correlations also reveal that while these ELCA and Episcopal clergy are almost uniformly more liberal than their congregations, clergy in conservative congregations are not as liberal as clergy serving liberal churches. These results are in part artifacts of congregational selection of their clergy staff. However, they likely reflect a perception bias from the clergy, who may tend to rate their congregations closer to their own views. This debate cannot be settled for certain without objective data from congregation members.

THE NATURE OF CONGREGATIONAL SUPPORT
FOR CLERGY POLITICAL ACTION

For scholars studying clergy politics, the most commonly utilized connection between clergy and their congregations is the congregation's approval of clergy political activity. There are three general hypotheses about why congregations would *not* support their clergy becoming involved in politics: first, because the political activity is deemed inappropriate for clergy to pursue, perhaps due to congregational beliefs about the proper mixing of church and state; second, because the congregation disagrees with clergy political views; and third, because engaging in political activity would detract from the clergyperson's ability to fulfill her main task—meeting the religious needs of the congregation. As one Episcopal priest commented, "there is another reason why I seldom preach about politics: these people need to hear how the gospel touches them and how it bears on their daily lives." The analysis in this section will address some additional explanatory factors to complement this existing set of hypotheses.

To begin, we utilize a set of questions asking about clergy approval and perceived congregational approval of fifteen different political activities. This question series was examined previously (see table 2.6); sample clergy were asked about the general *appropriateness* of these activities: "Do you approve of ministers participating in these ways? Would your congregation?" Note that clergy are not asked to discern how a majority of their congregation would feel, as in the policy issue statements. This series of questions allows us to evaluate how our sample clergy feel about clergy political activity *in general* and how these attitudes relate both to perceived congregational approval of the same activities and to *actual* clergy political activity levels reported in 1998. We found very little difference between ELCA and Episcopal clergy and congregations on these measures, and thus we present results for both sets of clergy combined.

Table 3.5.   Clergy and Perceived Congregational Approval of Clergy Political Action

Variable	Percent of Clergy Approving of the Activity	Rank of Clergy Approving of the Activity	Percent of Congregation Approving of the Activity	Rank of Congregation Approving of the Activity
Contact public officials	89.0	1	67.7	3
Urge church to register and vote	87.2	2	83.4	1
Publicly take a stand on an issue	81.4	3	50.8	5
Publicly offer prayer on an issue	80.9	4	69.0	2
Organize a study group in church	77.9	5	63.9	4
Participate in a protest march	68.8	6	27.9	10
Contribute money to party, PAC, candidate	64.8	7	25.7	11
Take a stand on an issue while preaching	63.6	8	38.0	6
Join a national group	60.3	9	35.4	8
Organize a social action group in church	57.0	10	37.2	7
Engage in civil disobedience	49.5	11	15.2	12
Publicly offer prayer for candidates	39.1	12	34.4	9
Actively campaign	35.5	13	12.0	13
Publicly endorse candidates	25.9	14	11.0	14
Endorse candidates while preaching	7.1	15	6.9	15

Source: 1998 ELCA/Episcopal Church Clergy Study. Number of cases varies.

Table 3.5 displays the percentage of clergy who approve ("strongly" and "not strongly" combined) of each political activity, the percentage perceived congregational approval of each, and 1–15 rankings (1 = most approved, 15 = least approved) for clergy and perceived congregational approval of the activities. There is a general congruence between the clergy and congregational rankings. The five most approved activities (over 75 percent clergy approval) are the same for the clergy and congregants, albeit in slightly different order: contacting public officials, urging the congregation to register and vote, publicly offering prayer on an issue, publicly taking a stand on an issue, and organizing a public affairs study group in the church. Direct partisan activity—campaigning, endorsing candidates in or outside the church—is clearly the least approved by clergy and their congregations.

It seems clear from this brief examination of rankings in table 3.5 what the preferred roles of ELCA and Episcopal clergy are in politics—clergy should get people involved but should not offer overtly partisan opinions whether acting as clergy or as private citizens. This pattern seems to conform to the perception of clergy as representatives who are enjoined from attempting to exert direct political influence and instead are encouraged to inform, mobilize, and represent.

Table 3.6 repeats the clergy and perceived congregational approval rankings of the fifteen political activities and adds three columns for further analysis of these responses. The first column reports the mean differences between clergy and perceived congregational approval of political activities (using the original 1–5 answer scale for each; see appendix A for coding details). Table 3.6 is organized from greatest mean difference to smallest, with positive values indicating that, on average, clergy approve of the act more than the congregation does.

The patterns in this column are not easy to discern. Some activities are strongly disapproved of by clergy and congregations (as perceived by clergy): public prayer for candidates and clergy endorsing candidates while preaching. The most approved acts and some of the most common acts tend to cluster at or below the overall average difference of one-half point—such as urging registration and voting, offering public prayer, and contacting public officials. But clergy and their congregations differ significantly on whether clergy should engage in unconventional activities such as protesting and civil disobedience. It is interesting to note that the high clergy–congregation gap for these unconventional activities is created by the high

Table 3.6. Average Difference and Correlation of Clergy and Congregation Approval of Clergy Political Action

Church Rank	Clergy Rank	Variable	Mean Clergy and Congregational Approval Difference	Correlation of Clergy and Congregation Approval	Percent of Congregtions Neutral in Approval
12	11	Engage in civil disobedience	0.99	0.49	23.4
10	6	Participate in a protest march	0.95	0.48	33.5
11	7	Contribute money to party, PAC, candidate	0.93	0.37	38.6
5	3	Publicly take a stand on an issue	0.72	0.47	22.6
8	9	Join a national group	0.68	0.53	46.2
13	13	Actively campaign	0.66	0.45	28.3
6	8	Take a stand on an issue while preaching	0.57	0.66	24.9
3	1	Contact public officials	0.52	0.47	21.7
7	10	Organize an action group in church	0.41	0.70	33.0
14	14	Publicly endorse candidates	0.38	0.59	20.4
4	5	Organize a study group in church	0.32	0.69	23.4
2	4	Publicly offer prayer on an issue	0.29	0.77	17.7
1	2	Urge church to register and vote	0.15	0.78	9.1
9	12	Publicly offer prayer for candidates	0.10	0.93	22.7
15	15	Endorse candidates while preaching	−0.02	0.70	5.6
		Overall average	0.51		

Source: 1998 ELCA/Episcopal Church Clergy Study. Number of cases varies.
Notes: The ranks signify the most approved of acts by clergy and their congregations in descending order—the most approved of act has the lowest ranking. The difference variable is calculated by subtracting congregation from clergy support: difference = (clergy approval) − (church approval). A positive mean indicates that the clergyperson approves more than the congregation. All correlations are significant at the $p < 0.01$ level; the correlations are calculated for approval of each activity by the clergy and congregation.

clergy approval of these actions, no doubt generated by the storied use of such strategies in the protest movements of several decades earlier. In fact clergy approval of these unconventional activities is strongly correlated with having an active social justice agenda.

The middle column of table 3.6 offers a different way to view the relationship of clergy approval to perceived congregational approval, using correlations between the two measures for each political activity. All correlations are significant and positive, indicating considerable congruence between clergy and congregation. The highest correlations are found at the bottom of the table, indicating again that our sample clergy perceive strong congregational agreement with their own perceptions of the appropriateness of several acts—public prayer on issues (acceptable) or for candidates (not very acceptable), and urging registration and voting (acceptable).

Table 3.6 also shows acts that clergy perceive the *least information* about congregation approval or disapproval. The percentage of clergy perceiving their congregations as neutral (last column) is a sign, as noted earlier, that clergy either have neutral congregations or do not have enough information to judge what their members believe. The pattern here is telling. Clergy perceive the most information (hence report the *lowest* perceived neutrality) from their congregations on activities that are obviously civic in nature (urging members to register and vote) or highly controversial (endorsing candidates while preaching). Clergy receive the most information on activities that rank either high or low in terms of clergy approval, and clergy receive decreasing information as the activity moves toward the middle of their approval rankings—protesting, joining a group, and contributing to campaigns. Some of these activities are private, and therefore clergy would receive little feedback or motivation from the congregation on them. Other activities, such as protesting and campaigning, are public acts, but a few clergy may participate at a safe distance from the church to avoid controversy.

Overall there is considerable diversity of opinion within the congregations served by our sample clergy. Some clergy work in churches whose members are perceived as strongly approving or strongly disapproving nearly every political action a clergyperson might take. But most clergy work in settings where overall congregational opinion of clergy political activity falls somewhere in the middle (mean perceived congregational approval of all activities = 3.06 on a 1–5 scale for ELCA clergy, 2.99 for Episcopal clergy). The measure of mean perceived congregational approval of clergy political activity has limited utility. The list of political activities clergy might pursue is varied, and lumping perceived congregational attitudes about all such activities into a mean score probably obscures our understanding of why congregations endorse or resist specific activities.

Nonetheless, a brief analysis of factors (statistical results not shown) affecting the mean perceived congregational view of clergy political activity reveals some intriguing patterns based on community and congregational characteristics, as well as clergy–congregation political relations (no clergy personal attributes are significant). For example, urban congregations are perceived to give significantly more approval to clergy political activity, while rural and southern churches are less supportive of ELCA clergy political activity. Congregations with a higher percentage of members involved in small groups are also perceived as more supportive of clergy political activity. Many clergy are involved in most activities sponsored by the church (many respondents wrote in "too many" or "all" when asked how many church groups they were involved with); social interaction between clergy and congregants builds credibility that clergy can expend on political action (Olson 1965) and generates a constituency that is supportive and may even make demands on clergy. We should not overlook the possibility that congregations with a high degree of involvement reflect a base of members in agreement. The degree to which members' political views fail to match official denominational positions, however, argues against a pure self-selection effect at work (Wald, Owen, and Hill 1988). Regardless, the positive effects of small group involvement, combined with the finding that clergy-congregation issues and ideological differences lead to less congregational approval of political activity, fits with our hypothesis that clergy more often move in synchronicity with their churches rather than in opposition to them.

Two additional measures affect mean perceived congregational approval of clergy political activity for Episcopal clergy only. Using questions comparing our sample clergy's congregation to other churches in their communities, we derived measures of isolation from the local community based on differing *beliefs* (theological views, political beliefs, minority membership, worship style, and amount of church activity) and isolation rooted in a lack of *activity* in the community (lower social status, less community involvement, and less political activity) (discussed at length in chapter 4). Activity isolation in Episcopal congregations leads to *less* congregational support for clergy political activity, while belief isolation leads to *greater* congregational support. When an Episcopal congregation can be considered a minority in its local community (which is often the case), even extensive community activity is less likely to be noticed, simply because the Episcopal presence is dwarfed numerically by neighboring churches. Belief isolation has a different impact; clergy may feel some pressure to make up for a representational deficit and hence congregations would wish clergy to speak for their distinctive religious views in public venues (Moore 1986; Morris 1984).

All these results demonstrate the salience of *location*—where the church is situated matters for what the church and its clergy do politically. A congregation's surrounding environment structures the composition of the congregation, the political culture of the area, and the opportunities for social and political action—all of which will shape how congregations view their clergy and how clergy feel about getting involved in politics. The traditional view—that congregational approval of clergy political involvement is driven by political disagreement and spiritual malnourishment—needs to make room for the salience of the other needs of congregations. Recent patterns of sustained and even increased levels of political action by mainline Protestant clergy suggest other forces at work. Our empirical analysis shows that congregational approval can flow from the social bonds forged between congregation members and clergy through church small groups and other avenues that bring ministers and members together.

THE POLITICAL IMPACT OF THE
CLERGY–CONGREGATION RELATIONSHIP

So far we have established that congregational approval of clergy political action is driven by the nature of the activity and how the activity corresponds to congregational perceptions of appropriate clergy political roles. We have also seen some evidence that the relationship of congregational approval to clergy activity depends on the status of the congregation in relation to its surrounding environment. Now we must examine whether these aspects of the congregation and clergy-congregation relationship substantively affect what clergy do—clergy approval of and engagement in various political activities, as well as clergy perceptions of their own political efficacy. We argue in this section that the necessary resources (public or private), target audience, and connection to governmental processes of the different political activities shape how congregants view each possible action and whether clergy feel empowered and possess the opportunity to engage in it.

Table 3.7 reproduces 1998 levels of clergy political activity for fifteen different acts (see table 2.6) and presents the correlation between the frequency of clergy engaging in each activity and perceived congregational approval of the activity. Performance of every activity is significantly related to congregational approval, suggesting that clergy agree with their members on

Table 3.7.   The Relationship between Clergy Political Action and Congregational Approval

Clergy Political Action	Percent of Clergy Engaging in Activity in the Past Year (1998)	Correlation of Clergy Action and Congregational Approval
Publicly offer prayer on an issue	55.8	0.268
Publicly take a stand on an issue	51.4	0.139
Take a stand on an issue while preaching	49.1	0.251
Urge church to register and vote	46.4	0.273
Contact public officials	39.8	0.174
Contribute money to a party, PAC, candidate	25.5	0.089
Organize an action group in church	23.8	0.235
Publicly offer prayer for candidates	20.5	0.399
Organize a study group in church	13.7	0.224
Join a national group	12.3	0.178
Publicly endorse candidates	11.3	0.161
Participate in a protest march	7.9	0.177
Actively campaign	6.1	0.113
Engage in civil disobedience	1.7	0.119
Endorse candidates while preaching	1.4	0.082

Source: 1998 ELCA/Episcopal Church Clergy Study. Number of cases varies.
Note: All correlations are significant at the $p < 0.01$ level.

occasion and can feel constrained by the amount of support offered by their members. There is considerable variation in the strength of the connection. Activities related to worship—public prayers on issues or for candidates and position taking while preaching—show the strongest relationship between congregational approval and clergy action, along with informational acts such as organizing study or action groups and urging registration and voting in the church.

In contrast, controversial activities and private activities have weaker relationships with congregational approval. Recall that according to table 3.5, contributing money was ranked by clergy as the seventh most approved activity (out of 15), but clergy ranked congregational approval of this activity eleventh. Contributing is the sixth most common political activity of clergy in 1998. There is a clear disjuncture here, no doubt driven by the private nature of the act and external mobilization by parties, candidates, and interest groups.

We focus next on the link between clergy–congregation opinion differences on issues and the average frequency that clergy report speaking publicly on the issue in question. These correlations and averages are presented

Table 3.8.   Correlations between Clergy-Congregation Opinion Differences and the Frequency of Clergy Speaking Out on the Issue during 1998

Clergy–Church Opinion Difference	Correlation with Clergy Addressing the Issue	Mean Frequency of Clergy Addressing the Issue
We need a federal law or amendment to prohibit all abortion unless necessary to save the life of the mother.	−0.24***	2.4
Capital punishment should be abolished.	−0.19***	2.4
More environmental protection is needed, even if it raises prices or cuts jobs.	−0.13***	3.3
Blacks and other minorities need special government help to achieve an equal place in America.	−0.11***	3.3
Homosexuals should have all the same rights and privileges as other American citizens.	−0.11***	2.5
The federal government should do more to solve social problems such as unemployment and poverty.	−0.09***	3.0
The U.S. should spend more on the military and defense.	−0.04*	2.0
We need a federal law or amendment to permit prayer as a regular exercise in schools.	−0.04*	2.2
The impending budget surplus should be used to give citizens a tax cut.	−0.01	2.0

Source: 1998 ELCA/Episcopal Church Clergy Study. Number of cases varies.
***$p < 0.01$; **$p < 0.05$; *$p < 0.10$
Note: A negative correlation suggests that a larger opinion difference drives down clergy speech.

in table 3.8. For the congregation to have an effect on the amount of clergy speech, clergy have to be aware of congregational opinions; media attention and denominational discussion of controversial issues would logically lead to greater congregational effects on clergy speech frequency. This is exactly what we find. The correlations for this selection of issues are significant (with one exception) and negative—*clergy speak less often about issues on which they have a large difference of opinion with their congregation.* Contentious issues such as abortion and capital punishment have the largest correlations, meaning that clergy speak about these issues infrequently (the mean frequency of 2.4 is closest to "rarely" on the speech frequency scale). Congregational effects are considerably weaker for less controversial issues and issues the clergy discussed very infrequently in 1998.

Finally, in table 3.9 we pull together the numerous explanatory factors utilized in this chapter to investigate their relationships to three dependent

Table 3.9.   Congregational Influences on Clergy's Efficacy, Political Activity, and Approval of Political Activity (bivariate correlations)

Variable	Clergy Capacity to Influence Church	Clergy Average Frequency of Congregation-Based Political Acts	Clergy Average Approval of Political Activity
Clergy–Congregation Tension			
Perceived congregational approval of clergy political activity	0.208***	0.326***	0.614***
Attitudes of my congregation discourage action	−0.169***	−0.136***	−0.079***
Attitudes of potential members discourage action	−0.120***	−0.140***	−0.098***
Church–clergy ideological differences	−0.017	0.066***	0.199***
Clergy Attributes			
The duties of my position discourage action	−0.127***	−0.104***	−0.150***
Years in the ministry	−0.099***	0.168***	−0.036
Tenure length at present church	−0.018	0.077***	−0.085***
Episcopal clergy	0.070***	0.091***	0.013
Congregational Characteristics			
Congregation is theologically divided	−0.104***	0.008	0.045*
Congregation is politically divided	−0.063***	0.018	0.015
Percent of church involved in groups, activities	0.058***	0.073***	0.024
Church size	0.005	0.063***	−0.001
Congregation–Community Relationship			
Belief isolation	0.058***	0.081***	0.095***
Activity isolation	−0.014	−0.029	−0.001

Source: 1998 ELCA/Episcopal Church Clergy Study. Number of cases varies.
***$p < 0.01$; **$p < 0.05$; *$p < 0.10$

variables: clergy political efficacy, the frequency of church-based clergy political activity (organizing political discussion groups and social action groups, urging members to register and vote), and general clergy approval of political activity. The explanatory factors in table 3.9 are divided into four categories: measures of tension between clergy and congregation, clergy personal attributes (including denomination to capture differences between ELCA and Episcopal clergy), congregational characteristics, and congregation–community relationships. Our analysis in table 3.9 is structured around these four sets of factors.

Clergy–Congregation Tension

The strongest and most consistent relationships driving clergy political behavior are direct political tensions between clergy and congregation. To evaluate these effects on clergy political efficacy, frequency of church-based political activity, and approval of political activity, we utilize four measures of tension: perceived congregational approval of political activity (previously discussed in table 3.5 and table 3.7), discouraging attitudes of the congregation toward clergy political activity (table 3.2), discouragement based on reactions of potential members (table 3.1), and general ideological differences between clergy and congregation as perceived by clergy.

Table 3.9 demonstrates that clergy who feel they have the support of their congregation are more politically efficacious, are more politically active, and strongly approve of political activity. Some of the latter relationship is surely due to a projection effect in which clergy assume their attitude matches the views of the congregation. However, if clergy had experienced disapproval from the congregation, it would surely register in considerations of these relationships.

The measures that ask clergy their opinion on whether congregational attitudes and the reactions of potential members discourage their political action also relate to decreased political efficacy, activity, and approval. To an extent, however, these relationships are misleading. Majorities of sample clergy were neutral on these points, which suggests they have little information about how their congregations feel and even less about what potential members might think. This is reflected in the effect of clergy–congregation opinion differences, which are not related to clergy efficacy but are positively related to activity and approval. Clergy seem to take seriously their prophetic mission to give voice to needs and beliefs not being heard. *But clergy are less politically active when they are in greater ideological agreement with their congregants.*

Clergy Attributes

Some of the direct conflict between clergy and their congregations is mitigated by clergy attributes such as tenure on the job, duties of the position, and denominational affiliation. For instance, one new pastor suggested that politics was not a high priority: "I have not been at this church that long and have other more immediate issues to address." But these factors are not always consistent predictors, and the direction of the relationships cannot be easily assumed. For example, clergy who have served more years in the ministry are more politically active but believe they have less capacity to influence their congregation. Clergy with longer service at their present church are' also more politically active in the church (though the relationship is weaker than that between years in the ministry and the frequency of political activity), but long-serving clergy are *less* approving of clergy political activity.

These results make more sense than might appear at first glance. Serving in a church is thought to allow clergy to build credit (Djupe 2001; Guth et al. 1997, 179), or political capital, that they can then expend on political activity. Table 3.9 shows this is exactly what occurs, even as clergy become more skeptical of political activity and of their own ability to affect congregational attitudes. Moreover, decreases in political efficacy, political activity, and clergy approval of political activity are also associated with clergy beliefs that the duties of their position discourage political action, indicating that clergy are busy people but also probably reflecting an underlying belief that politics and religion should be mixed with caution.

Table 3.9 also shows that Episcopal clergy are more efficacious and more politically active in church, though not more approving of political activity, than ELCA clergy. We have seen evidence previously that Episcopal clergy are more engaged in politics. The relationships observed here reflect both greater comfort among Episcopal clergy with political action and the belief isolation Episcopal congregations are more likely to witness, which as we have already seen leads to greater congregational support for Episcopal clergy political activity.

Congregational Characteristics

Clergy must be attuned to the internal dynamics of their congregations. Internal conflicts can be exposed and exacerbated by clergy political activity. Horror stories abound about congregations dividing over minor or major theological issues, splitting over political issues such as gay rights, and falling to pieces because of the actions of a pastor or other church official. Therefore, we would expect clergy to avoid politics when the congregation is divided. Table 3.9 shows that perceived theological and political divisions in the church reduce clergy political efficacy—it is obviously harder to persuade a divided group—but these same divisions *do not affect* the frequency of church-based clergy political activity. Interestingly, theological division also leads to higher clergy approval of political activity in general, while political divisions have no effect.

Table 3.9 also shows, not surprisingly, that larger churches have more church-based political activity. Large congregations simply have more capacity—more people, more resources, and often more visible concerns to tackle in urban neighborhoods—for undertaking political or social action, and large congregations also tend to have more than one pastor or priest to facilitate and participate in such activities. The fact that clergy in large churches do not approve more or have more efficacy provides further evidence that political action within churches is constituency based. Another way to view this relationship is through the effects of high member involvement in church groups and activities, which promotes more clergy efficacy and more political action in church. A supportive, organized congregation can promote, and sometimes demand, clergy to take political action whether clergy approve of it or not—neither church size nor group involvement levels affect clergy approval of activity.

Congregation–Community Relationship

In the United States, churches have always been an alternative institutional route to furthering the political desires and status of numerous groups (Finke and Stark 1992; Moore 1986). When political representation is lacking, churches can provide or build that political representation and assist in the development of social capital—civic skills, political acumen, and interpersonal trust—within their congregations (Djupe and Grant 2001; Leege 1988; Peterson 1992; Putnam 2000; Rosenstone and Hansen 1993). Undertaking such tasks requires some knowledge of the local community in which churches and members reside, especially if political activity includes electoral politics. Paralleling well-known political science findings (Finifter 1974; Key 1949), we thus expect that underrepresented groups—in our case, ELCA and Episcopal congregations with some form of minority status or isolation in their communities—will band together through available institutions and leaders (their churches and clergy) to magnify their voice and protect their interests.

To assess this hypothesis, we again utilize the measures of belief and activity isolation discussed earlier in this chapter. The churches judged by their clergy to be unlike their surroundings were more likely to be located in urban settings, while churches judged to be quite similar to their communities are largely in rural, northern areas. Table 3.9 shows that while activity isolation has no impact (simply doing less than one's neighbors does not alter clergy perceptions or activity levels), belief isolation has a significant effect on the variables of interest—leading to greater clergy political efficacy, more church-based political activity, and higher approval of clergy political activity. Therefore, *when the church constitutes a minority locally, clergy tend to act to fill the representation gap by becoming more active in politics and mobilizing the congregation to add its voice to the public sphere.* This is the basic dynamic that has driven African American clergy to become politically active, but we find it here, somewhat unexpectedly, for ELCA and Episcopal sample clergy.

CONCLUSION

In this chapter we have presented a wealth of data examining the relationship between ELCA and Episcopal clergy and their congregations in order to understand why clergy engage in political activity. Our analysis illuminates the subtle, multifaceted nature of this relationship and indicates that existing, straightforward theories about clergy–congregation interrelationships are not adequately specified.

Instead of merely thinking about the ramifications of disapproval for politically active clergy, we know that the political activities and roles clergy engage in result from a complex interplay of forces among clergy, congregation, and community. Clergy engage in political activity when they have personal and theological beliefs that suggest political activity is appropriate. Extended time in the ministry and at one church seems to teach clergy what levels and types of political activity are deemed appropriate by congregations, and how much activity is feasible given the time and energy constraints of the job. However, somewhat independently of these considerations, we find that clergy also take up political activity when their congregations are not well represented in their communities.

Congregations have differential effects on clergy behavior, depending on the type and visibility of the political activity as well as the issues involved. Our evidence shows convincingly that the relationships clergy build with congregations over time can promote or inhibit clergy and congregational political activity, and the political messages and actions of the clergy contribute to the health (or lack thereof) of this relationship in a dynamic process. As scholars of many religious traditions have noted, organized congregations can make demands of clergy and empower clergy to take further action, instead of merely acting as a brake on clergy activism.

It is clear from this discussion that context matters. Hence in the analyses to follow, it is imperative to keep in mind the need to examine specific participatory modes and issue specific activities whenever possible (Salisbury 1975). Incorporating these elements and performing more empirical analyses will no doubt improve our understanding of how clergy rely on and are deterred by congregational resources for political action. In chapter 4 we develop this understanding by considering community characteristics in greater detail, and in chapters 5–8 we utilize these findings to examine specific clergy political activities with more sophisticated methodological tools.

NOTE

1. The Equal Rights Amendment is a moot issue, probably accounting for the lukewarm support found. There is no evidence to suggest our sample clergy oppose equal rights for women, which almost all Americans support.

4

COMMUNITIES OF CONCERN:
THE CONTEXT OF CLERGY
POLITICAL ACTIVITY

Clergy live, work, and make political decisions within distinctive communities based on numerous attributes, including professional ties,
spiritual beliefs, geographical proximity, and common interests. But few
scholars have paid significant attention to whether and how these communities affect the political behavior of clergy, focusing instead on individual
(primarily theological) motivations for clergy politics. As our theoretical
ideas and empirical evidence in earlier chapters have intimated, we believe
firmly that one of the more important factors shaping the nature of a clergyperson's ministry and political activity is the *community in which the clergyperson lives and works.*

While clergy have personal goals for their ministry—conditioned by
their background, seminary training, and specific interests and beliefs—the
actual field practice of ministry usually must adapt to the wishes and needs
of the people found within and beyond the church walls. Members have
spiritual and personal needs that must be addressed. Congregational programs demand direction and leadership. Local organizations call on the clergyperson's time and energy in myriad ways—to attend Lions Club or Rotary meetings, preach at the ecumenical Thanksgiving service, or represent
the congregation at a civic gathering. All of these ministerial functions require the clergyperson to act in different ways using a diverse array of skills.
More important to the thrust of our argument, most of these activities offer opportunities for clergy to comprehend the cultural, political, and economic norms of the community—essential information if clergy wish to
pursue political agendas as part of their ministries and personal lives.

In this chapter we investigate the motivations and inspirations, as well
as the constraints and barriers, that arise from the character of the communities in which ELCA and Episcopal clergy minister. Do clergy respond to

the needs and opportunities found in the local community? How do pressures from their self-constituted communities complement and counter each other? Do these communities have an effect on clergy political beliefs and actions?

THE NATURE OF COMMUNITY FOR CLERGY

The first question to address is, What is community? In today's world the term clearly transcends geographic boundaries. Community thus has many different meanings and forms. Since no single measure can incorporate the multiple meanings of community, we adopt several measurement strategies. The primary distinction we make in constructing measures of the local community is between the *impersonal* and the *personal*—between the environments or *social contexts* and the *social networks* that clergy are involved in. Political scientists Robert Huckfeldt and John Sprague explain the difference:

> Contexts are structurally imposed while networks are individually constructed. Contexts are external to the individual even if the composition of the context depends on the makeup of the individuals contained within it. In contrast, networks represent the product of myriad choice made by people who compose the net, but choices that are circumscribed by the opportunities and constraints imposed by context. (1987, 1200)

We must also incorporate measures of non–geographic based communities, primarily in the form of group associations, whether professional (the denomination), political, or social. These forms of association have become central in building the social capital that undergirds American democracy (Putnam 2000; Wuthnow 1998).

Though a step removed from the daily lives of clergy, social contexts play a role in structuring their social and political choices. Numerous scholars have shown how the religious environment, measured by county concentrations of denominational membership, has an effect on religious commitment (Finke and Stark 1992), donations to political candidates (Green et al. 1996), vote choice (Gilbert 1993; Gilbert et al. 1999; Lopatto 1985), and party competition and majority party support (Djupe et al. 1997; Kleppner 1970). This research demonstrates conclusively that citizens take cues and seize opportunities for political action from the political, social, and economic makeup of their local environments. These cues and opportunities may include the stimuli from heightened party competition; the incidence of poverty, homelessness, and hunger; or a textbook controversy within a local school system. We will examine several aspects of the local environment for our sample clergy, using first the county as the unit of analysis and then the self-described and self-defined environments perceived by clergy.

THE RELIGIOUS ENVIRONMENT

In their seminal work on religious competition throughout U.S. history, sociologists Roger Finke and Rodney Stark (1992) find that successful churches place high demands on members and devote themselves to the spiritual needs of parishioners. They assert no role for political involvement in the maintenance and growth of religious organizations, but U.S. history indicates that political power may be at least incidental to religious success, and occasionally instrumental. Despite the historical separation of church and state, religious groups and government cannot help but interact on numerous fronts—local zoning ordinances, social service delivery guidelines, and regulation of church-sponsored educational institutions, to name just a few. All of these activities provide opportunities and motivation for congregation-based political and social action to influence government decisions.

The local religious environment—how many people belong to what kinds of churches in the community—is one factor that can affect a specific congregation's opportunities and motivation to engage the political process. Thus it is important to understand the religious nature of the places where ELCA and Episcopal clergy and their congregations reside. Table 4.1 presents a snapshot of the religious environments of ELCA and Episcopal sample clergy, compared to the entire United States. Figures in the table present the religious

Table 4.1. Religious Environments of Sample ELCA and Episcopal Clergy (percent)

Religious Adherence	ELCA	Episcopal Church	United States
Religious adherence	58.3	54.4	59.2
Roman Catholic	21.9	21.7	12.9
Evangelical Protestant	13.3	15.5	26.7
Mainline Protestant	19.3	11.0	15.4
ELCA	8.9	2.3	3.7
Episcopalian	1.0	1.3	1.0
Number of cases	1,333	894	3,103

Source: 1998 ELCA/Episcopal Clergy Study and 1990 NCCC Church Census.
Note: Cell entries signify the average concentration of each group in counties within which ELCA and Episcopal clergy reside.

composition of the average county in which our sample clergy are located, as well as the average religious composition of all U.S. counties.

The typical ELCA pastor and the typical Episcopal priest do not work in identical settings. The average level of religious adherence (church membership) in a county with a sample ELCA church is 58.3 percent, quite close to the national average (59.2 percent), while our sample Episcopal clergy work in counties with somewhat fewer church members (54.4 percent). Both Episcopal and ELCA sample clergy work in counties with substantially higher percentages of Roman Catholics than the average U.S. county, as well as substantially lower percentages of evangelical Protestants.

Strikingly, ELCA clergy are much more likely to live among other members of their denomination (average ELCA in county = 8.9 percent), while the average Episcopal clergyperson in our sample lives in a county that is just over 1 percent Episcopalian. This reflects the fact that the two denominations are concentrated in different regions of the country, as well as the fact that the ELCA has over twice as many members as the Episcopal Church. The most important implication of these patterns is that in many places (e.g., upper midwestern states) ELCA clergy can count on having several denominational colleagues and a substantial numerical presence in the local community. Although some parts of the United States (especially northeastern urban areas) have many Episcopal churches, the Episcopal population of any area is rarely very large relative to the overall population.[1]

These patterns have political implications besides the potential "strength in numbers" ELCA churches possess in many upper midwestern communities. While some aspects of religious competition (e.g., disputes over infant versus adult baptism) have little consequence for politics, political competition and activity may be a natural by-product of religious competition, due to the clash of values inherent in religious competition as well as the innate tensions and boundaries created in the drive for adherents (Djupe et al. 1997; Finke and Stark 1992; Iannaccone 1994, 1996; Kleppner 1970). Moreover, a congenial religious environment may provide a safe political haven of friends and fellow travelers with whom clergy can comfortably engage public issues.

At first glance, the political–religious competition hypothesis appears to be persuasive. Table 4.2 presents bivariate correlations of religious environmental measures and our summary measure of how frequently clergy engage in nineteen political activities (see appendix A for a full activities list). Political activity levels among sample Episcopal clergy are unaffected by any measured aspect of the county religious environment. But ELCA clergy appear to respond to environmental stimuli. ELCA clergy in counties with

Table 4.2. The Connection between Religious Environment and Clergy Political Activity (bivariate correlations)

Religious Adherence	Average Political Activity Frequency	ELCA Political Activity	Episcopal Political Activity
Percent religious adherence	−0.070***	−0.088***	−0.046
Percent ELCA	−0.046**	−0.076***	0.036
Percent mainline Protestant	−0.067***	−0.102***	0.002
Percent Evangelical Protestant	−0.006	0.039	−0.054
Percent Roman Catholic	−0.019	−0.037	−0.003
Number of cases	2192	1317	875

Source: 1998 ELCA/Episcopal Clergy Study and 1990 NCCC Church Census.
***$p < 0.01$; **$p < 0.05$; *$p < 0.10$

higher religious adherence rates are *less* inclined to participate in politics, as are those who are surrounded by more ELCA Lutherans and mainline Protestants. In such communities, ELCA clergy minister in a relatively agreeable religious environment, and individual ELCA pastors have fewer incentives to participate for two reasons: a consensus on key political issues is more likely to exist among religiously similar people. One or two (probably senior) pastors may do most of the political work (recall table 3.9), leaving newer colleagues to concentrate on different aspects of their ministry.

The flip side of this is that ELCA clergy, according to table 4.2, engage in *more* political activity when residing among fewer ELCA Lutherans, fewer mainline Protestants, and fewer religious adherents in general. Taken together, these results point to the prophetic role of clergy. *Clergy appear to be motivated to engage the public sphere and mobilize their members to action when they are confronted with a more secular population or theologically distinctive religious groups, both of which bring different values to public debate.* Religious environments clearly shape the contours of clergy engagement with the political sphere.

COMMUNITY PROBLEMS: INCIDENCE OF POVERTY

Clergy of many denominations and faith traditions engage in political activity to address pressing community needs. Such actions include leading or participating in strikes (Earle, Knudsen, and Shriver 1976; Lazerow 1995; Pope 1942; Wolcott 1982), spearheading pro- and anti-integration efforts (Campbell and Pettigrew 1959; McGreevy 1996; Thomas 1985) and attempting to meet the various psychological, social, and material needs of congregants and communities. Hunger and poverty in particular are two societal problems with which nearly all religious organizations are involved. Nearly all clergy speak out about these problems during a typical year (Kohut et al. 2000). One factor that might lead clergy to take more action concerning hunger and poverty is the incidence of poverty in the local community; with the problem more visibly in the midst of the church, clergy calls to action resonate more with congregants. Moreover, communities with widespread poverty tend to have fewer organizations to speak on behalf of the poor and powerless, a void clergy and congregations already fill in many cities (Olson 2000).

Clergy have numerous methods to attack hunger and poverty, including social service delivery, participation on local councils and boards devoted to the issue, and speaking out publicly to raise awareness about the scope and importance of the problem. We asked our sample clergy about the public, congregational, and personal methods they use to address hunger and poverty issues: how often the clergy publicly addressed hunger and poverty in the last year; whether they held adult education sessions on the issue; whether they personally belonged to a group devoted to addressing the issue (represented here by Bread for the World and Habitat for Humanity); and whether they participated on local councils and boards (which might be involved with hunger and poverty, though this question was not issue specific).

Table 4.3 presents the relationships between community poverty rates (percentage of county residents below the official poverty line in 1995; U.S. Census Bureau 1996) and the several forms of clergy responses we inquired about, broken down by denomination. Although none of the correlations is extremely high, the results show clearly that *clergy actually engage hunger and poverty issues less often when they are surrounded by poverty in their communities.*

Table 4.3.   Selected Clergy Belief and Activity Connections with County Poverty Rates (bivariate correlations)

	Poverty Rate		
Responses	Combined Sample	ELCA	Episcopal
Local political activity	−0.005	0.016	−0.020
Spoke out on hunger, poverty	−0.100***	−0.121***	−0.107***
Held adult education on poverty, hunger	−0.066***	−0.041	−0.095**
Belong to Bread or Habitat	−0.059**	−0.074**	−0.027
Government should do more to solve social problems	0.071***	0.085***	0.077**
Number of cases	1824	1088	724

Source: 1998 ELCA/Episcopal Clergy Study and U.S. Census Bureau (1996).
***p < 0.01; **p < 0.05, *p < 0.10

Other researchers have proposed that citizens in high-poverty areas may seek relief from enduring social problems in church, with an attendant focus by the clergy on spiritual healing rather than political mobilization (e.g., Cheal 1975; Stark 1964). While the results in table 4.3 support that contention, overall levels of clergy engagement imply that regardless of county poverty levels clergy take their prophetic role seriously, engaging hunger and poverty issues in a variety of ways. There appear to be slight differences between the denominations' responses, with the ELCA more likely to hold adult education sessions and Episcopal clergy more likely to join Bread for the World or Habitat for Humanity, whether or not poverty is severe locally. Overall clergy engagement on these issues is substantial: roughly 75 percent of sample Episcopal clergy and 81 percent of sample ELCA clergy spoke out about hunger and poverty often or very often in 1998, and three-fifths of ELCA and Episcopal churches held at least one adult education session on hunger and poverty.

The last response to poverty we examine is the possibility of attitude change, shown in the last row of table 4.3. ELCA and Episcopal clergy in communities with higher poverty rates are more likely to agree with the statement "the federal government should do more to solve social problems such as unemployment and poverty." Overall, clergy in the two denominations do not differ significantly in their view toward government action on social problems. We conclude from this analysis that ELCA and Episcopal clergy challenge their congregations to address poverty and related issues, with the direction of that challenge derived in part from conditions in the local community.

THE POLITICAL ENVIRONMENT

The local political context may constrain or expand the choices and opportunities clergy have for influencing local and national politics. Though certainly the rise of interest group politics and direct avenues of communication from citizens to national politicians has made us reconsider former U.S. House Speaker Tip O'Neill's famous phrase "all politics is local," several modes of influence clergy utilize will be affected by local political conditions.

Clergy, more than most citizens, have a bewildering array of opportunities and methods to affect the political process. These are most succinctly broken down into *direct* and *indirect* methods (see chapter 6 for an extended discussion of direct and indirect methods of political activity). Clergy directly affect the political process when they attempt to persuade decision makers through letter writing, lobbying, running for office, participating on lōcal boards and councils, and contributing to campaigns and political groups. Indirect methods are more common and include mobilizing church members to register and vote, endorsing candidates, speaking out on issues connected with candidate races or ballot measures, and mobilizing members by praying for candidates. Through indirect pathways the prophetic visions clergy hold for society may be realized into public policy via calls to action and activism aimed at parishioners. Indirect political activities may affect religious and secular audiences in several ways; Jelen (2001) suggests that, using these methods, clergy can at times influence opinions, set agendas, and empower and mobilize their parishioners.

What leads clergy to undertake direct or indirect methods of political influence? The political environment, like the religious environment, offers clergy both opportunities and constraints. Clergy may assume a prophetic role when their views are not being heard in the community, or clergy may become active when they sense an opportunity to make a difference. In electoral terms, this opportunity exists when the margin of victory is likely to be close. Clergy who mobilize their parishioners may tip the scales for a preferred candidate.

Table 4.4 displays selected measures of the political environments of ELCA and Episcopal sample clergy. Comparing the average ELCA and Episcopal clergyperson's county to the average county in the United States, the average Episcopal priest's county is several percentage points more Democratic, while the average ELCA pastor's county is slightly more Democratic. Both average denominational counties have 1992 voter turnout rates marginally higher than the average U.S. county.

Table 4.4. Political Environments of ELCA and Episcopal Church Clergy (percents)

Political Environment	ELCA	Episcopal Church	United States
Average 1996 Clinton vote	46.8	50.3	43.8
Average 1996 Dole vote	41.9	39.5	44.8
Average 1996 Perot vote	9.8	8.3	10.2
Average 1992 Clinton vote	40.5	44.2	39.8
Average 1992 Bush vote	38.3	36.9	40.0
Average 1992 Perot vote	21.2	18.9	20.2
Average 1992 turnout	45.2	44.0	43.9
Percent in congruent voting counties	54.0	60.5	—
Percent in competitive counties	41.3	35.2	—
Number of cases	1,329	889	3,103

Source: 1998 ELCA/Episcopal Clergy Study and 1998 *World Almanac*.

On the whole, sample ELCA and Episcopal clergy tend to reside in politically compatible areas. That is, roughly three-fifths of sample clergy voted for the same candidate as did the plurality of fellow county voters in 1996; we label this situation a *congruent voting county*. About two of every five sample clergy reside in *electorally competitive counties*—those counties with a difference between the 1996 Clinton and Dole vote percentages of less than ten points. ELCA clergy are somewhat more likely to reside in an electorally competitive county, while Episcopal clergy are somewhat more likely to reside in congruent voting counties.

To evaluate the influences of political environments on clergy political activity, table 4.5 examines the relationship between clergy political activity and three measures of the political environment: electoral competition, the extent of Democratic Party dominance, and whether clergy reside in a congruent voting county. Clergy political activity is broken down here into six categories based on the type of activity (appendix A has full details).

The correlations presented in table 4.5 reveal several consistent trends in the relationship of the political environment to clergy political activity. Clergy political activity in general is related positively to all three measures of competition. Clergy perform more activities when electoral competition is low and when surrounded by more Democrats; clergy political activity (including electoral activity) is even more strongly related to residing in congruent voting counties. These same environmental conditions also lead to a greater likelihood of clergy organizing a political discussion or social action group in their church, as well as a greater likelihood of clergy marching or protesting. Table 4.5 also shows that more clergy public speech about politics is likely in less electorally competitive counties.

Table 4.5. The Connection between Political Environment and Clergy Political Activity (bivariate correlations)

Political Activity Indices	Electoral Competition	Democratic Dominance	Congruent Voting County
Average frequency of activity	0.043**	0.040*	0.082***
Electoral activity	0.034	0.022	0.047**
Candidate support	0.015	0.000	0.003
Church organizing	0.047**	0.049**	0.046**
Public speech	0.060***	0.028	0.022
Marching/protesting	0.080***	0.091***	0.048**
Local activity	−0.002	−0.002	0.033

Source: 1998 ELCA/Episcopal Clergy Study and 1998 *World Almanac*. Number of cases varies.
***$p < 0.01$; **$p < 0.05$; *$p < 0.10$

It should not be surprising that *clergy political activity in general rises when clergy reside in areas that "fit" their political viewpoints*. Recall the investigation of church approval of clergy political activity in chapter 3; approval grew when the congregation was united on political matters, which is more likely in a politically homogenous community.

Table 4.5 reinforces the implications of those earlier findings and demonstrates the inherently partisan cast to these relationships. For most of our sample clergy, a "congruent voting county" means a county that supports Democrats more than Republicans. But congregational voting patterns, especially for Episcopal clergy, are likely to favor Republicans over Democrats. Hence greater clergy electoral activity in congruent voting counties may be viewed as a rational response to congregational preferences for Republicans. Public speech about issues is *not* more prevalent in such situations; activities of a civic nature are more appropriate avenues of persuasion. Finally, marching and protesting often involve issues of social justice, which in recent decades are more likely to be pursued by liberals; thus political environments with more Democrats would be more conducive to protesting issues that ELCA and Episcopal wish to engage. Clergy may use this tool in order to speak prophetically to a monolithic electorate or, perhaps more likely, because the action takes place in a politically safe environment.

Organizational mobilization also plays a role in structuring the connections found in table 4.5. Analysis of other aspects of our data shows that our sample clergy were more likely to be contacted by a religious/moral concerns organization in 1996 when Democrats were locally dominant, and they were more likely to receive a contact from a political party when Republicans were locally dominant.

In summary, from the evidence in tables 4.1–4.5 it appears that clergy respond to their political environment differently than to their religious environment. Inimical religious majorities lead clergy to more political activity, whereas antagonistic political majorities offer less motivation. The political community appears to most strongly affect clergy politics through organizational ties in homogeneous (especially Democratic) communities. Perhaps most important, our analysis reveals that *only rarely do clergy respond to and take advantage of electoral political opportunities* (see chapter 6 for more on this point).

This finding may not be surprising, given the policy concerns of most clergy as well as the trepidation with which ELCA and Episcopal clergy engage the electoral process. These clergy care about public policy issues that reflect their values and beliefs (which might be better labeled social or civic concerns) and are wary of campaigns and elections. This distinction makes our sample clergy different from those in other denominations who have come to care deeply about the electoral arena and participate frequently in it. For instance, the Kohut et al. (2000) study on the connection between religion and politics in the United States found that about a fifth of American parishioners heard their clergy talk about candidates and elections from the pulpit. In our sample, a smaller percentage of clergy reported having done so.

There are other meaningful ways to measure the political environment, in particular conceptions of the political environment as larger than the local community. Public policy researchers have analyzed the salience of national policy communities, events that destabilize such communities, and organizations and entrepreneurs who take advantage of "policy windows" (Baumgartner and Jones 1993; Kingdon 1995). Clergy belong to some of these organizations that lobby, mobilize, and campaign at crucial "windows" of political opportunity, and such groups encourage clergy and other members to rally allies and lobby decision makers. Hence a full analysis of determinants of clergy political activity must also account for the issues, events, and actors that might encourage clergy to participate on specific issues.

SELF-DEFINED COMMUNITY

As demonstrated in chapters 2–3, clergy perceptions of their congregations and communities offer insight into determinants of clergy political beliefs and actions. Similar to our thoughts about the effects of the religious and political environment, we wanted to know how well clergy and their churches were integrated into their communities, using a host of measures to rate their level of integration. In addition, we asked clergy to assess how well their churches were integrated into their respective denominations. These perceptions are presented in table 4.6.

Interestingly, on many factors, sample churches are more like their local communities than they are like other churches within their denominations. On the whole and not surprisingly, sample churches are more like the denomination than the community for religious matters only, though this is by no means true for all sample churches. Only *half* of ELCA and less than half of Episcopal churches believe that their worship and music styles are the same as those in the rest of the denomination; some perceive themselves as more traditional, some as more contemporary. These churches have ethnic/racial, socioeconomic, and church activity profiles somewhat more like their localities than their denominations. Clergy believe their churches are most

Table 4.6.   Clergy Perceptions about How Their Congregations Compare with Other Churches in the Community and with Churches within Their Respective Denominations (percents)

Bases of Comparison	Same as Community ELCA	Same as Community Episcopal	Same as other ELCA Churches	Same as other Episcopal Churches
Worship and music styles	42.4	34.9	47.7	45.6
Theological beliefs	46.3	33.8	65.2	52.0
Members' church activity	62.7	54.5	59.7	49.8
Members' community involvement	63.6	55.2	62.0	54.5
Political beliefs	66.6	53.0	65.0	58.7
Income and social status	69.5	54.8	57.8	52.8
Ethnicity/race	74.1	66.9	55.4	51.9
Members' political activity	77.5	69.2	76.6	70.0

Source: 1998 ELCA/Episcopal Church Clergy Study. Number of cases varies.

like their communities *and* denominations in their political activity levels, racial and ethnic composition, and social status.

These data indicate the roots of denominational diversity and the persistence of regional settlement patterns for both denominations. As noted earlier, Episcopalians are found more in the urban Northeast and do not dominate any locality. Perhaps because they lack the reinforcing effects of a relatively large community presence, Episcopal churches tend to be less like their denominations than ELCA churches are. In addition, these results suggest that a significant number of ELCA and Episcopal congregations constitute a minority in their communities. Minority status affects how adherents and their representatives relate to their surrounding religious, social, and political environment.

How does isolation from the community relate to clergy political activity? On the one hand, clergy of churches that are in the minority might feel marginalized and have difficulty penetrating community power networks; such clergy may then seek comfortable and supportive environments in which to act—in church. On the other hand, clergy of minority churches may take on a prophetic role, representing their congregation's needs to the community and attempting to mobilize their congregations to participate fully in public decision making. Similarly, some see their pastoral role through working with people; one ELCA pastor commented: "I am a shepherd who must aid people to determine God's leading."

The evidence already offered in this chapter, investigating the effects of religious and political environments on clergy actions, offers some support for both hypotheses. Other studies have found evidence to support the second notion. For instance, Thomas (1985) found that during a Boston busing crisis, clergy of the numerically dominant Catholic Church were less active than were the minority Protestant clergy. Olson's study of urban clergy makes a similar point, that economically distressed neighborhoods are more isolated from government institutions, leaving clergy (especially in African American neighborhoods) in a strong position to mobilize congregants for action (Olson 2000, 53–54).

In order to test these hypotheses, we will again use indices derived from clergy assessments of congregational *isolation*, which we first introduced in chapter 3. The *belief isolation index* includes differences in theological views, political beliefs, minority membership, worship style, and level of church activity; the *activity isolation index* incorporates lower social status, less community involvement, and less political activity by the congregation, as perceived by clergy. The higher the isolation index score, the more isolated a church is from its community.

Table 4.7 explores the relationships between our three measures of isolation and five measures of clergy political activity. Almost uniformly, *the more isolated the congregation is perceived to be from the community, the more politically active clergy are.* This relationship holds for all three specific activity types: clergy organize in their churches, speak out in public on political matters, and engage in electoral activities more often when isolated from the community. As seen in our examination of overall clergy political activity (chapter 3), *belief isolation* is a more salient factor affecting clergy political activity. Activity isolation is weakly related to more public speech and church organizing, as well as to less overall activity.

The results in table 4.7 help clarify clergy motivations for participating in political activities. Clergy must be understood, in part, as organizational representatives of their members—the congregation's agent in the public square. *Clergy engage in direct political action more often when their congregations*

Table 4.7.   Church Isolation from the Community and Modes of Clergy Political Activity (bivariate correlations)

Isolation Measure	Past Year Political Activity	Frequency of Political Activity	Public Speech	Church Organizing	Electoral Activity
Community isolation	0.089***	0.056**	0.074***	0.076***	0.083***
Belief isolation	0.096***	0.084***	0.073***	0.071***	0.085***
Activity isolation	0.029	−0.039*	0.043**	0.046**	0.026

Source: 1998 ELCA/Episcopal Church Clergy Study. Number of cases varies.
***$p < 0.01$; **$p < 0.05$; *$p < 0.10$

are isolated from the broader community, but clergy also attempt to bridge the repre sentation gap through mobilizing their churches (indirect action). Though this relationship must be submitted to further testing for a full account of clergy motivations for political activity, our findings mark a departure in the social scientific understanding of how clergy relate to their churches, respond to their environments, and live out their calling.

EFFECTS OF SEMINARY TRAINING

Many clergy are born into their denomination and are gradually socialized into its theology, practices, and customs. The decision to take up the ministry, however, entails something altogether different from confirmation rites and courses taken during youth. Beatty and Walter (1988) argue for a group theory of religion and politics in which denominational socialization and norms constitute the most powerful influence on the political behavior of clergy.

The educational process has always exerted significant pressures shaping the worldview of those exposed to it (e.g., Alwin 1976). It surely is no different for clergy and is perhaps more meaningful (Carroll and Marler 1995), although most ELCA and Episcopal clergy today enter and complete seminary in their forties and fifties, thus coming to a second (or third or fourth) career as ministers with extensive life experiences less easily altered by seminary training. The salience of seminary training can be assessed indirectly by observing the fights to control denominational seminaries in the Southern Baptist Convention and the Lutheran Church, Missouri Synod (Ammerman 1990; Finke and Stark 1992).

At issue, however, is whether clergy receive distinctive training depending on the particular seminary they attend, and whether such distinctive training has political implications. Numerous factors determine where future clergy choose to receive their seminary education, one of which may be the theological orientation of the seminary. Table 4.8 displays theological conservatism, political ideology, and political activity measures of sample ELCA and Episcopal clergy divided by seminary attended.[2]

Table 4.8 reveals that graduates of ELCA seminaries have similar theological views and political ideologies, and markedly similar levels of political activity. If there is a politicization effect of ELCA seminaries, it appears to differ little from school to school. The modest differences observed most likely result from self-selection by prospective clergy and their local synod advisory boards in the seminary admissions process.

Table 4.8. Theological and Political Attributes of Selected ELCA and Episcopal Seminary Graduates (mean scores)

ELCA Seminary	Political Ideology	Theological Conservatism	Frequency of Political Activity	Frequency of Public Speech
Seminex (35)	2.4	3.5	2.4	2.8
Chicago (110)	2.5	3.4	2.4	2.6
Gettysburg (126)	2.6	3.6	2.3	2.7
Philadelphia (85)	2.6	3.3	2.4	2.7
Pacific (60)	2.6	3.5	2.4	2.7
ELCA average (1,329)	2.7	3.6	2.3	2.7
Luther (427)	2.7	3.6	2.3	2.7
Southern (56)	2.7	3.5	2.2	2.5
Wartburg (140)	2.8	3.6	2.3	2.6
Trinity (174)	3.0	3.7	2.3	2.7

Episcopal Seminary	Political Ideology	Theological Conservatism	Frequency of Political Activity	Frequency of Public Speech
Episcopal Divinity (30)	2.2	3.0	2.4	2.9
General Theological (93)	2.3	3.0	2.3	2.8
Berkeley at Yale (54)	2.3	3.2	2.4	2.9
Pacific (62)	2.4	2.8	2.4	2.8
Harvard (16)	2.4	2.6	2.6	3.0
Episcopal average (889)	2.6	3.2	2.3	2.7
Seabury-Western (83)	2.6	3.0	2.4	2.7
Virginia Theological (106)	2.7	3.3	2.4	2.8
Sewanee (71)	2.8	3.2	2.2	2.6
Nashotah (63)	2.8	3.4	2.2	2.7
Bexley Hall (17)	2.8	3.2	2.5	3.0
Southwest (25)	2.8	3.1	2.2	2.3

Source: 1998 ELCA/Episcopal Church Clergy Study. Number of cases in parentheses.

The story is a bit different for Episcopal seminary graduates (bottom half of table 4.8). There is somewhat wider variation in all the attributes displayed, compared with ELCA clergy. The most theologically liberal seminary graduates (from Harvard Divinity School, which is nondenominational) differ by nearly a full point from the most theologically conservative (Nashotah House). Although there are differences in political activity and public speech frequencies, it would be a stretch to conclude that clergy from some seminaries are highly politicized or markedly apolitical. Once again, the selection of seminaries depends on the individual predispositions of the prospective Episcopal clergyperson, whose diocesan bishop also has considerable input on the choice of seminary.

What does table 4.8 tell us about the effect of seminaries on clergy political and religious attitudes? For one thing, we cannot make strong inferences about the content of seminary education from the data; for example, the fact that Episcopal Divinity School (EDS) graduates have the most liberal political views is probably due in part to the training and worldview offered by EDS, but also due to preexisting beliefs that attracted seminarians to EDS in the first place. A further investigation of the effects of seminary education will be presented in chapter 9. At this point, we can say that there are no obvious politicization effects from specific ELCA and Episcopal seminaries. However, the fact that these seminaries have differing curricula and emphases in training future ministers implies that clergy with more or less interest in politics can self-select seminaries that will reinforce their perceptions about the appropriateness of such activity in their clergy careers. Other clergy will receive greater or fewer political messages as a byproduct of attending a particular seminary, whether they want to or not.

PROFESSIONAL CONTACTS

Professional socialization does not end with seminary but continues through lifelong learning from peers (Guth 2001). Whether through local clergy councils, synod or regional meetings, or the national meetings of the church, clergy maintain friendships with peers and may at times discuss the appropriateness of political involvement. These interactions serve to convey norms and expectations about political involvement throughout the clerical ranks (Wald, Owen, and Hill 1988). Evidence to support this claim is scarce, but Shupe and Wood (1973) found, with a limited sample, that clergy felt their political activism was maintained by supportive denominational policies as well as like-minded colleagues in the ministry.

Clergy interactions are not limited to colleagues of the same denomination, however; as one Episcopal priest noted, "I have much more effective clergy colleague friendship and support with non-Episcopal rather than Episcopal clergy." Primarily through community associations, both secular and religious, clergy come into contact with significant numbers of clergy from other denominations and sometimes maintain relationships with them. These types of associations are common in most professions—lawyers know and associate with attorneys from other firms, college faculty get to know colleagues at nearby institutions, and small-town business owners regularly interact with other businesspeople at local functions.

We investigate the significance of professional contacts with clergy in and outside of the denomination in table 4.9 and table 4.10. Where do ELCA and Episcopal clergy find their intradenominational contacts? How does association with the local Catholic priest or Methodist pastor affect ELCA and Episcopal clergy political activity? Table 4.9 and table 4.10, along with additional analysis of denominational cues, offer some insight into these questions.

Table 4.9 displays the frequency of discussion with clergy of the same denomination, as well as the sources of clergy contacts. Almost all clergy have a contact of some sort within their own denomination (96 percent for the ELCA; 97 percent for Episcopal clergy), and clergy of both denominations average talking "often" with colleagues of their own denomination (2.2 on the 5-point scale). Clearly the lines of communication—and hence socialization—among clergy are open.

The patterns of intradenominational professional contact sources in table 4.9 show other interesting variations. For example, the dominant source of contacts differs by denomination: ELCA clergy are more likely to find colleagues through local clergy meetings (61.7 percent versus 43.2 percent for Episcopal clergy), and more Episcopal clergy find contacts in local diocesan meetings (58.5 percent, versus 42.4 percent for ELCA clergy). Such variations are almost certainly due to the geographical concentration of ELCA Lutherans in the upper Midwest. Even small towns often have more than one ELCA congregation, and thus interaction with other ELCA ministers is almost unavoidable. Episcopal clergy are more likely to be the only ones in their town and therefore tend to rely on diocesan meetings for such interaction—one priest's experience is fairly typical in small towns: "I am fairly isolated from other Episcopal clergy, the nearest being [over 30] miles away." If having local support structures and amenable social networks

Table 4.9.   The Source of and Discussion with Professional Contacts of ELCA and Episcopal Clergy and Their Political Activity

Same Denomination Colleagues	ELCA	Episcopal Church
Average discussion level	2.2	2.3
Met in seminary	34.6	31.3
Met in college	6.7	2.7
Met in a community organization	11.9	9.0
Met at a synod/diocese meeting	42.4	58.5
Met at a denominational meeting	33.9	32.2
Met at a local clergy meeting	61.7	43.2
Met through pulpit sharing	15.1	13.7
Colleagues more politically active on average	17.4	20.5
Colleagues similarly active on average	67.9	57.4

Source: 1998 ELCA/Episcopal Church Clergy Study.

facilitates clergy political activity, table 4.9 indicates that ELCA clergy would have more opportunities than their Episcopal counterparts.

THE DENOMINATIONAL CONTEXT

Denominations exert largely diffuse and indirect pressures to carry out ministry in particular ways. This is not surprising, since denominations exist to support worship and beliefs that are distinct from others. Moreover, denominational leaders (the national office, synod/diocesan bishops) are manifest to clergy at all career stages—directing seminary placements, approving prospective clergy for ordination, influencing clergy job placements, setting social action priorities for the local synod/diocese. Table 3.1 showed that our sample clergy believe the attitudes of denominational leaders and the norms/culture of the denomination are more encouraging than discouraging of clergy political activity, although substantial percentages of sample clergy perceived no effect.

Clergy who think that denominational leaders encourage their political activity are also encouraged by the culture of their denomination.[3] Perceived encouraging attitudes of denominational leaders and clergy actions contribute modestly to more clergy political activity. Denominational messages evidently can suggest that political activity should not crowd out the core religious activities clergy are employed to provide. Episcopal clergy feel more encouraged by the culture of their denomination than ELCA clergy, though there is no difference in the effect of the perceived attitudes of their denominational leaders, which are just slightly encouraging of clergy political activity levels. More religiously conservative clergy feel more discouraged by the attitudes of denominational leaders,[4] though there is no relationship between theological conservatism and the encouragement felt from the denominational culture.

Consequently, like the religious environment of the community, the denominational community plays an important (if secondary) role in promoting certain behaviors in its clergy. Campbell and Pettigrew (1959) found that the denomination was one of the important forces affecting the political decisions of clergy, and our data on ELCA and Episcopal clergy concur nearly forty years later.

LOCAL PROFESSIONAL CONTACTS

As noted earlier, clergy mix with colleagues from other denominations on a regular basis at local clergy councils, community boards, informal gatherings, and community groups and political organizations. Such interaction capitalizes on collective organizational resources, experience, and moral authority to deal with shared community problems and issues. For clergy in some denominations, theological particularism may prevent or discourage such associations (Quinley 1974, 249), but this factor rarely restricts ELCA and Episcopal clergy.

Table 4.10 shows that while ELCA and Episcopal clergy interact a bit less often with clergy of other denominations than with denominational colleagues, roughly three-fourths of clergy in each denomination associate with colleagues from other denominations. The largest number of these contacts are made in local clergy meetings, and ELCA clergy are ten points more likely to do so than Episcopalians. The small-town roots of the ELCA help account for this difference. ELCA clergy appear more likely to attend local clergy meetings, perhaps in part because other ELCA colleagues will

Table 4.10.   Contacts with Clergy Colleagues from Different Denominations

Different Denomination Colleagues	ELCA	Episcopal Church
Percent who regularly associate with other denominations' clergy	77.7	70.5
Average discussion with those clergy	3.5	3.5
Percent met at a local clergy meeting	54.7	42.2
Percent met in a community organization	35.5	34.2
Percent met through pulpit sharing	9.6	7.5
Percent met in seminary	1.3	3.3
Percent met in college	0.9	1.3
Top denominational source	United Methodists (22%)	Catholic Church (37%)
Second denominational source	Catholic Church (22%)	ELCA (36%)
Third denominational source	United Church of Christ (21%)	United Methodists (34%)

Source: 1998 ELCA/Episcopal Church Clergy Study.
Note: Denominational sources should be read as the percent of clergy who named the denomination as a source of at least one discussion partner. Clergy could list as many denominations as fit their circumstances and as many discussion partners who share that denominational connection; in practice the longest list included six different denominations. Because clergy reported that several discussion partners often came from the same denomination, these figures doubtlessly understate contact with the top denominations.

be present; as a consequence ELCA clergy would have more opportunities to meet colleagues from other denominations and faith traditions.

The denominational content of the contacts also differs between ELCA and Episcopal clergy, as shown at the bottom of table 4.10. Regional membership patterns again lie behind these differences, as Episcopalians in urban areas would have many more Catholic priests to meet. Catholics and United Methodists appear on both lists (with much higher percentages among the Episcopal sample clergy), and Episcopal clergy report ELCA pastors as their second most frequent contact outside Episcopal circles. No evangelical Protestant denominations or non-Christian faith traditions appear in the top three for either group.

DISCUSSION PARTNERS: THE SOCIAL NETWORK

As social elites and opinion leaders in their communities, clergy should have relatively stable preferences for political action. But they may be influenced by the people with whom they live, work, and discuss politics. We envision several varieties of influence that the social network may have on clergy. The most likely form of influence stems from the concept of cross pressures (Berelson et al. 1954). A clergyperson may face significant social and professional consequences when raising and taking stances on controversial public issues with which friends and congregants disagree. Quinley (1974) found that clergy who were active in the civil rights movement in the 1960s in California sometimes faced membership losses, rancor within the congregation, and even loss of their job due to their activism on disagreeable matters. Alternatively, clergy may undertake controversial activities in spite of social approbation, preferring (personally and professionally) to live out their beliefs regardless of the consequences.

As a first look at the influence of political discussion partners, table 4.11 presents data on the political discussion partner networks of ELCA and Episcopal clergy (respondents could name several) and shows striking parallels between the two denominations. Approximately 90 percent of clergy named at least one political discussion partner. Nearly 60 percent of clergy named a church member as a discussant; the next greatest source named is a clergy colleague (40 percent). Roughly 60 percent of clergy also named a family member (immediate and extended) as a discussion partner.

What beliefs and attributes are the political discussion partners of ELCA and Episcopal clergy bringing to these conversations? On most measures, though a majority of discussion partners are perceived to share similar political

Table 4.11.   ELCA and Episcopal Clergy Contact with Discussion Partners and Their Perceived Political Attributes

Discussion Partners	ELCA	Episcopal Church
Percent clergy with a discussion partner	88.4	91.1
Percent church members	58.9	58.2
Percent family members	37.8	37.7
Percent relatives	23.6	22.5
Percent neighbors	24.0	21.9
Percent group/club members	12.4	15.8
Percent other clergy	41.4	44.1
Average discussion frequency	3.5	3.5
Percent same level of political activity	58.9	56.9
Percent same party affiliation	57.2	57.2
Percent same school prayer position	56.1	63.3
Percent same religious ideology	48.7	48.6
Percent same abortion position	47.8	62.8
Percent same political ideology	45.2	47.7

Source: 1998 ELCA/Episcopal Church Clergy Study. Number of cases varies.

opinions and behaviors with sample clergy, slightly less than half of clergy have discussion networks that differ from them in some way, thereby creating significant room for influence. The possibility of influence is known to increase with the existence of differences between discussants, since difference drives the contextual influence process (Huckfeldt and Sprague 1995; McPhee 1963). The greatest differences shown in table 4.11 exist on abortion attitudes and political ideology for ELCA clergy, whereas religious and political ideology show the most differences in the social networks of Episcopal clergy. It is not only difference that matters, however; a network in which people hold similar positions and behaviors indicates clergy have a supportive environment that can help reinforce a political position or behavior (Shupe and Wood 1973).

Another form of influence that the social network may exert stems from its political content. It is a long-standing finding that the environment shapes the content of the social network, providing supply constraints on the choice of discussants for even the most selective citizen (Huckfeldt and Sprague 1995; Putnam 1966). That is, if the sole Republican social worker is going to have political discussion at work, it will have to be with one of the Democrats she works with (Huckfeldt and Sprague 1995). Quinley (1974) found that clergy with many church member social contacts were more conservative and less likely to participate in politics. The effect is to create a network closed to the community climate of opinion (Granovetter 1973; Huckfeldt et al. 1995).

Those with closed networks are less likely to participate in the community and to mirror community opinion. This may, of course, be a conscious choice by clergy, yet it carries significant behavioral consequences. We expect that clergy will exert some selectivity concerning the composition of their discussion networks, though the local environment will also exert an effect.

Table 4.12 presents the percentage of clergy who indicate that their discussion networks hold the same political partisanship as themselves in a fairly complex combination of church and county partisan environments. It is clear that the church partisan environment exerts the strongest influence over the content of the discussion networks of clergy, though it is certainly not conclusive. Republican clergy in pro-Clinton churches and Democratic counties have the same network partisan content as Republican clergy in pro-Clinton churches and Republican counties. However, agreeable county environments can boost the effects of a consonant church context—14 percent more Democratic clergy in Clinton churches and Democratic counties have homogeneous networks than Democratic clergy in Clinton churches and Republican counties. Whatever the effects may be over the long run, the political environment does appear to affect the content of this political information source for sample ELCA and Episcopal clergy.

RELIGIOUS AND MORAL
PUBLIC AFFAIRS ORGANIZATIONS

Clergy also express themselves politically through involvement in local and national political and social organizations. The Moral Majority specifically

Table 4.12.   The Effect of County and Church Political Environments on the Partisan Content of Clergy Political Discussion Networks (percents)

	Disagreeable County	*Agreeable County*
Clinton Church		
Democratic clergy	60.5	74.1
Republican clergy	47.6	47.5
Dole Church		
Democratic clergy	46.3	49.7
Republican clergy	65.0	72.8

Source: 1998 ELCA/Episcopal Church Clergy Study.
Note: Cell entries are the percent of clergy social networks that are judged to have the *same* partisanship as the respondent in relationship to the 1996 county and church vote. Therefore, 60.5 percent of Democratic clergy in pro-Clinton churches and Dole counties had discussion networks that were largely Democratic. "Agreeable" and "disagreeable" refer to the presidential vote of the county in 1996; "agreeable" means that the clergy voted for the candidate who carried the county.

targeted clergy, thinking that their action would lead to the mobilization of church members (Liebman 1983). While the Christian Coalition explicitly avoided that tactic, the Interfaith Alliance has embraced it, targeting and gaining the support of a number of mainline Protestant clergy. Like average citizens, clergy with organizational contacts should be mobilized to partic- ipate on issues of interest to the organization and to participate generally at increased levels. Forty-six percent of sample clergy claimed membership (whether active or merely "checkbook") with at least one group, and many claimed more memberships; table 4.13 shows clergy group affiliations in detail.

The pattern of ELCA and Episcopal clergy group affiliations reveals something about their political beliefs as well. The most common mem- bership is in Habitat for Humanity (34 percent), while the second most common is Bread for the World (BFW) (17 percent), which was founded by Lutheran social activists and clergy. All other groups have membership rates in the low single digits—not surprising for many of the listed groups, since the ELCA and Episcopal Church are not very supportive of conser- vative political causes.

ELCA and Episcopal clergy organizational attachments are best char- acterized as nonpartisan with an emphasis on social justice—providing housing and serving people in need. These groups often have chapters run through local congregations, providing volunteers, funds, and organization (Chaves 1999). Thus we might understand clergy membership in Habitat

Table 4.13. Group Affiliations and Affinities of ELCA and Episcopal Clergy

Organization	Percent Claiming Membership	Average Closeness
Habitat for Humanity	34.2	4.3
Bread for the World	17.1	3.5
Focus on the Family	5.1	1.9
Promise Keepers	4.9	2.3
The Interfaith Alliance	3.6	2.7
Operation Rescue	1.8	2.2
American Family Association	1.1	1.6
The Christian Coalition	0.9	1.3
Americans United for Separation of Church and State	0.8	2.0
National Association of Evangelicals	0.7	1.9
Traditional Values Coalition	0.1	1.5
Other groups	9.9	—
At least one group membership	45.7	—

Source: 1998 FLCA/Episcopal Church Clergy Study.

and BFW as not only a reflection of personal interests but also an extension of organizational duties and responsibilities. Few of these sample clergy appear engaged in the "culture wars" (Hunter 1991) and few devote themselves to the cause of maintaining or loosening church–state boundaries. Moreover, sample clergy feel close only to BFW and Habitat, giving no other organization an overall "close" rating. The next closest groups (Promise Keepers, Interfaith Alliance, Operation Rescue) all receive evaluations between "neutral" and "far" (i.e., hostile). These ratings also suggest a diversity of voices and outlooks within these two denominations, though only on the margins.

CONCLUSION

In this chapter, we have explored a variety of ways to conceive of the environment surrounding clergy and its connections to clergy political activism. The social context—ranging from the intimate relationships of family, friends, and congregants to the impersonal political and religious composition of the county—provides clergy with stimuli for their decisions about whether and how to engage the political process.

The analysis in this chapter supports our argument that clergy often enter the political process as representatives of their congregations. *Clergy care about how their congregations fit within the community social and political structure and they act accordingly, attempting to supply a voice where it is lacking and to mobilize the voices of their congregants for public action.*

These findings are significant in several ways. The environment of clergy action has been overlooked by researchers for too long, though this has been changing in recent years (Crawford and Olson 2001; Olson 2000). Utilizing research conducted by others, this chapter demonstrates that the environment beyond church walls matters and helps shape clergy conduct. Our findings point toward a renewed understanding of clergy as primarily organizational actors who represent a faith tradition and a particular community of believers wherever that prophetic role may lead, including at times into the political process.

In the next four chapters, we apply the theoretical and empirical framework laid out thus far to a series of important political activities in which clergy can engage: public political speech (chapter 5), electoral activities (chapter 6), local political activity (chapter 7), and contacting government representatives (chapter 8). In the final empirical chapter (chapter 9), we delve into the internal politics of these two denominations, exploring clergy opinion and speech about full communion between the ELCA and Episcopal Church, a move with serious repercussions for both denominations.

NOTES

1. The average county population is also much smaller for ELCA clergy— 150,000 fewer people (1990 population data) than the average Episcopal county. More opportunities to make a meaningful political impact likely exist in smaller counties.

2. In this and other tables dividing our sample by the seminary our sample clergy attended, we use only the seminaries with enough cases (generally at least 10 graduates) to sustain the statistical analyses employed.

3. Correlation $= 0.251$; $p = 0.000$; n $= 1432$.

4. Correlation $= 0.066$; $p = 0.015$; n $= 1351$.

5

THE POLITICAL VOICE OF CLERGY

As we demonstrated in chapters 2–4, the primary mechanism ELCA and Episcopal clergy utilize for political action—whether attempting to set congregational agendas, influence member opinions, or mobilize groups for action—is public speech. In this respect our sample clergy closely resemble ministers in other denominations and faith traditions. Hence it is not surprising that numerous social scientific inquiries have examined the nature, frequency, and ability of clergy to speak their minds to their members and the public (Campbell and Pettigrew 1959; Crawford and Olson 2001a; Guth et al. 1997; Hadden 1969; Jelen 2001; Koller and Retzer 1980; Olson 2000; Quinley 1974; Stark et al. 1971; Thomas 1985). Scholars have observed differences in configurations of clergy public speech rooted in theology and ideology (Stark et al. 1971), as well as differences based on resources and opportunities (Crawford and Olson 2001a; Guth et al. 1997; Olson 2000). But few scholars have collected the data necessary to investigate the *congregational, denominational, and community characteristics* that might motivate or limit clergy public political speech.

In this chapter, we seek to concentrate the theoretical and empirical findings we have presented previously, in order to derive a comprehensive understanding of the political voice of clergy. We observed in chapter 2 that clergy are publicly engaging important contemporary political issues both inside and outside church, thus providing parishioners and sometimes the surrounding community with theologically oriented perspectives on political questions. A principal reason ELCA and Episcopal clergy speak publicly about political topics is to offer a prophetic voice, whether directed *inward*— to help members draw connections between their faith and their political opinions and actions—or *outward*—to explain denominational perspectives on pressing issues to the general public, especially if sample clergy perceive their congregations to have minority status in the broader community.

But clergy are not limited to the prophetic role when speaking out or taking action in the political arena. A multifaceted test of the possible inducements and deterrents to clergy public speech on political topics is necessary to see how prophetic impulses and numerous other stimuli come together to shape the political voice of clergy. In this chapter we ask, How often and why do ELCA and Episcopal clergy speak out on contemporary political topics? What roles do they envision taking on when they address political issues in public? How might the prophetic voice of clergy be amplified or muted by other factors present in each clergyperson's own background and her immediate congregational, denominational, and community surroundings?

In exploring answers to these questions, we will offer a detailed five-part categorization of factors affecting clergy public speech. This typology will guide our inquiries into the different forms of clergy political activity analyzed in chapters 5–9. But discerning the answers to the critical questions we pose in this chapter must begin with an understanding of how previous research has illuminated the determinants of clergy public speech.

UNDERSTANDING CLERGY PUBLIC SPEECH:
AN OVERVIEW

At the outset of chapter 3, we summarized the two contrasting emphases of previous social scientific studies examining clergy political activities, including public speech. A study of clergy responses to the Little Rock desegregation crisis of 1957 posited that *congregational support* was the most compelling influence on their political activity (Campbell and Pettigrew 1959). But as we indicated previously, following the Campbell and Pettigrew study researchers turned away from the congregation and community, instead giving primary attention to the *theological roots* of clergy political beliefs and actions. The dominance of this theological emphasis—an individualist approach to understanding clergy political speech and activity—has obscured some key lessons drawn from the Little Rock study for over three decades.

This is not to say that theological factors are irrelevant. Indeed, the dominance of the theological approach within this literature stems from the persuasiveness and clarity of its findings. Researchers in the 1960s found clear differences in clergy political activity levels based primarily on theological characteristics. For example, Hadden (1969), Stark et al. (1971), and

Quinley (1974) all found that theologically modernist clergy were more willing than theologically conservative (also termed orthodox) clergy to speak and act politically. The denominational differences in clergy political activity uncovered by Stark et al. stemmed clearly from otherworldliness clergy focused on the importance of the afterlife (conservative or orthodox clergy) were less likely to speak out on politics than liberal clergy more focused on this life. On the basis of these findings, many scholars suggested that theologically based political activity differences were enduring, instead of constituting an artifact of the particular opportunities for public expression in the 1960s, which favored theological and political liberals.

These clergy studies emphasizing theological orientations did not ignore other motivations. Hadden and Quinley also suggested that clergy decisions about engaging in political activity were tied closely to keeping their jobs—another factor identified previously by the Campbell and Pettigrew Little Rock study. Many clergy faced church boards that withheld funds, members who left, and even termination when they involved themselves in politics (especially racial politics) in the 1950s and 1960s.

As part of an influential series of studies of anti-Semitism in America, Rodney Stark and colleagues (1971) focused specifically on political speech of Protestant clergy. Using a sample of California clergy interviewed in 1968, Stark and colleagues examined the nature and amount of political speech from the pulpit. They called what they found the "silent pulpit," a recurrent refrain in later studies as well. They estimated that 6 percent of sermons delivered in California in 1968 dealt primarily with political issues (1971, 90). Almost all sample clergy claimed to have touched on a political issue in the pulpit, and a strong majority (70 percent) claimed to do so in at least 10 percent of their sermons. However, *overwhelming majorities indicated that they had never taken a specific position on a political issue during a sermon.* These findings indicated to Stark and colleagues that clergy were likely to bring up current issues but were not likely to dwell on them or make an explicit connection between religion and public affairs for their parishioners. The inevitable conclusion of the Stark California study was that clergy could not exert a significant influence on the political attitudes and values of their parishioners.

Research on clergy political speech and activity since the late 1960s has uncovered increased levels of clergy political activism of all sorts. Koller and Retzer (1980) found that North Carolina clergy mentioned nearly twice as many political issues in sermons than clergy in the Stark study did. Using more extensive data from national samples of several denominations in the late 1980s and early 1990s rather than state-level samples, Guth et al.

(1997) also found more political messages in sermons, and they reported high levels of political engagement outside the pulpit as well. As we have shown already and will demonstrate again, our sample clergy are similarly politically engaged in more ways and at higher levels than clergy studied in the 1960s.

Guth and colleagues also reported in the *Bully Pulpit* that while theologically modernist clergy were found to participate more than theologically conservative clergy in the course of their careers, the gap in political activity between the two camps had diminished considerably by 1988 (Guth et al. 1997, 162–73). The gradual softening of theological barriers that might bar political action by conservative clergy, as well as explicit recruitment efforts by political activists and organizations (Guth 1996; Martin 1996), have contributed to reducing the political activity gap between modernist and conservative clergy.

These shifts suggest that theology does not play the same role today that it once did in stimulating most kinds of clergy political activity. Based on their findings, Guth and colleagues posited that

> psychological resources, especially interest in politics, have a pervasive influence [on clergy political activity], . . . A minister's understanding of the propriety of various activities has an enormous effect on action, as do a variety of ideological factors, including agenda, beliefs, and partisanship. On the whole, the organizational context is a good bit less important . . . (1997, 180)

THE DETERMINANTS OF CLERGY PUBLIC SPEECH: A FIVEFOLD TYPOLOGY

Our perspective on the determinants of clergy public speech, and clergy political activity more generally, utilizes many of the same components quoted above, but with far different emphases based on a more comprehensive set of explanatory factors. Our survey of ELCA and Episcopal clergy was designed to capture their theological beliefs, personal orientations toward politics, and the range and frequency of political activities clergy engaged in as clergy and as private citizens—in effect to test the existing theories on a new set of denominations. However, our data—supplemented with additional information about the political and social characteristics of the local communities where responding clergy live and work—also allow for a much deeper consideration of congregational, community, and denomina tional influences on clergy political beliefs and actions than in previous studies.

We have asserted repeatedly that the congregation, community, and denomination have not received due attention as salient influences on clergy, and we have already presented evidence that clergy sometimes play a prophetic role, directly implicating the congregation, community, and denomination in clergy political activities. If theological orientation has declined as a significant predictor of clergy political activity, consideration of other possible catalysts becomes even more essential.

A comprehensive framework from which to understand clergy public speech, and clergy political activity in general, requires several components. Campbell and Pettigrew suggested three systems affecting clergy political choices: the personal, the professional (or denominational), and the congregational (1959, 87). We have expanded this typology, dividing one category and adding another. In order to understand clergy public speech and political activity we must examine the effects of and interrelationships among five different sets of factors: the *personal attributes of clergy, political and theological orientations, congregational resources, denominational cues,* and *community influences.* We turn now to a detailed consideration of how each set of factors affects what clergy say and do in the political realm, including specific hypotheses to be tested in this and the four succeeding chapters.

Personal Attributes

Several personal attributes shape whether clergy will address public policy issues and become politically active. Generally speaking, more educated clergy are more likely to understand the political process and to perceive the freedom to address political issues (Campbell and Pettigrew 1959). All of our sample clergy are highly educated, and we expect little difference between clergy with a master of divinity (M.Div.) degree and those with a doctoral degree. Gender is another salient characteristic; table 2.8 showed that women clergy addressed social justice issues more often, while male clergy were more likely to discuss moral reform agenda items. Interestingly, recent studies have found little difference in rates of activism between male and female clergy (Crawford, Deckman, and Braun 2001).

Ministerial experience in general, as well as tenure at the present church, may also play a significant role. Figure 2.3 showed that sample clergy ordained from the 1960s on were more politically active; we would expect such clergy to speak more about policy issues as well. Clergy who have served in their present churches for extended periods (which we term tenure length) tend to find fewer professional risks in political action—the "building credit" theory we noted in chapter 3. The differences between clergy based on experience are complicated by the fact that newly ordained ELCA and Episcopal clergy tend to be middle-aged or older (Wheeler 2001); only 6.1 percent of ELCA pastors and 3.9 percent of Episcopal clergy are under age thirty-five (Wood 2001, 18). The combination of greater life experience before ordination (which may include decades of voting and other political activities) and professional socialization into a more politically active corps of clergy means that clergy public speech frequencies and political activity levels are not likely to be dramatically affected by ministerial experience or tenure length.

Our detailed examination of clergy public speech in this chapter, as well as specific clergy political activities in chapters 6–9, will not include many other personal attributes of clergy. With only slight differences in these indicators among our sample clergy, we hypothesize that *personal attributes will not play a strong role in influencing levels of clergy political speech or activity.*

Political and Theological Orientations

The authors of *The Bully Pulpit* concluded that political and theological orientations were the most significant factors affecting the political actions of clergy, echoing three decades of research, albeit with more weight given to political ideologies and interest. Having already seen significant diversity among our sample clergy on basic indicators of political and theological orientations (chapter 2), we also expect several such indicators to affect what clergy discuss and what they do politically.

ELCA and Episcopal clergy are highly educated and typically bring to their jobs thoughtfully considered personal views on religious and political topics, in addition to specific skills such as public speaking and organizing. Clergy thus possess the resources and motivations to understand complex issues, to care about addressing them, and to move others to act. All of the social science literature indicates that citizens with high political efficacy, greater political interest, strong partisan identification, and clear ideological stances are more active in politics (Rosenstone and Hansen 1993; Verba and Nie 1972; Verba, Schlozman, and Brady 1995). Accordingly, our analysis of clergy speech and activities will include measures of *political interest, Democratic or Republican partisanship,* and *liberal or conservative political views.* Tables 2.3, 2.9, and 2.10 summarize these indicators for our sample clergy. We expect that many of these factors, especially partisan identification, will have relatively weak effects on producing clergy public speech in accord with the practice of one ELCA pastor, who commented: "I generally restrict myself to public prayers concerning broad social justice issues (e.g., hunger, homelessness, abuse, racism) rather than party agendas."

In addition, clergy can draw from theological orientations to politics that have been found to distinguish politically active from inactive clergy (Jelen 1995; Wilcox, Linzey, and Jelen 1991). As noted earlier, the modernist orientation of most ELCA and Episcopal clergy establishes some predisposition to greater public speech and political activity, although religious conservatism now presents fewer theological barriers to political participation, according to recent studies of clergy and laity (Guth 1996; Guth et al. 1997). Our measure of *theological conservatism* (table 2.1) will test the degree to which theological beliefs affect speech and activities among ELCA and Episcopal clergy.

Guth and colleagues also found that clergy approval of political activity is strongly related to actual clergy activity (1997, 146–50). We incorporate this concept in different ways depending on the clergy activity being studied. For speech, greater *political efficacy* (whether ministers believe they can influence the political views of their congregants and understand politics well enough to accomplish political goals; see table 2.4) should lead to more discussion, while for activities *the clergyperson's approval of an act* (table 2.6) is likely to be salient, although the direction of causation is not easily established.[1]

We believe that political and theological orientations will influence the public speech and political activity of our sample clergy, just as they would affect what ordinary citizens say and do in the political milieu. Once again this hypothesis conforms to existing research emphasizing the salience of such factors. However, personal attributes and political-theological factors are not adequate by themselves to explain clergy political speech and activity. Due to the nature of their jobs, clergy are not simply ordinary citizens, and much of what they might say and do in politics must be carefully considered in light of the status they hold inside and outside their congregation.

Congregational Resources

In the first chapter we asserted that ELCA and Episcopal clergy took on prophetic, representative roles for their congregations—speaking out and taking action based in part on theology and personal conscience but also as a means of expressing what the church believes. Because their congregations have some control over clergy job status, ELCA and Episcopal clergy must balance the potential benefits of political activity with the needs and desires of members (Wald 1997, 38–40). This balancing act should not be concep tualized as a one-way street with the congregation in control, as noted in chapter 1. The congregation may strongly affect the political activity of clergy by its approval or disapproval of certain actions; moreover, the con gregation may have strong preferences about the level and targets of clergy political participation, and make its own views known. However, it is sim ply wrong to believe that clergy serve passively, registering the temperature of the congregation and doing what the congregation wants or allows them to do.

The reality of the clergy–congregation relationship, and its impact on levels and modes of clergy public speech and political action, is more com plex and interesting than the congregation-controlled model. In chapter 3 we saw that our sample clergy hold political views that are distinctly more Democratic and liberal than their congregations', and we have observed high levels of clergy public speech and political activity despite the partisan gap between clergy and congregation. We know from other research that congregations sometimes demand that clergy take on political leadership roles (Lincoln and Mamiya 1990; Morris 1984), and that clergy have risked political activities even in tense and risky environments (Campbell and Pet tigrew 1959).

The clergyperson holds some degree of influence over the congrega tion and vice versa when it comes to clergy political activity. Describing the interplay between the two, and how it relates to clergy decisions about pub lic speech and political action, means focusing on what the congregation has to offer—what we term *congregational resources.* These include opinions (pro or con) on potential forms of clergy political expression, opinions about po litical issues, a sense of how the Christian faith teaches members to live their lives (structured and reinforced regularly by sermons and other educational opportunities offered by the church and clergy), their needs and general lack of resources, and tangible assets—a building that can be the center of activ ity and the members themselves, whose energies and talents can be utilized for political ends.

These congregational resources are captured in our survey data by sev eral indicators. First, the *size and location of the church,* the *activity levels of its members,* and *member loyalty to the denomination* may affect clergy political speech and activity. Large churches tend to have more programs and activ ities, and larger congregations tend to be found in urban and suburban ar eas. Both should lead to higher levels of clergy speech and actions, due to proximity to pressing social problems (especially in urban areas) and larger clergy staffs, which may free up time for clergy political action. Regional traits may also lead congregations to have more or less interest and incentive to influence clergy actions on specific issues; we test for this possibility using variables denoting specific regions of the United States.

Size and location alone are not sufficient congregational resources to compel clergy actions. Mobilizing members to act in support of the political goals desired by clergy will not occur if members tend to be quiescent and disengaged. Accordingly, we asked clergy to estimate what percentage of members were involved in church activities, reasoning that clergy speech and actions were more likely in an already engaged environment with high percentages of members involved. Clergy also reported to us that they were personally involved in nearly every church group, meaning that clergy have even more regular access to the already engaged members. *Heightened member activity in existing groups is likely to enhance levels of clergy public speech and political activity.*

Brand loyalty—whether members grew up in the denomination versus converted to it, as perceived by clergy—may also influence clergy speech and political activity. In mainline Protestant churches, lifelong denominational adherents have often decried the political involvement of some clergy as divisive—especially locally visible, controversial activities. By contrast, high member turnover creates a congregation of primarily newer members with few political expectations of their clergy, which serves to enhance the freedom of clergy to be politically active (Campbell and Pettigrew 1959; Djupe 1999). While previous research makes clear that most citizens do not join churches for political reasons (Wald, Owen, and Hill 1988), the heightened politicization of churches and clergy in recent years may well lead new members to have a greater expectation (whether they like it or not) of clergy engaging in political activity. We expect that *congregations with fewer members who grew up in the denomination* (or parent denominations for the ELCA) *should be more likely to support clergy politicking.*

Perhaps the most salient congregational resources that may bear on clergy decisions about political action are member opinions about political issues that clergy might choose to engage, the propriety of clergy political activity in general, and specific forms of political activity. The prevailing finding in the literature is that political disagreement between the clergy and the congregation is likely to inhibit clergy activism (Campbell and Pettigrew 1959; Guth et al. 1997; Hadden 1969; Quinley 1974). Clergy whose political views differ from the congregation's may feel pressure to remain quiet on political matters, while clergy who match their congregation's politics would be encouraged (or at least not be constrained) by member opinions. Moreover, political divisions within the congregation may force clergy to downplay politics to avoid a schism and the consequent loss of members (or their jobs). We expect this hypothesis to apply especially to partisan, controversial, and visible political activities.

It would be naive to assume, however, that congregations only hinder the political activity of clergy, or that all forms of clergy political activity should be reduced by the existence of congregational disapproval. Alternatively, as leaders and representatives of a specific organization, clergy may lead the congregation on certain matters, fulfilling a prophetic role by engaging in more public speech and more political activities. If clergy feel strongly enough about a specific issue due to theological or personal beliefs or are highly motivated to perform a particular political action, then ideological differences with the congregation may actually spark more clergy speech or action, not less. Alternatively, clergy who disagree with their members may favor participatory forms that are private (such as contributing money or joining a national group) or nonpartisan (working in local civic organizations). These possibilities more fully reflect the prophetic role clergy are frequently encouraged to play in challenging the views held by congregants and society.

The nature of the political activity must also be considered. While the prophetic role fills a representative function, clergy have other outlets for political self-expression. We expect that clergy who hold ideologies that differ from their congregants' will be more likely to contact public officials. Choosing to send a message to government allows clergy to witness their personal and theological beliefs (though not necessarily in public), and to satisfy their need to express political views; contacting public officials instead of focusing their efforts on their congregation also avoids a potential backlash of member sentiment. Finally, local activities that clergy might engage in often evade ideological categorization, have civic rather than political goals, and may work directly for the church's benefit. Hence participation on a local council or board should not be strongly related to congregational opinions.

The potential effects of congregational opinions on clergy public speech and political activity thus depend not just on agreement or disagreement, but on the clergyperson's predispositions and the nature of the activity being examined. We can test for both hypotheses—that clergy–congregation disagreement reduces clergy politicking *and* that clergy–congregation disagreement might spark *more* clergy public speech and political activity—by using several variables. First, for the speech or activity being examined, we utilize the clergyperson's perception of congregational approval of clergy political speech and various political activities. Generally congregational approval should lead to more clergy speech and disapproval should equate with less speech. But we remain open to the possibility that clergy will speak or engage in a particular activity more frequently if they perceive disagreement, especially if the activity can be done in ways (particularly private or nonpartisan acts) that are less likely to provoke congregational objections.

Second, for speech and opinions on public policy issues, we use measures comparing the clergyperson's view on issues with the congregation's perceived view—greater disagreement may lead clergy to engage in less speech on the issue (to avoid controversy and division), or more speech in an attempt to persuade the congregation and to teach the appropriate theological viewpoint if one exists.

Finally, we asked clergy whether their church was generally politically divided or united. Again, the traditional hypothesis is that political division in the church should reduce clergy political speech and activity, but divisions may also enhance clergy speech and activity, according to the prophetic hypothesis.

Regardless of which hypotheses are determined to apply, our analysis of congregational resources affecting clergy speech and political activity will establish again that congregational influences must be considered in detail if we are to develop a complete understanding of clergy political activity. These congregational effects are part of the broader environment in which clergy work, an environment that also includes the denomination to which clergy belong and the community in which they work.

Denominational Cues

Denominations constitute distinctive cultures, prescribing boundaries around actions in the long run and encouraging specific behaviors in the short term. In their professional lives clergy come to identify with one denomination and are socialized into it through personal beliefs, religious practices, seminary training, calls to denominational pulpits, and regular meetings with peers. Denominations also take public stances on important societal issues, hoping to receive support from constituent clergy and their members in public and in private. Denominational public agendas suggest sermon topics and church activities dedicated to addressing a constellation of public policy issues. Therefore, one would expect the denomination, through its many layers of contact with clergy (especially true for the ELCA and Episcopal Church), to exert powerful socializing effects on clergy behavior.

One of the clearest findings from past research on clergy political activity, that clergy in certain denominations and religious traditions are more comfortable mixing religion and politics, has now become clouded and murky. Wuthnow (1988) describes this transformation as the breakdown of denominationalism and the realignment of American religion into two camps, mirroring two-party politics. The theologies that built and sustained distinctive denominational traditions and histories of political engagement have been transformed to accommodate mobilization efforts by political activists and evolving traditions of political activity (Martin 1996). To compete with these influences, denominations still provide the lion's share of socialization for new clergy, primarily from seminaries but also from interaction with local clergy colleagues and in regional and national meetings. *Denominational norms communicated through colleagues thus should help to shape the amount of clergy public speech and political activity.*

We incorporate the influence of the denomination through four main variables to be utilized in chapters 5–9: whether the clergyperson is ELCA or Episcopal, whether the clergyperson believes her denomination is supportive of clergy political roles and activities, the activity levels of clergy colleagues, and the clergyperson's evaluation of her local denominational unit (the synod for ELCA pastors, the diocese for Episcopal priests and deacons). Based on data we have presented so far (especially chapter 2), we expect Episcopal priests and deacons to be somewhat more politically active than ELCA pastors. We also hypothesize that greater perceived denominational support for clergy politicking and more political activity by clergy colleagues should enhance speech and activity, and that dissatisfaction with the denomination—measured by the evaluation of the unit closest to the clergyperson—may affect clergy speech and activities on issues related to denominational affairs (see chapter 9).

With membership levels in the ELCA and Episcopal Church declining in recent decades, the interest a denomination has in maintaining itself has the potential to send mixed messages to clergy: keep people in the pews but also witness on important issues when members may disagree with the denomination's message delivered by clergy. Our analysis will help discern just how, in this changing environment and with the future of the denomination in mind, the denomination affects decisions by ELCA and Episcopal clergy about public speech and political activity.

Community Influences

Clergy are involved in national and local groups as well as activities outside of their churches and profession, and they minister to congregations in communities with distinctive political and social traits, all of which may carry political ramifications (Crawford and Olson 2001a, 2001b; Olson 2000). Therefore, when analyzing clergy public speech and political activity, we include factors that reflect how clergy relate to the secular community (whether locally or nationally based) outside of their church and profession, and how their congregations differ from others in the local community and in the denomination as a whole.

We capture clergy orientations toward the secular community through measures of public affairs group affiliations and contact, as well as media usage. Just under half of our sample clergy belong to at least one public affairs group with a religious motivation or affiliation, such as Bread for the World or Habitat for Humanity. These organizations can act as an additional influence on clergy political action, a force seen as crucial for mobilizing the political participation of citizens (Guth 1996; Guth et al. 1997; Rosenstone and Hansen 1993; Verba, Schlozman, and Brady 1995).

Some groups have recruited clergy specifically, including the Moral Majority in the 1980s (Liebman 1983; Martin 1996) and the Interfaith Alliance beginning in the late 1990s (Interfaith Alliance 2002). In 1996, 86 percent of our sample clergy reported at least one contact from a political party or campaign, religious or moral concerns organization, denominational agency, or a group of laity from their congregation; 68 percent were contacted in 1998, a midterm election year. The most common sources of contact were political parties and candidates (59 percent), followed closely by moral concerns organizations (49 percent); about 10 percent of clergy were contacted by denominational agencies or congregation-based groups for political purposes. ELCA and Episcopal clergy are perceived as useful allies for many political and civic groups, and *we expect clergy activity to rise with the frequency and greater extent of contacting from such groups.*

Clergy also receive inspiration for public political speech and activity from media sources, both secular and religious in nature. We asked our sample clergy a host of questions about what they read, viewed, and listened to on a regular basis. The effects of these sources are not so much in telling clergy what to think and say, but rather indicating what clergy might think and talk about when preaching or interacting in and outside of their congregations. The ability of national media sources to set audience agendas is well established by social science research (Graber 2002). Using measures of newspaper reading, radio and television usage, and periodical subscriptions, we expect that the more numerous and diverse the information sources clergy utilize on a regular basis, the more they will speak and act on public policy issues.

In chapter 4 we found that congregational support for clergy political activity among Episcopal clergy was greater when clergy perceived their congregations to be isolated from other local churches in terms of beliefs (theological views, political opinions, minority membership, worship style, level of church activity); congregational support was lower when clergy perceived their congregations to be isolated in terms of activities (social status, community involvement, political actions). Location and orientation to location matter and perceptions of isolation or integration with the local community must be incorporated into any full analysis of clergy speech and activities.

Why should isolation affect clergy political actions? Regardless of whether one approves of clergy and congregations mixing religious beliefs and political ends, clergy sometimes find themselves, by choice or accident, engaged in local political issues as the spiritual representatives and leaders of their churches. A lack of political representation may make it difficult for the church and church members to thrive in a community through adverse zoning decisions, school board policies, and other undesirable social policies. Such situations may result from the minority status of the congregation's beliefs in the community and/or the underinvolvement of the congregation in the community. These two problems often appear together but are in fact independent of each other—a group can have beliefs representative of the community but not participate fully in civic life. Since most clergy have a strong civic orientation and realize that a healthy democracy requires robust citizen participation, they are already predisposed to induce members to vote and engage in politics through other means.

From a clergy-centered view, then, one might argue that clergy would participate more often in politics in communities with like-minded people—a politically safe environment but also one in which agreeable, mobilizing organizations also exist. Of course, the involvement of congregants in public affairs is another way to ensure the representation of church beliefs and the maintenance of relevant community standards. We test for this effect by using measures of the percentage of residents in each clergyperson's county who belong to the ELCA and the Episcopal Church.

Yet the strongest motivation for clergy political speech and action is likely to be the relative *absence* of their congregation's voice and their own beliefs in community decision making. We argue that in situations where the congregation is *not* well represented in the local community—small in numbers and perhaps politically distinct as well—the clergy can dictate the congregation's public voice directly and indirectly. *Where their churches are incongruent with the surrounding community, clergy will more likely speak out about political issues, get involved in elections, attempt to influence member opinions directly, and motivate members to act themselves.* An analogous effect has been found in studies of the D.C. lobbying offices of national denominations; while these offices surely hope to influence legislation in Congress, they also serve to present publicly the faith-inspired viewpoints of the denomination's membership, which are often perceived to be underrepresented in Washington (Hertzke 1988; Hofrenning 1995). Such an expressive act of prophetic witnessing is seen as worthwhile in and of itself, and clergy in local communities are well positioned to fill this same role for their congregants.

Hence clergy in congregations that are *unlike* the rest of the local community should be more active in order to represent the church in the public sphere. We attempt to capture this effect by utilizing the *belief isolation* and *activity isolation* measures introduced in chapter 3, and sometimes adding a third measure to capture the differences a clergyperson perceives between her church and others in the same denomination. It is not obvious whether greater *denominational isolation* should lead to more or less clergy political activity, although we suspect that clergy who see their church as unlike others are probably isolated on the other measures as well, and thus clergy in these churches are more likely to engage in public speech and political activity.

THE FREQUENCY AND CONTENT
OF CLERGY PUBLIC SPEECH

In the Stark study of California clergy (1968), 64 percent of Episcopal priests took a stand from the pulpit on a political issue at some point in their careers. Contrast this figure with the 88 percent of our 1998 nationwide sample of Episcopal priests and deacons who took a stand at some point in their career, and the 47 percent who did so in 1998. Our evidence suggests that Episcopal clergy have become more politically active from the pulpit over the last thirty years.

Stark also found in 1968 that California clergy of the American Lutheran Church (ALC) and the Lutheran Church in America (LCA), the two large bodies that merged in 1988 to form the ELCA, differed significantly in their political public speech levels—63 percent of LCA clergy had taken a stand on a political issue in the pulpit during their career, versus only 38 percent of ALC clergy. According to our 1998 data, of those ELCA clergy who have been in their present churches since the merger (eleven years), 50 percent of clergy in former LCA churches took a stand from the pulpit during 1990 alone, while only 39 percent of clergy in former ALC churches did so. Thus a small gap remained in 1998 between clergy in formerly LCA and ALC churches. Overall, 90 percent of ELCA clergy took a stand on a political issue at some point in their careers, and 56 percent took a stand in 1998. Like Episcopal clergy, ELCA clergy also appear to have become significantly more comfortable mixing religion and politics since the late 1960s.

There are many ways clergy can make their views known in public. Table 5.1 shows that the most common mode of speech clergy utilize to address political and social issues during 1998 is *public prayer*—54.6 percent of clergy prayed publicly on a political or social issue during 1998, with ELCA clergy 12 percentage points more likely to do so than Episcopal clergy. A majority of ELCA and Episcopal clergy have publicly taken a stand on a political issue, and about half have taken a stand on an issue while preaching. By contrast, just under a fifth of clergy have prayed for candidates in public, while just over a tenth have publicly endorsed a candidate. Clearly sample ELCA and Episcopal clergy feel more comfortable addressing public policies and problems rather than parties, candidates, and elections.

Stark and colleagues found that California clergy were relatively unwilling to deal with the issues that were ripping the country apart in 1968, including the war in Vietnam, the assassinations of Martin Luther King Jr. and Robert Kennedy, and race riots (Stark et al. 1971). Are modern clergy more or less likely to take up important issues of the day? We addressed this question in chapter 2 (table 2.7), which introduced two categories of public policy issues: a *moral reform agenda* and a *social justice agenda*. Table 5.2 combines ELCA and Episcopal clergy responses to give the overall percentage of sample clergy who report speaking at least once in 1998 about these sixteen issues. As noted in chapter 2, social justice issues are discussed more

Table 5.1. Percent of Clergy Who Exercised Political Voice in 1998

Variable	Total	ELCA	Episcopal Church
Publicly (including preaching) pray on a political/ social issue	55.7	60.5	48.9
Publicly (not preaching) take a stand on a political/ social issue	51.5	51.4	51.6
While preaching take a stand on a political/social issue	48.9	49.7	47.8
Publicly (not preaching) pray for candidates	20.5	22.1	18.4
Publicly (not preaching) endorse a candidate	11.3	10.2	13.0
Number of cases	2,146	1,260	888

Source: 1998 ELCA/Episcopal Church Study.

often than moral reform issues: 80 percent or more of sample clergy addressed six of the eight social justice issues, versus two of eight moral reform issues discussed by at least 80 percent of sample clergy. Nearly every clergyperson publicly addressed at least one of the sixteen issues in 1998.

Table 5.1 and table 5.2 indicate that in 1998, our sample clergy are clearly willing to go beyond merely mentioning current events in passing, as was more common in the late 1960s. Our sample clergy take stands on important public issues and thereby connect faith and public policy for their constituent publics. Moreover, clergy have clearly become more politicized over the last thirty years, perhaps leading or perhaps following the trend of religious adherents nationwide becoming more comfortable with exploring the political implications of their religious beliefs (Kohut et al. 2000).

PREDICTING CLERGY PUBLIC SPEECH

With these initial explorations in mind, we now turn to a detailed test of our fivefold typology, examining overall levels of clergy public speech in 1998 and the frequency of 1998 clergy public speech on four specific political issues. Our choice of dependent variables—these two measures that we will analyze—and the methods we will use require some explanation.

Dependent Variables

The distinction between overall public speech and specific comments on issues is important. It is possible that levels of public speech are not

Table 5.2.   Percent of Clergy Addressing Specific Public Policy Issues in 1998

Social Justice Issues	Percent	Moral Reform Issues	Percent
Hunger and poverty	98.4	Family problems in America	95.3
Environment	93.0	Homosexuality	80.0
Education	92.8	Capital punishment	75.7
Civil rights	91.8	Current political scandals	74.3
Women's issues	89.4	Abortion	73.0
Unemployment, the economy	87.0	Gambling laws	66.1
Gay rights	74.0	Prayer in public schools	66.0
Budget deficits, government spending	60.9	National defense	61.7

Source: 1998 ELCA/Episcopal Church Clergy Study. Number of cases = 2,146
Note: For each issue, the question asks: "How often have you addressed the following issues publicly in the last year? Very often, often, seldom, rarely, or never." The cell entries report the combined responses for all categories except "never."

issue-specific, but rather stem from a common set of factors regardless of the content of the speech. Thus our first analysis will utilize an index that combines the three most common forms of 1998 clergy speech (see table 5.1): publicly praying about a political or social issue, taking a policy stance in public, and taking a policy stance while preaching. Scores on the public speech index range from zero (doing none of the activities in 1998) to three (doing all three in the past year). Thirty-five percent of our sample clergy spoke in all three ways and 31 percent, one or two; 34 percent took no policy stances and offered no public prayers on political or social issues during 1998.[2]

It is equally plausible to suggest that content matters. Among other goals, political speech intends to provide some information to the audience. Hence the nature of the issue, the salience of the issue to the congregation (especially religious and moral dimensions of the issue), and the cues offered by the political environment may all affect whether and how often clergy address a specific public policy or societal issue.

Accordingly, our second analysis will use the frequency with which our sample clergy publicly addressed four issues during 1998: abortion, school prayer, gay rights, and the environment. Abortion and school prayer are part of the moral reform issue agenda of ELCA and Episcopal clergy, while gay rights and the environment fall on the social justice agenda (see table 5.2). All four issues were mentioned by at least two-thirds of sample clergy in 1998, with the environment being mentioned often or very often by 46 percent of sample clergy; 24 percent discussed gay rights often or very often, and less than 15 percent mentioned abortion and school prayer often. Using issue-specific dependent variables from both agendas will allow us to assess whether clergy use different calculations in deciding what policy issues to address publicly.

Statistical Methods

Overall, the contrasts between factors that predict our two *dependent variables*, overall clergy speech and issue-specific speech, should help to identify the processes by which clergy enter the public arena to engage political issues through their speech. Performing this analysis with the five sets of potential explanatory factors we have discussed—termed *independent variables*—requires a sophisticated statistical method, known as ordinary least squares (OLS) regression analysis, or simply *regression.*

Regression analysis allows us to incorporate and test for the effects of many independent variables simultaneously on one dependent variable; this full test is termed a *regression model*. Essentially the regression procedure is a complex sorting mechanism, calculating the separate, distinct impact that each included independent variable has on the dependent variable. The tables of regression results we are about to analyze (table 5.3 and table 5.4) give two essential pieces of information for each independent variable:

- the *coefficient*, a measure of the *direction* (positive or negative) and *strength* (the change in the dependent variable based on a one-unit change in the independent variable) of the relationship between each independent variable and the dependent variable
- an assessment of whether or not the relationship is *statistically significant*, indicated by the asterisks in the table

Although the regression coefficients in table 5.3 and table 5.4 are not precisely equivalent to the correlations we presented in Chapters 3 and 4, *the measures of statistical significance presented are interpreted exactly as in the previous correlations.* Hence one asterisk means at least 90 percent confidence that the independent variable is statistically related to the dependent variable (the standard minimum necessary confidence level to claim a relationship between the two variables); two asterisks equates to 95 percent confidence; and three asterisks indicates at least 99 percent confidence—a virtual certainty that the independent variable is related to the dependent variable. Zero asterisks would indicate that no statistical relationship exists between the independent and dependent variables—that the former has no effect on the latter.

As already noted, appendix B offers a more detailed, technical description of the OLS regression procedure. Our discussion of the regression model results will focus on the substantive implications—whether our initial hypotheses for the five sets of independent variables thought to influence clergy public speech are confirmed or not confirmed by the regression analysis.

Determinants of Overall Clergy Public Speech

Table 5.3 presents the results of a regression analysis predicting 1998 overall ELCA and Episcopal clergy public speech, using the public speech index as the dependent variable. A positive sign on an independent variable coefficient indicates that clergy public speech increases as the independent variable increases in value; a negative sign means that public speech decreases as the independent variable increases in value. The independent variables are broken down into the five categories discussed earlier to facilitate comprehension of the regression model results. Significant relationships are found with thirteen independent variables, including at least two in each of the five categories.

Table 5.3.   Estimated Clergy 1998 Overall Public Speech
(OLS regression estimates)

Variable	Coeff.	(S.E.)
Personal Attributes		
Doctoral degree	0.107	(0.050)**
Male	−0.051	(0.088)
Years in the ministry	−0.013	(0.003)***
Tenure length at present church	−0.005	(0.005)
Political and Theological Orientations		
Strong partisan	−0.000	(0.036)
Strong political ideology	0.097	(0.051)*
Political interest	0.089	(0.055)
Political efficacy	0.051	(0.021)**
Theological conservatism	−0.076	(0.039)*
Congregational Resources		
Average congregational approval of clergy speech	0.275	(0.038)***
Clergy ideological difference with church	0.168	(0.047)***
Church is politically divided	−0.022	(0.041)
Church size	0.000	(0.000)
Less brand loyalty in congregation	0.085	(0.048)*
Rural church	−0.095	(0.073)
Southern church	−0.052	(0.079)
Denominational Cues		
Denomination perceived as supportive of clergy politicking	0.019	(0.042)
Colleagues' political activity	0.292	(0.057)***
Episcopal clergy	−0.351	(0.075)***
Community Influences		
Memberships in public affairs groups	0.073	(0.026)***
Newspaper reading	−0.015	(0.015)
Periodical subscriptions	0.060	(0.019)***
Belief isolation	0.279	(0.120)**
Activity isolation	0.153	(0.138)
Constant	0.550	(0.444)
Number of cases		1,563
Adjusted R^2		0.136

Source: 1998 ELCA/Episcopal Church Clergy Study.
***$p < 0.01$; **$p < 0.05$; *$p < 0.10$

Table 5.3 shows that two personal attributes of clergy are statistically related to overall clergy public speech. Clergy with doctoral degrees are more likely to speak publicly, while public speech decreases the more years a clergyperson has been in her profession. Neither gender nor tenure at the present church are significantly related to overall public speech. As expected, personal attributes are not dominant factors determining levels of clergy speech.

Three political and ideological factors are related to overall clergy public speech as well. Clergy speak more often if they have a strong political ideology (liberal or conservative) and if they believe ministers can have a political impact (political efficacy). The negative sign on the theological conservatism measure means that more theologically conservative clergy speak less often, while theologically liberal clergy speak more often; this fits with the historical patterns depicted by existing research. Partisanship and interest in politics are not significant predictors of overall clergy speech. While *The Bully Pulpit* asserts that factors in this category are dominant in affecting levels of clergy political activity, we find that for ELCA and Episcopal sample clergy, political and theological orientations are relatively weak predictors of overall public speech, when other potential explanatory factors are accounted for.

The balance of factors affecting levels of 1998 clergy public speech come from extrapersonal sources: the congregation, the denomination, and the community. The primary congregational influences are the perceived congregational approval of clergy public speech and the existence of ideological differences between the clergy and her congregation. *Clergy public speech is greater when clergy-congregation disagreement is stronger and when the congregation is believed to approve of clergy speech.* Rather than feel constrained by a political gulf separating themselves and their congregations, clergy seem willing to undertake a prophetic role to bridge it. Moreover, we find a significant effect from the brand loyalty of the membership—less brand loyalty in the congregation allows for more clergy politicking while greater brand loyalty constrains clergy speech—exactly as we anticipated. Though the point should not be taken too far, aggregated over forty years and many denominations, the shifting denominational memberships of U.S. churchgoers (Bromley 1988; Djupe 1999; Wuthnow 1988) presents one reason why clergy have become more politically engaged since the 1960s.

The model results in table 5.3 also reveal that denominational cues affect clergy public speech levels. Episcopal clergy speak out significantly less often than ELCA clergy (about one-third of a point less on our 0 to 3 index); table 5.1 shows the primary difference between the two denominations to be frequency of public prayer on a political or social issue. While the perception of support from denominational leaders does not affect sample clergy speech levels, the political activity cues provided by denominational colleagues encourage more clergy public speech. There is certainly some self-selection occurring here; politically active clergy may well seek out the support and friendship of others who are also politically engaged. But self-selection does not explain the regression model result, which demonstrates the explanatory power of this statistical method: *the speech-encouraging effect of having politically active ELCA or Episcopal colleagues is independent of all other factors in the model.* Hence our sample clergy are not just speaking out frequently and consorting with like-minded peers because they are predisposed to do so. Their frequency of public speech rises *because* they have like-minded peers who are politically active.

Finally, three community influences affect sample ELCA and Episcopal clergy public speech levels. It is not surprising to see the positive influence of public affairs group memberships on the public speech of clergy, which squares with long-standing research into the determinants of political participation (Verba and Nie 1972). The effect of periodical subscriptions is also positive and significant. Clergy who receive more journals have or want more information, and they find ways to present some of this material to their members in public forums.

The most important relationship in the clergy public speech index model is the positive effect on clergy speech from congregational belief isolation. This finding strongly supports our contention that *clergy are more likely to fulfill a prophetic role, in this case praying or taking issue stances more often, when they believe their congregation holds beliefs unlike other churches in their community.* Public speech is a way for ELCA and Episcopal clergy to offer a neglected perspective. If done directly—speaking in the community outside the congregation—clergy become the public representatives of their congregations, in addition to serving as spiritual representatives. When the speech takes place within the congregation in sermons and other gatherings, clergy can use their church's perceived minority status to spur members to speak up and act themselves—exactly what researchers have found to occur in other minority groups embedded in contrary social contexts (Finifter 1974; Key 1949).

The regression model results presented in table 5.3 offer strong support for all elements of our fivefold typology of influences on overall clergy political speech. We turn now to an exploration of speech content—whether the same factors affect the likelihood of clergy discussing four often contentious political and social issues

PREDICTING CONTENT-SPECIFIC CLERGY SPEECH

Our four chosen issues—abortion, prayer in public schools, gay rights, and the environment—possess important attributes that will assist in sorting out the determinants of issue-specific clergy public speech. First, as noted earlier, two issues (abortion and school prayer) are moral reform agenda issues for ELCA and Episcopal clergy, while gay rights and the environment fall in the social justice category. Second, while all four issues were potent, public, and present in American politics during 1998, the two social reform issues received more coverage. Gay rights entered the national agenda primarily through growing national and state-level debates over same-sex marriage, as well as the murder of Matthew Shepard (an Episcopalian) in Wyoming. The environment was also a prominent issue during this midterm election year, fueled by Democratic Party criticism of what they believed to be a less-than-green Republican Congress.

Each of these issues has a unique history within each denomination. The ELCA has lobbied on behalf of hate crimes legislation, yet it has become embroiled in internal controversy over the ordination of gays and lesbians, which occurred despite church rules that forbid it ("Ordained against the Rules" 2001). At its 2001 General Assembly, the ELCA voted to undertake a four-year study of issues surrounding sexuality, sexual orientation, and the church, leading to a definitive resolution no earlier than 2005 (Religious News Service 2002). The Episcopal Church, by contrast, has provoked controversy domestically and within the worldwide Anglican Communion by quietly supporting the ordination of gays and lesbians in many dioceses; Episcopal congregations generally have been perceived as more welcoming and tolerant of gay and lesbian relationships than most U.S. denominations ("Prelates and Provocations" 2001; Solheim 1998). In early 2000, nine Episcopal bishops joined nine hundred U.S. religious leaders in signing a statement endorsing same-sex blessing rituals and the ordination of gay and lesbians (McCormick 2000).

Less controversy has been generated on the other issues under study here. Both denominations have affirmed the need for greater environmental protection, and faith-based perspectives on environmental concerns continue to increase in visibility within U.S. denominations (Fowler 1995; Keizer 2001). Both denominations also oppose prayer in public schools, although the Episcopal Church appears more open about advocating "church partnership with government" (Episcopal Public Policy Network 1995); the ELCA's 1991 social statement "The Church in Society" offers a more qualified endorsement of church–state interactions (ELCA 1991b). The Episcopal Church has

officially favored access to abortion since the mid 1980s, reaffirming this
stance in a 1994 resolution opposing legislation that would limit abortion
rights (Episcopal Public Policy Network 1994). The 1991 ELCA social statement on abortion challenged the sexualization of U.S. culture and bemoaned
the number of abortions performed, concluding that abortion should be legal in specific circumstances (ELCA 1991a).[3]

These institutional connections to the four issues being analyzed are
reflected in how often ELCA and Episcopal clergy address these issues.
There is no difference on the frequency of addressing abortion or the environment (table 2.7), but Episcopal clergy address gay rights more frequently
while ELCA pastors talk about prayer in public schools more often. The
majority of our clergy would also be presenting liberal or Democratic positions on these four issues (table 2.11); hence our regression models test
whether Democratic and liberal clergy address these issues more often than
conservative and Republican clergy.

The OLS regression results predicting the frequency of discussing each
issue are presented in table 5.4. Once again we have divided the independent variables into our familiar five categories of potential influences, and
our discussion of model results is also ordered by these five categories.

Personal Attributes

We expected that clergy personal attributes would have limited effects
on the frequency of clergy speech. Table 5.4 shows that years in the ministry has a consistent significant effect. More time served leads to more discussion of all four issues, whereas table 5.3 showed that more time in the
ministry related to *less* overall public speech, taking numerous other factors
into account. These results suggest that the most experienced clergy (who
are almost all men) feel less constrained in tackling contentious issues than
newer clergy. More experienced clergy were socialized to be politically active (recall figure 2.3), and experience teaches veteran clergy how to raise
sensitive subjects in appropriate ways. Interestingly, tenure length at the present church does not affect speech frequencies on any issue, suggesting that
clergy holding their posts longer do not perceive additional impetus to political speech from "credit" or goodwill they may have built over the years.

Table 5.4 also shows that clergy with doctoral degrees are less likely to
discuss abortion publicly, and male clergy discuss the two social justice issues less often than female clergy (recall table 2.8). This last result reflects the
feminist orientations of female clergy in these denominations (Crawford,
Deckman, and Braun 2001, Olson, Crawford, and Guth 2000)

Table 5.4. Estimated 1998 Frequency of Clergy Public Speech on Selected Issues (OLS regression estimates)

Variable	Abortion		School Prayer		Gay Rights		Environment	
	Coeff.	(S.E.)	Coeff.	(S.E.)	Coeff.	(S.E.)	Coeff.	(S.E.)
Personal Attributes								
Doctoral degree	−0.088	(0.041)**	−0.028	(0.042)	−0.023	(0.041)	−0.000	(0.040)
Male	−0.084	(0.075)	0.006	(0.076)	−0.203	(0.075)***	−0.214	(0.073)***
Years in the ministry	0.015	(0.003)***	0.012	(0.003)***	0.008	(0.003)***	0.013	(0.003)***
Tenure length at present church	0.003	(0.004)	0.004	(0.004)	−0.003	(0.004)	0.000	(0.004)
Political and Theological Orientations								
Democrat	0.008	(0.031)	0.011	(0.032)	−0.009	(0.031)	−0.066	(0.031)**
Republican	0.040	(0.037)	0.102	(0.037)***	−0.028	(0.037)	−0.094	(0.036)***
Liberal	−0.015	(0.051)	0.059	(0.051)	0.427	(0.051)***	0.136	(0.049)***
Conservative	0.224	(0.070)***	−0.006	(0.071)	−0.264	(0.070)***	−0.393	(0.068)***
Political interest	0.102	(0.049)**	0.129	(0.050)***	0.082	(0.049)*	0.101	(0.048)**
Political efficacy	0.021	(0.019)	0.074	(0.019)***	0.074	(0.019)***	0.024	(0.019)
Theological conservatism	0.181	(0.040)***	0.156	(0.040)***	−0.276	(0.040)***	0.021	(0.039)
Congregational Resources								
Average congregational approval of clergy speech	0.222	(0.033)***	0.093	(0.034)***	0.252	(0.033)***	0.132	(0.033)***
Clergy issue stance differs from congregation's issue stance	−0.123	(0.024)***	−0.025	(0.023)	−0.030	(0.026)	−0.042	(0.014)***

(continued)

Table 5.4. Estimated 1998 Frequency of Clergy Public Speech on Selected Issues (OLS regression estimates) *(continued)*

Variable	Abortion Coeff.	(S.E.)	School Prayer Coeff.	(S.E.)	Gay Rights Coeff.	(S.E.)	Environment Coeff.	(S.E.)
Church is politically divided	−0.021	(0.035)	−0.001	(0.036)	0.021	(0.035)	0.037	(0.034)
Church size	−0.000	(0.000)	−0.000	(0.000)	−0.000	(0.000)	−0.000	(0.000)
Percent of members active in church								
small groups	0.002	(0.001)*	0.003	(0.001)**	0.001	(0.001)	0.001	(0.001)
Less brand loyalty in congregation	−0.023	(0.040)	0.007	(0.041)	0.039	(0.040)	−0.057	(0.039)
Rural church	0.091	(0.061)	0.220	(0.066)***	0.021	(0.061)	0.213	(0.059)***
Southern church	0.016	(0.065)	0.173	(0.066)***	−0.050	(0.065)	0.056	(0.063)
Denominational Cues								
Denomination perceived as supportive of clergy politicking	−0.017	(0.035)	−0.008	(0.035)	−0.028	(0.035)	−0.032	(0.034)
Episcopal clergy	−0.021	(0.065)	−0.196	(0.067)***	0.149	(0.065)**	−0.032	(0.064)
Community Influences								
Memberships in public affairs groups	0.077	(0.021)***	0.049	(0.022)**	0.063	(0.021)***	0.049	(0.021)**
Newspaper reading	−0.000	(0.012)	0.009	(0.012)	0.032	(0.012)***	0.001	(0.012)
Periodical subscriptions	0.041	(0.015)***	0.003	(0.015)	0.038	(0.015)**	0.029	(0.015)~
Belief isolation	0.041	(0.100)	−0.138	(0.102)	0.248	(0.100)**	0.167	(0.097)*
Activity isolation	0.233	(0.116)**	0.062	(0.118)	0.129	(0.116)	0.028	(0.114)
Constant	0.662	(0.354)	0.177	(0.357)	1.551	(0.354)	2.475	(0.343)~
Number of cases	1,645		1,638		1,632		1,642	
Adjusted R²	0.155		0.084		0.310		0.112	

Source: 1998 ELCA/Episcopal Church Clergy Study.
***$p < 0.01$; **$p < 0.05$; *$p < 0.10$

Political and Theological Orientations

The effects of explicitly political and theological measures vary depending on the issue in question, according to table 5.4. The only consistent finding for all four issues is that clergy interest in politics leads to more speech, just as one would expect. Theological conservatism affects speech on three issues but not on the environment, where theological perspectives do not break down neatly along conservative-modernist lines.[4] On the moral reform issues of abortion and school prayer, theological conservatives speak more often, while theological liberals are more vocal on gay rights. Table 5.4 also shows that greater political efficacy leads to more speech only on school prayer and gay rights.

For the four political orientation variables included in the table 5.4 models, we find expected relationships and we observe that *political orientations are more important predictors of clergy speech on social justice issues*. Republican clergy speak more often about school prayer (part of the GOP agenda since the early 1980s), but no other political orientations predict school prayer speech. Conservatives discuss abortion more often, again the only significant political orientation variable. By contrast, on gay rights and the environment, liberal sample clergy speak more often while conservative clergy are less vocal. Democratic and Republican partisanship also predict less speech on the environment; the liberal and conservative variables account for stronger influences than these partisan measures. From this pattern of results, it seems clear that gay rights and the environment were more salient issues in 1998, with cues available for all sides, whereas forces motivating abortion and school prayer discussion appear to affect conservatives and Republicans only.

Congregational Resources

The role of the congregation in shaping clergy political behavior lies at the intersection of congregational approval of clergy public speech and ideological agreement with the clergy. While approval of activity may allow clergy to act, opinion differences will shape the issues on which they can be active without drawing the congregation's enmity. The table 5.4 models reveal that congregational approval of clergy speech always leads to more speech about each issue. As we found consistently with a more general measure of ideological differences, clergy who are more liberal than their congregations on each issue (as perceived by the clergyperson) speak out more often on the issue. This effect is significant only for abortion and the environment, although the direction is consistent across all four issues.

Some other congregational resources affect levels of clergy speech on these issues in 1998. Greater congregational group activity leads to more speech on abortion and school prayer. Pro-life and pro-choice organizations in particular have always relied on congregational mobilization to help achieve their aims (Craig and O'Brien 1993). Having a more involved congregation may also promote the clergy addressing issues that concern some of the small groups directly. In addition, clergy speech on school prayer and the environment is higher in rural churches, and clergy in southern churches talk more about school prayer. We attribute these results to the nature of interest in the issues—southern and rural Americans have tended to support school prayer as a states rights issue (Gilbert et al. 1999), and environmental concerns are always of interest to rural areas dependent on agriculture for their economic livelihoods.

No other congregational resource affects clergy discussion of gay rights in 1998. This issue has become very contentious in many denominations besides the ELCA and Episcopal Church, with the relatively liberal stances of clergy and denomination clashing against general congregational discomfort or even hostility. Political orientations and community influences—the impact of national debates over gay rights in 1998—affect clergy speech on gay rights, but many congregations seem to wish the issue would disappear altogether. Clergy discussions of gay rights and sexual orientation issues therefore fit with a prophetic role.

Beyond the congregational approval and clergy–congregation difference variables, few congregational resource factors are salient in table 5.4. Political divisions within the congregation may encourage clergy to downplay politics to avoid a schism and the consequent loss of members, but this proposition finds no support in our models. Moreover, church size and member brand loyalty have no effect on issue-specific speech.

Denominational Cues

Table 5.4 shows that denominational cues seem to have little impact on clergy issue-specific speech. Episcopal clergy spoke out on gay rights more often and ELCA clergy spoke on school prayer more often—a reflection, perhaps, of greater ELCA ambivalence toward church–state separation issues. Interestingly, perceived support from the denomination for clergy political activity did not inspire speech on any issue. The connection to denominations is largely a product of socialization and should also be long-term in nature. It may not be surprising, therefore, that patterns of the everyday political life of clergy are not motivated by our measures of denominational influence, except in special cases (see Findlay 1993).

Community Influences

The table 5.3 model of general clergy public speech showed that group memberships and clergy reading habits sparked more clergy speech, as did belief isolation—the perception that the clergyperson's congregation does not believe what most others in the community believe. The Table 5.4 models also show that public affairs group memberships and reading habits affect specific issue speech. More group memberships spark more speech on all four issues, while the effects of periodical subscriptions (significant on three issues) and newspaper reading (significant on one) are almost always positive—more reading material and actual perusal equates with more clergy speech.

The effects of the two isolation measures—belief and activity isolation—are not the same across the four issues. *For both social justice issues, greater belief isolation leads to more clergy public speech*; belief isolation does not affect clergy speech on abortion and school prayer. Clergy leadership on these issues represents the local manifestation of national movements that, as we indicated earlier, were more active and visible in 1998. The events of 1998 (gay marriage debates, the Shepard murder, and growing discussion of how sexual orientation should be dealt with in public and private venues) threw the sexual orientation policy community equilibrium off balance, leading clergy to believe they had an opportunity to effect change (cf. Baumgartner and Jones 1993). Therefore, clergy were more vocal on the issue when a prophetic voice was called for, when their own and their congregation's beliefs were not in the community mainstream.

Table 5.4 also shows that *activity isolation is a significant predictor only of clergy speech about abortion*, which as we noted earlier has more congregation-based mobilization for political action than any of the other issues. Combined with the other abortion model results, it appears that conservative clergy are more vocal about abortion and more likely to spur members to act when perceiving the congregation to be less engaged in the local community. The results for the isolation measures in table 5.4 show yet again that in communities where the congregation is not well represented the clergy can dictate the congregation's public voice directly and indirectly.

CONCLUSION

In this chapter we have explored the nature, frequency, and determinants of clergy public speech. We find that it is relatively pervasive and conveys significant normative judgments about the workings of the policy process. Our regression models largely confirm existing notions about the determinants of clergy speech. But the significance in our models of previously excluded factors, especially the congregation's relationship with the community, suggests that factors external to the clergy and church cannot be overlooked as potent influences in these and other types of clergy political activity. There is no question that clergy political behavior cannot be understood in a vacuum, but rather should be considered a product of personal motivation situated in an environment conducive to action, including the pressures exerted by the congregation, the denomination, and the community.

Interestingly, and perhaps most importantly, we find that clergy engage in more public speech (both in general and on specific issues) when their congregations constitute a minority within the community in terms of beliefs or involvement levels. In such situations clergy represent their congregations in the public sphere and motivate members to add their distinctive voices to public debate. Church involvement is an important avenue through which minority voices can be represented in public decision making, and ELCA and Episcopal clergy help to spur their members to act through the amount and content of their public pronouncements and political activities. The process by which clergy are encouraged to become representatives in the public square is driven in part by local church–community relations.

Finally, we find that the patterns of clergy addressing substantive policy issues are shaped by the opportunities presented by the nature of the policy community. Clergy become active participants in a policy debate when they sense an opportunity for change and when they are encouraged to participate by their secular ties and agreeable congregations. Together, these findings suggest the religious roots of public opinion and policy change, for many public opinion shifts over time are not solely the accumulation of individual reactions to events. Instead, we must view public opinion and policy changes as the product of conscious action on and discussion of issues within highly localized social networks, a form of political influence that American churches exert on members in regular and highly significant ways.

NOTES

1. Clergy role orientations, such as approval of some political activity, are extremely close to activism itself; hence, some caution is warranted in establishing the causal order of the relationship. It is just as likely that some clergy get involved in a

political activity at the behest of colleagues, friends, congregation members, or groups, and then begin to find it an appropriate activity in which to engage.

2. One might question whether all three of these variables in fact belong together. Our investigations show that the three variables tap a common factor (results not shown). We looked further for evidence that might suggest a difference in the participants or their motivations for each mode and venue of public speech. We found little to no difference, except for very modest differences in perceived congregational support for the three activities (higher for public prayer). Thus we are confident in combining these three forms of speech into the public speech index.

3. "The position of this church [the ELCA] is that, in cases where the life of the mother is threatened, where pregnancy results from rape or incest, or where the embryo or fetus has lethal abnormalities incompatible with life, abortion prior to viability should not be prohibited by law or by lack of public funding of abortions for low income women. On the other hand, this church supports legislation that prohibits abortions that are performed after the fetus is determined to be viable, except when the mother's life is threatened or when lethal abnormalities indicate the prospective newborn will die very soon" (ELCA 1991a).

4. Robert Booth Fowler's important 1995 book, *The Greening of Protestant Thought*, examines the growing theological awareness of environmental concerns in U.S. Protestant circles.

6

LEADERS OF THE FLOCK OR LONE RANGERS? CLERGY IN ELECTORAL POLITICS

The preachers gave it to Reagan.

—Rev. James Robison (Martin 1996, 220)

During the course of American political history, clergy have been credited with fulfilling or dashing the electoral hopes of numerous candidates and organized interests. Most notably, clergy have played roles in moral crusades that spilled over into the electoral arena through issues and candidates (Kleppner 1970, 1979). In the nineteenth and early twentieth centuries, issues such as abolition and prohibition, and candidates such as William Jennings Bryan and Al Smith, represent just a few examples that drew clergy into the electoral arena in a more prominent fashion. Today, inspirations for clergy to become active in campaigns and elections have multiplied. Issues such as abortion, school prayer, gay rights, and affirmative action, and figures such as Ronald Reagan, Pat Robertson, Jesse Jackson, and Jimmy Carter, have all engaged religious leaders' attention. As a result, the overall electoral activity of U.S. clergy appears to have increased since the 1960s (Guth et al. 1997).

Like ordinary citizens, clergy understand that engaging in electoral politics is one way to express policy preferences, whether through supporting candidates with similar viewpoints on key issues or backing a local ballot measure. Since advanced education is known to be a strong predictor of political participation (Wolfinger and Rosenstone 1980), it is not surprising to find that clergy care more about politics than average citizens, and that clergy are highly involved in political and electoral activities. Because U.S. clergy have the potential to mobilize, set agendas, and shape the voting patterns of large numbers of American citizens, we need to understand what motivates and what limits clergy participation in electoral activities.

125

Two principal questions will be explored at length in this chapter. *How and how much do ELCA and Episcopal clergy engage in electoral activities?* And more importantly, *why do clergy get involved in elections?* This second question is fundamentally about representation. That is, do clergy, like average citizens, act primarily to satisfy *personal* political preferences, or should they be considered first and foremost as *representatives* of their faith and their members, acting out of duty to those to whom they minister or concern for them? Answers to both questions will provide a clear and more comprehensive understanding of the role of clergy in electoral politics, allowing us to assess a third critical question: *just what difference does clergy political activity make in the U.S. electoral system?*

Three perspectives, not all mutually exclusive, stand out as ways to approach these questions. First, we could conceive of ELCA and Episcopal clergy as *political elites* with well-formed ideologies, clear issue agendas, and strong habits of civic participation. The elite perspective would lead us to conclude that clergy desire to have their agendas fulfilled and will pursue that mission doggedly through electoral politics. Clergy who adopt this perspective can be termed *straight policy seekers.*

Second, with finite resources, not to mention consideration of the personal and professional risks and rewards inherent in electoral activities, clergy can be viewed as balancing choices about electoral activities with the other demands created by their work and their status in the congregation and community. Such clergy can be termed *strategic policy seekers* and their behavior could then be understood using the *rational actor model* (Downs 1957), in which citizens become active and distribute their personal political resources for greatest effect.

The last point is related to a third perspective—clergy might be conceived as *prophetic representatives* of their congregations and denominations, placing the needs of their faith community above or in tandem with their own agendas. In this model, clergy political activity constitutes a natural extension of ministry and may preclude some personally desired political actions. For instance, representative clergy in congregations that constitute a minority locally would be more involved in electoral and local politics, in order to present their faith tradition's viewpoints and ensure their unique voice is heard in the public square, setting aside "winning" as the only or primary goal of electoral activity (Hofrenning 1995).

The potential electoral impact of clergy depends on three closely related factors: the nature of their activities, their role, and the resources they can muster for the cause. These factors can be utilized in two basic types of clergy electoral activity: those with direct effects and those with indirect effects. *Direct effect activities* include campaigning, contributing money, and voting; in all three clergy act and are counted with the same weight as average citizens. *Indirect effect activities* include mobilizing church members to register and vote, endorsing candidates, speaking out on issues connected with candidate races or ballot measures, and mobilizing members by praying for candidates. All of these actions are aimed at congregants, influencing electoral outcomes through the political beliefs and choices of church members.

We will demonstrate that clergy in our sample, like other mainline Protestant clergy, act like interested and involved policy-seeking partisans in elections—an orientation that is individualistic and largely distinct from their behavior in their official duties. Very few clergy attempt to influence the partisan opinions of congregants or mobilize members behind specific parties or candidates, because either there is little support for such activity or there are concerns about the propriety of such activities. Instead, ELCA and Episcopal clergy pursue electoral activities that are primarily *civic* in nature—encouraging members to be informed citizens and to vote.

In terms of political impact, straight policy-seeking clergy and representative clergy pursue their ends without much regard for the possibility of influence. Hence these clergy may have a relatively light impact on the electoral process. On the other hand, strategic policy seekers will pour their energies into contests in which they are likely to make a difference, increasing their potential impact. Moreover, indirect effect activities can have a greater impact on the electoral process due to the larger numbers of potential voters involved.

Clergy have at their disposal numerous resources—including congregations, moral authority, church publications, and civic skills—that can be utilized in electoral politics, though tapping these resources often proves difficult. Members may be intransigent due to their desire for nonpolitical clergy efforts, low political interest or efficacy, and disagreement with the clergyperson's agenda. Clergy often have few monetary resources to contribute to parties, candidates, and causes, and little time outside of their ministerial duties to expend on campaigns and political meetings. This is not to mention the potentially detrimental effects of congregational disapproval of active, public electoral politicking by clergy: job loss, shrinking membership, and a more hostile work environment.

Therefore, *clergy are likely to have the greatest impact in elections when strong motivations coincide with an inviting electoral context—competitive elections and strong political parties—and a high resource base of information, money, and interest in both personal and congregational terms.* To evaluate this claim, we empirically investigated ELCA and Episcopal clergy electioneering with a look at the amounts, types, and targets of clergy activities, leading to an analysis of the determinants of clergy electoral activity. We will conclude this chapter with a discussion centered on the question of what impact ELCA and Episcopal clergy make on U.S. electoral politics.

TYPES AND AMOUNTS OF CLERGY ELECTIONEERING

As previous U.S. national surveys have shown, not all clergy act alike in electoral politics. Clergy in certain traditions, namely white and black evangelical Protestants, are more comfortable addressing and involving themselves in partisan politics (Kohut et al. 2000). Nevertheless, a nontrivial number of sample ELCA and Episcopal clergy do participate in electoral politics in several ways. These activities showcase the various roles that clergy fill during elections, and they provide clues for interpreting the impact of clergy electoral involvement.

Table 6.1 summarizes the type and frequency of clergy electoral involvement for seven activities. Our survey asked clergy whether they had engaged in these activities *in the past year* (1998), and whether they had ever done so *in their careers*. The percentage of clergy who reported engaging in electoral activities during 1998 is significant, and there are few sizable differences between the two denominations. Forty-six percent of all clergy reported urging their congregations to register and vote during the year. Just over one-quarter contributed to parties, political action committees, or candidates (slightly higher among Episcopal clergy), and 21 percent prayed for candidates (many sample clergy indicated praying for *all* candidates, often as part of the normal Sunday

Table 6.1.   The Types and Incidence of Clergy Electoral Activity by Denomination (percent)

Electoral Activities	Overall Past Year	Overall Career	ELCA Past Year	ELCA Career	Episcopal Church Past Year	Episcopal Church Career
Urge church to vote	46.4	87.2	47.6	87.6	44.7	86.5
Contribute money	25.5	60.8	23.4	57.1	28.5	66.0
Pray for candidates	20.5	48.7	22.0	52.2	18.4	43.8
Endorse candidates publicly	12.1	41.9	10.3	41.6	13.0	43.0
Registration drives	10.3	—	10.3	—	10.2	—
Campaign	6.2	41.3	4.9	37.8	7.9	46.1
Endorse candidates while preaching	1.3	6.2	1.3	5.7	1.4	7.0

Source: 1998 ELCA/Episcopal Church Clergy Study. Number of cases varies.

liturgy, and not using prayer in a partisan way). This ELCA pastor's view of the use of prayer is common: "Regarding political prayers in church, throughout my years in ministry I have regularly prayed for the president regardless of party—the same for national and local legislators." No other electoral activities (publicly endorsing candidates, running voter registration drives, campaigning) were engaged in by more than 15 percent of sample clergy. The impact of such activities can still be significant. Although only 10 percent of ELCA and Episcopal churches in our sample participated in voter registration drives in 1998, this translates into approximately 1,800 congregations nationwide attempting to engage new voters in the electoral process.

Over their careers, our sample clergy engage in these activities more frequently and in patterns identical to past-year activities. Seven out of eight clergy have urged their congregations to vote, and three in five have made a monetary political contribution. Nearly half have prayed for candidates and over 40 percent have endorsed candidates publicly or have engaged in campaigning. Endorsing candidates from the pulpit is rarely done.

The findings in table 6.1 confirm what we have assumed about mainline Protestant clergy involvement in elections—they are involved but in relatively low-cost ways in any given election cycle. Nearly half attempt to foster civic participation in their congregations by urging members to vote in elections; other partisan activities pursued by the clergy are generally obscured from the congregation's view (contributing money) or are done infrequently (endorsing and campaigning). This pattern is reflected in a comment made by an ELCA pastor: "I feel very much restricted as a pastor in taking part in political campaigns—I feel a strong need to remain 'neutral' in public."

The most common partisan activity identified in table 6.1 is contributing money, which clergy do far more often than the general public (26 percent, versus just 7 percent of the public, according to the 1996 National Election Study). Few clergy campaign or endorse candidates, and almost no clergy do so while preaching. Though figures in these categories appear small, the general public, again, is far less likely to engage in such activities—half as likely, in fact, to work for a campaign. Our sample ELCA and Episcopal clergy can only be described as quite politically active, relative to the general population.

THE ROLE OF CLERGY IN DIRECT DEMOCRACY: BALLOT INITIATIVES

Though certainly not a new phenomenon, legislating by ballot initiative has gained in both notoriety and attractiveness for groups and social movements

with limited access to established political networks, and for well-funded interest groups in states with easy ballot access (Sabato, Ernst, and Larson
2000). Ballot measures frequently deal with issues that draw out citizens
with moral reform and social justice concerns, including clergy. Politicking
on ballot measures has the added advantage of being an officially nonpartisan political activity (not dealing with parties or candidates), and therefore
it does not incur the threat of revocation of a church's tax exemption as
would endorsing candidates.

Moreover, clergy do not face the same repercussions from their congregation for talking about social and political issues as they might for explicitly partisan activities. Fifty-three percent of our sample clergy believe
their congregations agree that it is appropriate for clergy to take a stand
publicly on a political or social issue (25 percent perceive disapproval), and
39 percent perceive their churches to agree that it is appropriate for clergy
to take such a stand while preaching (36 percent perceive disapproval). Contrast these relatively high approval figures with the 8 percent of clergy who
perceive approval from their congregations for clergy to campaign for a
party or candidate (63 percent perceive disapproval).

A 1999 ballot initiative in Alabama provides a good example of how
clergy can participate in ballot initiatives, thus avoiding the usual approba-
tions surrounding involvement in candidate elections. With a platform con-
sisting almost solely of instituting a state lottery to benefit public education,
as has become common in many states, Democrat Don Siegelman won, 58
percent to 42 percent, over Republican incumbent Fob James in the 1998
Alabama gubernatorial election. Clergy did not have a high-profile role in
the 1998 election; evangelical voters, however, strongly supported Governor
James due to his advocacy of posting the Ten Commandments in public
places (Manuel 1998). Many clergy played prominent roles in the 1999 legislative referendum opposing the constitutional amendment to institute
Governor Siegelman's promised lottery (Manuel and Mantius 1999). In this
special election, the lottery proposal was defeated 55 percent to 45 percent.
The active engagement of clergy reflects their comfort with reframing the
lottery issue from benefiting education (1998) to promoting sinful behavior
and regressive taxation (1999). The shift in clergy involvement from 1998
to 1999 also reflects the ambivalence of many clergy about engaging in partisan electoral activity and their willingness to talk about political issues.

Because of the diverse range of clergy political interests, a variety of
ballot measure issues may attract their attention. In an interesting switch
from the early 1990s, more states in 1998 had medical use of marijuana
measures (seven) than abortion measures (only two) on the ballot. A staple

issue that attracts news stories about clergy political activity is gambling, about which four states had ballot measures. Other issues, however, may pique interest and spark activity among clergy, such as education, the environment, gay rights, animal rights, and affirmative action; all of these issues were represented on the ballot in at least one state in 1998 (authors' calculations from Initiative and Referendum Institute data for 1999).

Initiatives and referenda give clergy the opportunity and motivation to speak out about issues of concern, and the presence of so many initiatives with clear moral reform dimensions enhances these opportunities. The single-issue nature of most referenda also enhances the likelihood of clergy involvement. Ballot initiatives allow clergy to present their own and/or the denomination's point of view on the issue in question, thus drawing a more direct tie from faith and belief to potential voter decisions than is often possible in a candidate-centered race with multiple issues in play. Clergy may perceive that congregants need or want more guidance because traditional cues (party labels, incumbency) are not supplied by ballot measures.

To investigate how clergy get involved in ballot measures, we attempted to discern whether sample ELCA and Episcopal clergy speak out more about an issue when there is a corresponding ballot measure—do they talk more to their congregation about education, for instance, if an education measure is on the ballot? The short answer is no: *ELCA and Episcopal clergy do not appear to take cues from the political opportunities that ballot measures present.* Clergy in states with ballot measures addressing abortion, education, and the environment did not speak out more often on those issues than clergy in states without such ballot measures. Clergy in states with a gambling measure on the ballot actually spoke out *less* about gambling than did clergy in states with no gambling-related ballot measure.[1] Gambling measures were held in New Jersey, Missouri, Arizona, and California; states from the North and West tend to have fewer theologically orthodox clergy than other states (theologically orthodox clergy oppose gambling at higher rates than others do). Missouri, New Jersey, and California have long established gambling traditions, which may mean residents are inured to the issue and to clergy and denominational opposition. Moreover, the measure in California pitted Native American gambling interests against the Nevada gaming industry, a more difficult issue frame since a "no" vote could be viewed as anti–Native American.

These results do not mean that clergy play less important roles on ballot initiatives; it is more likely that there is a standard amount of time clergy are willing to devote to political matters. If an issue is prominent in the political process, in whatever venue, many clergy will address it. Clergy do not expend twice the effort when an issue arises in two venues (i.e., national and state). Hence *clergy are not primarily strategic policy seekers*; when they have an increased opportunity to make a difference, here through direct democracy, they do not take advantage and increase their mobilization efforts. Instead clergy serve mainly as information conduits, linking their congregants to the electoral process in general rather than specific ways.

ESTIMATING THE DETERMINANTS OF CLERGY ELECTIONEERING

As we explained at length in chapter 5, clergy political activities in all their varied forms must be understood as responses to the political and social environments in which clergy live and work. We turn now to regression models assessing which factors motivate clergy to engage in specific electoral activities, using the fivefold typology of explanatory factors presented in chapter 5. We expect types and amounts of clergy electoral activity to be determined by a combination of personal attributes, political and theological orientations, congregational resources, denominational cues, and community influences. Evaluating these explanatory factors together should allow us to determine the degree to which our sample ELCA and Episcopal clergy are strategic policy seekers, straight policy seekers, or prophetic representatives when it comes to electoral activities.

One critical question to assess in evaluating these models of clergy electoral activity is whether clergy are motivated by any form of congregational isolation to act as prophetic representatives, an orientation found to explain levels of clergy public speech in chapter 5. We would expect this dynamic to be somewhat *less likely* to occur in the context of elections. Table 6.1 shows limited clergy enthusiasm for explicitly partisan activities involving the congregation, and other types of political involvement are more easily accomplished with far less risk attached. Moreover, while ELCA and Episcopal clergy and congregants may share core theological values and hold beliefs about social responsibility in common, they remain largely in opposite partisan camps.

In a basic test of the isolation–involvement hypothesis, we correlated clergy electoral activism with two measures of a congregation's relationship with the community: percentage secular in the county (an assessment of religious difference) and percentage mainline Protestant in the county (a measure of religious similarity for our two denominations). The correlations are weak but tell a consistent story: sample clergy are *less* likely to be involved in electoral activities in communities with similar religious populations, and *more* likely when they live in communities whose populations differ in religious terms.[2] These results confirm part of the religious competition thesis of Finke and Stark (described in chapter 4): so-called lazy monopolies feel less pressure to mobilize politically, while clergy representing a numerical minority feel more compelled to counter the prevailing religious–political environment, perhaps even to counter what are perceived as "rival" churches with opposing viewpoints and more members (see also Djupe et al. 1997).

Finally, table 6.1 shows few denominational differences in levels of electoral activity. Thus the models estimated in table 6.2 and table 6.3 combine ELCA and Episcopal clergy, with an independent variable capturing differences between them. Based on social class differences and other factors described below, we expect that Episcopal clergy would be slightly more active in most electoral activities than their ELCA counterparts.

Career versus Past-Year Activities

We will test our ideas on two sets of models explaining ELCA and Episcopal clergy electoral activities: a first set explaining the *career frequency* of four clergy electoral activities (table 6.2) and a second set of models predicting whether clergy engaged in four specific electoral activities *in the last year* (in this case, 1998) (table 6.3). From the first, more general approach, we can discern the factors shaping the contours of clergy electoral activism over time; from the second, more focused approach, we can identify the more immediate concerns and opportunities presented to sample clergy. We expect clergy orientations to electoral politics—embodied in such factors as partisanship, political interest, and political ideology—to factor strongly in shaping the career activism of clergy. We also expect that in the more immediate decision-making process of the past year, pressing concerns of the congregation and profession should play a stronger role.

Direct versus Indirect Activities

Table 6.2 and table 6.3 break down clergy electoral activity into two direct activities (*campaigning* and *contributing*) and two indirect activities (*candidate support,* which is an average of three different clergy actions aimed at support for candidates, and *mobilizing,* which is urging congregation members to register and vote) for both the career and the past year. One important thing to remember is that electoral politicking is the least frequent type of activity in which our sample clergy engage, and it is often done individually (campaigning or contributing) rather than under the church's auspices. We suspect, therefore, that ELCA and Episcopal clergy pursue direct electoral activities due to strong personal motivations and as a way to express their political views without church scrutiny. Sending a check to a candidate or party may be the most private political act of all, especially if the amount is too small to trigger federal or state reporting guidelines. In contrast to direct political activity, indirect political activity aims to influence the political process through the congregation, and hence more congregational factors should come into play.

CAREER-LONG CLERGY ELECTORAL ACTIVITY

Table 6.2 presents regression results explaining the frequency of direct and indirect electoral activities clergy report engaging in during their careers. A positive sign on a regression coefficient indicates that the frequency of the specific electoral activity *increases* as that particular independent variable increases in value; a negative sign means that the frequency of the specific electoral activity *decreases* as the independent variable increases in value.

Determinants of Career Levels of Campaigning and Contributing

The model results for the direct activities of campaigning and contributing (first two columns of table 6.2) are quite similar in many ways. Differences between the two models arise from the distinctive nature of each activity. Campaigning is a public act; although congregation members may not actually directly observe or know that their minister is campaigning for someone, the potential always exists for members to become aware of it, and over the course of a career both clergy campaigning and congregational awareness are more likely. Contributing, as we noted previously, is a private act. Unless the clergyperson's contribution to a federal or state campaign is large enough, no public report or record would exist and members would be unaware of the contribution unless the clergyperson chose to tell them.

In terms of personal attributes, clergy with longer service in the ministry have campaigned and contributed more than clergy who are newer to the ministry. Clergy with doctoral degrees have contributed and campaigned less often than clergy with only the standard M.Div. degree. This reveals only a modest distinction, however; as we established in table 6.1, our

Table 6.2. Estimated Career Frequency of Clergy Electoral Activity Participation (OLS regression estimates)

| | Direct Electoral Activity | | | | Indirect Electoral Activity | | | |
| | Campaigning | | Contributing | | Candidate Support | | Mobilizing | |
Variable	Coeff.	(S.E.)	Coeff.	(S.E.)	Coeff.	(S.E.)	Coeff.	(S.E.)
Personal Attributes								
Doctoral degree	−0.084	(0.030)***	−0.092	(0.037)**	−0.077	(0.020)***	0.015	(0.032)
Male	−0.070	(0.055)	−0.053	(0.066)	−0.068	(0.036)*	−0.022	(0.064)
Years in the ministry	0.006	(0.002)***	0.006	(0.003)**	0.002	(0.001)	0.017	(0.002)***
Tenure length at present church	−0.004	(0.003)	0.006	(0.004)	−0.002	(0.002)	0.002	(0.003)
Political and Theological Orientations								
Strong partisan	0.051	(0.021)**	0.109	(0.026)***	0.029	(0.014)**	0.025	(0.025)
Strong political ideology	0.064	(0.031)**	−0.043	(0.037)	−0.020	(0.020)	−0.046	(0.036)
Political interest	0.011	(0.034)	0.089	(0.042)**	−0.053	(0.022)**	0.010	(0.040)
Political efficacy	−0.008	(0.013)	−0.021	(0.016)	−0.023	(0.008)***	−0.023	(0.015)
Clergy approval of activity	0.202	(0.018)***	0.369	(0.022)***	0.324	(0.019)***	0.257	(0.044)***
Theological conservatism	−0.199	(0.024)***	−0.192	(0.029)***	−0.101	(0.016)***	0.119	(0.029)***
Social justice agenda speech frequency	−0.212	(0.032)***	−0.184	(0.038)***	−0.188	(0.021)***	0.109	(0.039)***
Moral reform agenda speech frequency	0.353	(0.032)***	0.265	(0.039)***	0.260	(0.021)***	0.205	(0.038)***
Congregational Resources								
Average congregational approval of activity	0.110	(0.021)***	−0.021	(0.021)	0.070	(0.013)***	0.194	(0.044)***
Clergy ideological difference with church	0.048	(0.028)*	0.000	(0.034)	−0.001	(0.019)	−0.023	(0.033)
Church size	−0.000	(0.000)	0.000	(0.000)**	−0.000	(0.000)	−0.000	(0.000)
Less brand loyalty in congregation	0.049	(0.029)*	−0.002	(0.035)	0.032	(0.019)*	−0.010	(0.034)
Urban church	0.066	(0.042)	0.012	(0.050)	0.002	(0.028)	−0.110	(0.048)**

(continued)

Table 6.2. Estimated Career Frequency of Clergy Electoral Activity Participation (OLS regression estimates) (continued)

| | Direct Electoral Activity | | | | Indirect Electoral Activity | | | |
| | Campaigning | | Contributing | | Candidate Support | | Mobilizing | |
Variable	Coeff.	(S.E.)	Coeff.	(S.E.)	Coeff.	(S.E.)	Coeff.	(S.E.)
Denominational Cues								
Denomination perceived as supportive of clergy politicking	0.065	(0.025)**	0.025	(0.030)	−0.019	(0.017)	0.111	(0.030)***
Colleagues' political activity	0.318	(0.042)***	0.645	(0.049)***	0.426	(0.026)***	0.465	(0.046)***
Episcopal clergy	−0.033	(0.046)	0.103	(0.055)	−0.105	(0.030)***	0.082	(0.053)
Community Influences								
Partisan contact sources in career	0.053	(0.018)***	0.078	(0.021)***	0.004	(0.012)	−0.005	(0.021)
Less 1996 county electoral competition	0.019	(0.037)	−0.024	(0.044)	0.028	(0.024)	−0.002	(0.043)
Memberships in public affairs groups	0.001	(0.016)	0.022	(0.020)	−0.005	(0.010)	−0.021	(0.019)
Periodical subscriptions	0.014	(0.011)	0.013	(0.014)	−0.002	(0.007)	−0.010	(0.013)
Belief isolation	0.096	(0.073)	−0.078	(0.087)	0.044	(0.048)	−0.086	(0.084)
Activity isolation	−0.226	(0.084)***	0.030	(0.102)	−0.038	(0.055)	0.167	(0.098)*
Constant	0.174	(0.255)	−0.336	(0.307)	1.066	(0.190)	−1.762	(0.291)
Number of cases	1,493		1,469		1,558		1,501	
Adjusted R^2	0.382		0.399		0.562		0.387	

Source: 1998 ELCA/Episcopal Church Clergy Study.
***$p < 0.01$; **$p < 0.05$; *$p < 0.10$

sample of highly educated clergy participates far more than the general population. Gender and tenure length at the present job have no relationship to the career frequency of direct activities.

Political and theological orientations are very important indicators of career campaigning and contributing; six of the eight independent variables are statistically significant predictors in each model. As one would expect, strong partisan affiliations lead to greater campaigning and contributing, and strong political ideology increases campaigning while greater political interest leads to more contributing. Clergy who approve of clergy campaigning (35 percent) and contributing (68 percent), not surprisingly, tend to engage in these activities more often. Political efficacy is not a predictor of either activity over a clergyperson's career; partisan viewpoints and personal motivations appear to matter more than a belief that participating will make a difference.

The three theological indicators reveal an interesting pattern as well. The models incorporate the frequencies with which sample clergy discuss moral reform and social justice agenda issues (see table 2.7), in addition to our measure of theological conservatism. Clergy who speak out more often on social justice issues engage in less direct electoral activity over their careers. Conversely, *clergy with strong moral reform agendas (speaking out on abortion and homosexuality, among other issues) have been more active in campaigns and have made campaign contributions more often.*

These results strongly suggest strategic thinking by politically active ELCA and Episcopal clergy. A focus on social justice issues leads clergy away from electoral politics, most likely into direct activism within their communities. Social justice–minded clergy are not indifferent to the electoral process, but they perceive a better and more immediate way to meet the needs they identify. Moreover, directly engaging the needs of their community is a more typical ministerial activity, one that congregation members would expect clergy to pursue; indeed, congregation members are likely to be found side by side with clergy in such endeavors.

By contrast, theological conservatism and the moral reform agenda that accompanies it have been directly infused into electoral politics since the rise of the Christian Right movement in the late 1970s (Martin 1996). Hence for a pastor, priest, or deacon who actively preaches on moral reform issues, campaigning and contributing are ways to support candidates (predominantly Republicans) who will enact favorable legislation. Holding conservative theological views is not enough to spark direct activities over a career; accounting for frequency of moral reform speech, conservative theology actually leads to *less* career campaigning and contributing. Add to this the heightened attention to moralistic issues in the wake of the 1998 Clinton scandals and impeachment. The kinds of messages radiating from candidates and their campaigns in 1998 resonated with and hence helped mobilize those who placed heavy emphasis on moral issues.

The major differences between the career campaigning and contributing models come in the variables measuring the relationship between clergy and congregation. Congregational resources have little bearing on the extent of clergy contributing, no doubt due to the private nature of writing checks. Hence only church size is significant; clergy in larger churches are paid more and thus have more money to contribute. In contrast, several factors affect clergy campaigning. Sensing approval from the congregation increases clergy campaigning, and congregations with low brand loyalty (and thus fewer expectations) appear to tolerate more campaigning by their clergy. Clergy may also approach campaigning as a prophetic act, as those with an increased ideological distance from the congregation tend to campaign more. On the other hand, this result could also mean that clergy who disagree with their congregation pursue their political ends elsewhere.

Clergy who have politically active denominational clergy colleagues are likely to campaign and contribute more often over their careers. Active colleagues provide cues about the appropriateness and the possibilities of political activity, cues that appear to be taken to heart. A perception of denominational support also leads to more campaigning (a potentially public act) but not to more contributing (a private act)—clergy perceive denominational cues when their activities would affect the public image of the denomination.

Interestingly, once we take into account other factors, there are no differences between ELCA and Episcopal clergy on either career direct activity, though the denominational effect barely misses statistical significance in the contributing model. Episcopal clergy report that they contribute more than ELCA clergy do, a function primarily of social class status—Episcopal clergy have higher incomes, more theological and personal comfort with electoral politics, and significantly more contacts with organized political groups. Higher concentrations of Episcopalians in eastern seaboard states with strong party organizations may also contribute to higher Episcopal clergy levels of direct activity (Mayhew 1986).

Finally, there are few direct community influences on the career campaigning and contributing levels of ELCA and Episcopal clergy. Clergy who receive contacts from political groups and organizations tend to campaign and contribute more frequently, much like average citizens (Rosenstone and Hansen 1993; Verba, Schlozman, and Brady 1995). Activity isolation equates to less campaigning by sample clergy, while belief isolation, electoral competition, group memberships, and reading materials have no impact on either direct activity. Taking into account all the other factors tested in these models, less active congregations offer clergy less motivation to engage in political activities, due perhaps to member apprehensions but also to clergy priorities—animating and revitalizing less active parishes may well take precedence over personal political goals.

Determinants of Career Levels of Candidate Support and Mobilization

The career candidate support and mobilizing models in table 6.2 reveal explanatory patterns that are often similar to the direct activity models. The nature of the two indirect activities used as dependent variables accounts for some important distinctions among the models as well. Urging congregation members to register and vote is a civic activity, and part of what we term candidate support—praying for candidates—is also a civic-minded gesture. But candidate support also includes candidate endorsements inside and outside the church, which are obviously partisan actions. These differences explain why the same factor sometimes encourages one type of indirect activity but discourages the other.

Theological conservatism and speaking on social justice agenda issues fit this pattern. Both are significant influences on career candidate support and career mobilizing activity. But theological conservatism and more frequent social justice speech discourage the former (and also discourage both direct activities) and encourage the latter. We argued previously that clergy focused on social justice tend to favor direct action addressing social concerns over electoral politics. This same reasoning would make such clergy less likely to endorse candidates, preferring not to tread in controversial waters for fear of disrupting their service mission activities. However, getting people involved in the political process through voter registration would be an appropriate long-term avenue for social justice–minded clergy to pursue as part of a broader strategy for social change.

Theological conservatism must again be linked with clergy speech on moral reform issues to understand its influence on indirect career activities. Clergy speaking frequently on moral reform issues are more engaged in candidate support and in mobilizing members. But as we observed with the direct activities, *simply holding a theologically conservative worldview does not compel clergy to engage more in any partisan activity*—such clergy contribute less, campaign less, and offer public candidate support (via prayer or endorsements) less. They do, however, encourage members to vote more often than theologically liberal clergy. These effects correspond to existing research showing that theological conservatives participate in politics more often through their congregations (Guth et al. 1997; Hadden 1969; Quinley 1974).

These explanatory factors predicting clergy support for candidates suggest the importance of a motivated speaker having a receptive audience. Hence other political and theological orientations are also key predictors. Strong partisans are more likely to engage in candidate support activities, while clergy who approve of the activities do them more often over their career. Greater political interest and political efficacy actually spark *less* candidate support and have no influence on mobilizing. Clergy with a strong awareness of political issues and their own ability to affect member viewpoints would likely shy away from candidate endorsements as too risky on many levels. The positive impact of political interest on mobilizing is seen in that model by the two speech agenda items—moral reform and social justice speech both predict more mobilizing activities, as interested clergy seek to get allies to the polls.

Both career indirect activity models also show the salience of congregational approval, which leads to more clergy support for candidates and mobilizing efforts. In the case of candidate support, the congregation's influence primarily works at the negative end of the scale—clergy whose members disapprove of candidate endorsements are less likely to do so. Beyond congregational approval, few other congregational resources affect indirect activities. We find that less member brand loyalty grants clergy more latitude to engage in candidate support activities, and that clergy in urban churches are less likely to urge members to register and vote, meaning clergy in non-urban churches do this more often. This latter finding is somewhat puzzling, although it would make sense that clergy in low-population areas would stress voting; with fewer total votes in a rural town or small city, the congregation's political voice can be amplified by high member turnout.

Denominational cues also affect career indirect activities. Colleague political activism is a strong predictor of more clergy candidate support and of mobilizing. Denominational approval also elevates clergy levels of mobilizing, while Episcopal clergy are less likely to engage in candidate support activities; denomination has no effect on urging registration and voting. Our sample ELCA and Episcopal clergy are clearly perceiving denominational norms, especially those favoring civic-minded actions by clergy over partisan activities. It is also clear that clergy who wish to be politically active seek out like-minded colleagues for support and confirmation of the propriety of their choices.

Finally, personal attributes and community influences are less important indicators of indirect career activities than of direct activities. More educated clergy engage in less candidate support activity, as do male clergy, while longer serving clergy are more likely to have mobilized members to register and vote. Activity isolation is also a marginally significant predictor of greater mobilizing activity over the career. This would be expected as a way to address the congregation's isolated position. But tenure length at the present church, electoral competitiveness, partisan contacts, group memberships, and belief isolation have no effect on either indirect activity.

CLERGY ELECTORAL ACTIVITY IN 1998

The final set of regression models examines the same four electoral activities only for the last year, which for our sample clergy was 1998; these results are presented in table 6.3. Because three of the four activities are measured for 1998 as either/or (clergy either did or did not engage in them), a different regression technique called *logistic regression* (or logit) must be utilized for the table 6.3 campaigning, contributing, and mobilizing models (see appendix B for more technical details). But the statistical significance and the signs on the coefficients in the three logit models are interpreted *exactly as the previous models we have analyzed were* (and in the table 6.3 candidate support model).

As would be expected, the more immediate concerns and motivations of an election year are reflected in the 1998 results, compared to the career activities analyzed in table 6.2. This explains why personal attributes such as years in the ministry do not affect electoral activism in the short run, except as a proxy for income differences. Moreover, the pattern of results in table 6.3 confirms the distinction between direct and indirect activities: direct activity reflects personal motivation and organizational mobilization, while indirect activity stems from personal motivations situated in an environment conducive to action.

Direct Activities in 1998

Clergy who actively campaigned for candidates in the 1998 elections were driven to act by six factors: personal interest in politics, personal approval of campaigning, congregational approval of campaigning, frequent speech on moral reform issues, working in an urban church, and frequent contacts from partisan organizations. All of these factors are positively associated with 1998 clergy

Table 6.3. Estimated 1998 Clergy Electoral Activity Participation (logistic and OLS regession estimates)

	Direct Electoral Activity				Indirect Electoral Activity			
	Campaigning		Contributing		Candidate Support		Mobilizing	
Variable	Coeff.	(S.E.)	Coeff.	(S.E.)	Coeff.	(S.E.)	Coeff.	(S.E.)
Personal Attributes								
Doctoral degree	0.080	(0.167)	−0.117	(0.105)	−0.004	(0.024)	0.158	(0.094)*
Male	0.400	(0.346)	−0.347	(0.190)*	−0.048	(0.042)	0.008	(0.164)
Years in the ministry	−0.018	(0.013)	0.016	(0.008)**	−0.002	(0.002)	0.007	(0.006)
Tenure length at present church	0.019	(0.017)	0.003	(0.011)	−0.001	(0.002)	−0.004	(0.009)
Political and Theological Orientations								
Strong partisan	0.166	(0.151)	0.304	(0.084)**	0.008	(0.017)	−0.041	(0.064)
Strong political ideology	0.223	(0.182)	0.082	(0.110)	−0.010	(0.024)	0.090	(0.093)
Political interest	0.886	(0.235)***	0.234	(0.127)*	0.087	(0.026)***	−0.027	(0.103)
Political efficacy	0.064	(0.077)	0.088	(0.046)*	0.015	(0.010)	−0.036	(0.039)
Clergy approval of activity	0.532	(0.101)***	0.654	(0.080)***	0.206	(0.022)***	0.307	(0.117)***
Theological conservatism	0.111	(0.145)	−0.187	(0.088)**	0.037	(0.019)**	−0.025	(0.076)
Social justice agenda speech frequency	0.241	(0.184)	−0.047	(0.114)	0.050	(0.024)**	0.126	(0.101)
Moral reform agenda speech frequency	0.397	(0.179)**	0.421	(0.113)***	0.033	(0.025)	0.419	(0.100)***
Congregational Resources								
Average congregational approval of activity	0.191	(0.111)*	0.009	(0.059)	−0.004	(0.015)	0.238	(0.114)**
Clergy ideological difference with church	0.206	(0.172)	0.076	(0.103)	−0.002	(0.022)	0.002	(0.086)
Church size	0.000	(0.000)	0.000	(0.000)***	−0.000	(0.000)	−0.000	(0.000)
Less brand loyalty in congregation	0.222	(0.160)	0.300	(0.102)***	0.023	(0.022)	0.220	(0.087)**
Urban church	0.404	(0.232)*	0.033	(0.146)	0.017	(0.033)	−0.284	(0.125)**

(continued)

Table 6.3. Estimated 1998 Clergy Electoral Activity Participation (logistic and OLS regession estimates) *(continued)*

| | Direct Electoral Activity | | | | Indirect Electoral Activity | | | |
| | Campaigning | | Contributing | | Candidate Support | | Mobilizing | |
Variable	*Coeff.*	*(S.E.)*	*Coeff.*	*(S.E.)*	*Coeff.*	*(S.E.)*	*Coeff.*	*(S.E.)*
Denominational Cues								
Denomination perceived as supportive of clergy politicking	−0.038	(0.150)	0.003	(0.088)	−0.027	(0.020)	0.128	(0.076)*
Colleagues' political activity	−0.269	(0.232)	0.015	(0.137)	0.051	(0.030)*	0.223	(0.113)**
Episcopal clergy	0.088	(0.265)	−0.302	(0.164)*	−0.061	(0.035)*	−0.390	(0.138)***
Community Influences								
Partisan contact sources in 1998	0.176	(0.102)*	0.330	(0.062)***	0.029	(0.014)**	0.075	(0.053)
Less 1996 county electoral competition	0.066	(0.223)	0.050	(0.133)	0.029	(0.029)	0.048	(0.110)
Memberships in public affairs groups	0.017	(0.087)	0.123	(0.053)**	0.014	(0.012)	0.002	(0.048)
Periodical subscriptions	0.029	(0.066)	0.120	(0.039)***	0.017	(0.009)*	0.099	(0.034)***
Belief isolation	0.513	(0.434)	0.514	(0.260)**	0.024	(0.056)	0.061	(0.219)
Activity isolation	−1.008	(0.623)	0.042	(0.301)	0.018	(0.065)	0.647	(0.253)***
Constant	−12.534	(1.647)	−7.468	(0.933)	−0.838	(0.198)	−5.940	(0.786)
Number of cases	1,584		1,580		1,602		1,594	
Percent of cases currently predicted	89.0		69.0		(Adjusted R^2 = 0.127)		55.9	

Source: 1998 ELCA/Episcopal Church Clergy Study.
***p < 0.01; **p < 0.05; *p < 0.10
Notes: Estimates for Candidate Support model are OLS regression estimates; all other coefficients are logistic regression estimates.

campaigning—more interest, more approval, and more contacting lead to more campaigning by clergy. Together these six elements predict 89 percent of clergy decisions about actively campaigning in 1998—a modest performance considering the low percentage of clergy campaigning. All of these factors make perfect sense—clergy are more likely to campaign when they want to, when they know members approve, and when some partisan source asks. Urban clergy have more races to get involved in, and they may also have been motivated by the 1998 Democratic Party push to regain the majority in the U.S. Congress, which required assistance to mobilize Democratic voters in urban areas.

Explaining whether or not our sample clergy made political contributions in 1998, unlike the 1998 campaigning model, involves factors from all five categories of potential effects. Contributing clergy were more likely to be female, Lutheran, more experienced at serving in larger churches (both equate to higher income), approving of the act, and serving in churches with less congregational brand loyalty. Contributing clergy also had more political interest and efficacy, stronger partisan views, more theologically liberal views, greater speech on moral reform issues, more partisan contacts (i.e., fund-raising appeals), more periodical subscriptions and group memberships, and a greater sense of congregational belief isolation.

This list reflects the fact that contributing clergy are not all motivated by the same influences, as was the case with the core set of six factors inducing 1998 clergy campaigning. The impetus to give money appears to stem from both ends of the political spectrum: clergy stressing moral reform probably gave money to Republicans and theological liberals most likely funneled their contributions to liberal and Democratic causes; partisan contacts surely targeted clergy in both camps. As expected, giving money is also demonstrated to be a personal choice: the congregation's approval does not affect clergy contributing, although having fewer lifelong adherents offers more liberty for clergy to act, as we have seen in previous models.

The fact that belief isolation led to a greater likelihood of clergy contributing in 1998, but not to more clergy campaigning, is also worth noting. If a congregation is isolated locally, campaigning is not particularly efficacious nor is it likely to bring positive attention to the church. But giving money allows clergy to assist causes—to exercise their political voice (personally or on behalf of members) when local conditions otherwise serve to suppress that voice.

Indirect Activities in 1998

In the 1998 indirect activity models, we see again that few personal attributes affect 1998 candidate support and voter mobilization activities.

Clergy with doctorates were more likely to try to mobilize congregants in 1998, but no other personal attribute matters. Instead the salient factors follow no obvious coherent pattern across the models, nor do they correspond precisely to the patterns in the table 6.2 career indirect activity models. The key exception is clergy approval of the activity in question, which predicts more indirect activity here just as it predicted more activity in every chapter 6 regression model.

Table 6.3 shows that 1998 candidate support is driven primarily by political and theological indicators, denominational cues, and information-based community factors; no personal or congregational measure affects candidate support. Clergy engage in more candidate support activities when they are more interested in the elections, more theologically conservative, and more vocal on social justice issues. Once again the pairing of likely opposing viewpoints from theological and political convictions shows that candidate support exists across the political spectrum occupied by clergy, not solely with Democratic or Republican ministers. Having politically active colleagues also sparks more candidate support, and ELCA pastors engage in more such activity than Episcopal priests and deacons; recall from table 6.1 that ELCA clergy prayed for candidates somewhat more often than their Episcopal counterparts did. The two community influences on clergy candidate support in 1998 are rooted in information. Clergy who are contacted more tend to give more candidate support, and clergy reading more publications also do more for candidates.

A different set of cues motivates 1998 congregational mobilizing activity, according to table 6.3. Three congregational factors are salient indicators, and political–theological forces matter far less, as we would expect for this civic activity. Clergy are more likely to mobilize if they believe the congregation approves, if fewer members are lifelong adherents, and if the church is located in a suburban or rural area. Colleague activity and denominational support also increase the likelihood of clergy mobilizing their members in 1998. Episcopal clergy are significantly less likely to attempt to mobilize members than ELCA clergy in 1998. Clergy also mobilize more when they have more periodical subscriptions, indicating again that having more information sources during the election year leads to more clergy electoral activity. The only remotely partisan cue to mobilization in 1998 comes from clergy stressing the moral reform agenda, who are more likely to attempt mobilizing efforts in their congregations.

Mobilization efforts by ELCA and Episcopal clergy in 1998 are also heightened by congregational activity isolation, which had a positive effect on career mobilization by clergy in table 6.2. This is a direct indicator of the civic orientation of ELCA and Episcopal clergy and helps explain why less brand loyalty also enhances election-year clergy mobilization efforts. We have observed broad perceived congregational support for clergy who wish to urge members to register and vote. Mobilizing members to do their civic duty is one safe way that clergy can get their church more involved with the local community when a perceived involvement deficit exists. Similarly, less brand loyalty suggests a weakened relationship to community organizations, which clergy can help restore through voter mobilization and other methods (Djupe 2000; Wuthnow 2000).

CONCLUSION:
THE IMPACT OF CLERGY ELECTIONEERING

The results presented in table 6.2 and table 6.3 tell us something about the ability of groups with partisan ends to target clergy effectively. ELCA and Episcopal clergy speak and act politically in public and in their congregations more than might be expected given the research on previous "storms" in mainline churches (Balmer 1996; Hadden 1969; Quinley 1974; Roof and McKinney 1989). Over their careers, ardently partisan clergy are likely to pursue many of these activities anyway, and external mobilization from groups serves to solidify party connections. Hence *partisan motivations and party contacts lead only to increased direct electoral activity*—those activities with the smallest impact on the electoral process and the least relationship to the clergyperson's church. This pattern holds in both the career and past year models—partisans engage in more contributing, campaigning, and supporting candidates, while explicitly partisan indicators do not affect clergy attempts to mobilize the congregation and wider public to vote or support specific candidates. These effects speak to the efficacy of intentionally working through the clergy to build a larger, grassroots movement. It is relatively easy to mobilize clergy who see quickly and clearly the connection of an issue to their core values. Our sample clergy appear to require more than simple group mobilization and issue consonance before involving their congregations in their preferred political causes.

In the previous chapter we observed that belief and activity isolation spur clergy to speak out more often on political issues. In this chapter we have observed weaker links between clergy electoral activities and measures of congregational isolation. The exceptions demonstrate the civic-mindedness of ELCA and Episcopal clergy in considering electoral action. Activity isolation causes clergy to increase their mobilizing efforts, and it reduces clergy campaign efforts over the career. Belief isolation only matters once, increasing the private act of giving money to a campaign or cause. *ELCA and Episcopal clergy do not perceive partisan politics as an effective means to increase representation in the community.* In fact, mobilization behind a losing candidate or unpopular cause may *increase* alienation with the community.

We began this chapter by describing three possible roles clergy could adopt in pursuing electoral activity: straight policy seekers, strategic policy seekers, and prophetic representatives of the congregation. The evidence we have presented in chapter 6 suggests that *in electoral activity ELCA and Episcopal clergy are most often straight policy seekers, and only clergy interested in a moral reform agenda tend to be strategic policy seekers.* Generally our sample clergy do not appear to respond to opportunities for increased electoral influence, save for those pushing moral reform issues, who are almost always spurred to greater career and 1998 activity levels. The regression models in table 6.2 and table 6.3 reveal that *clergy living in electorally competitive counties engaged in the same amount of electoral activity as their peers in congruent voting counties.* In fact, clergy engage in more activity when they reside in counties whose voting patterns are amenable to clergy personal preferences. Isolation of the congregation may drive clergy to civic activities, but a lack of personal political isolation actually motivates clergy to act politically—to be straight policy seekers.

These results by no means diminish the potential impact of clergy electoral activities. By our calculations, the mean population of electorally competitive counties was smaller (roughly 145,000 residents) than the mean population of congruent voting counties (about 245,000). *An average-sized ELCA or Episcopal congregation thus accounts for roughly 1 percent of the winning margin in electorally competitive counties*—ten times as large as the effect of an average congregation in congruent voting counties. Moreover, extrapolating our survey responses to the full membership of these two denominations, ELCA and Episcopal clergy urged roughly 1.2 million people (about one out of every six members) to register and vote before the 1998 midterm elections.

Electioneering is not the principal method by which ELCA and Episcopal clergy engage the political process, nor is it an activity that often has a direct connection to congregational needs and mission. Rather, ELCA and Episcopal clergy function in elections much like average citizens, albeit with a greater civic resource base on which to draw, leading to higher levels of civic participation in multiple forms, especially direct activities. In considering actions that attempt to engage the congregation (indirect activities), clergy again appear motivated by personal goals and orientations, with limits imposed by the congregation's often negative attitudes toward clergy electioneering.

The empirical evidence and anecdotal reports from our sample clergy lead us to conclude that *civic* is the most appropriate term to describe the role of ELCA and Episcopal clergy in the electoral process. In denominations with a clearer integration and acceptance of electioneering activities, we suspect that congregational factors would become more apparent throughout and that more clergy would engage in electoral activities. The evidence from these two denominations would not support the assertion that clergy can "deliver" electoral success to any candidate or party except in unusual circumstances.

NOTES

1. Correlation = −0.103; p = 0.000; n = 2046.

2. Correlations between the religious difference measure and four electoral activities (career campaigning, frequency of contributing money, registration drives in 1998, and church-based registration drives during the career) were positive and statistically significant with 90 percent confidence or better. Correlations between the religious similarity measure and the same four electoral activities were all negative and statistically significant with 95 percent confidence or better. None of these correlations had an absolute value greater than 0.10. We found no significant correlation between religious difference/similarity and two electoral activities: publicly supporting a candidate and urging congregants to vote.

7

LOCAL PARTICIPATION OF ELCA
AND EPISCOPAL CLERGY

The Bully Pulpit and many other recent investigations of U.S. clergy politics have overlooked explicitly local forms of civic and political participation by clergy. The social scientific study of clergy political action began with analysis of clergy responses to local racial controversy—a
community problem with national implications (Campbell and Pettigrew
1959). With few exceptions the literature then moved to a broader national
focus on pressing issues of the time—declining membership in mainline
Protestant churches, the civil rights movement, and the rise of the Christian Right and countervailing movements. Only recently have scholars renewed their focus on local clergy civic and political activities, reflecting the
community-oriented focus of most ministries (Crawford and Olson 2001b;
Day 2001; Olson 2000; Thomas 1985; Wolcott 1982).

Local forms of civic and political action are central modes of clergy
political expression. For example, faith-based community organizations play
a crucial role publicly addressing, facilitating action on, and solving community political and social problems (Matovina 2002, 12–17; Roozen,
McKinney, and Carroll 1984, 70–78; Wortman 2002, 6–11). Moreover,
most national issues also have local dimensions, giving clergy the opportunity to offer their opinions and advocate for desired public policies. Thus
the participation of clergy in local politics and civic life carries significance
at multiple levels of U.S. politics.

Clergy can participate in the civic and political life of their communities in many ways. Our survey asked about three of the most common
forms: *involvement with clergy councils, work on local councils and boards, and participation in local community groups.* In 1998 nearly half (45 percent) of sample
ELCA and Episcopal clergy participated on a local clergy council, 31 percent served on a local board or council, and 25 percent were active in a

local community or political group. ELCA clergy were slightly more active (five percentage points more) on clergy councils; otherwise participation rates were identical between the two denominations.

Local participation thus ranks as one of the most common activities in which sample ELCA and Episcopal clergy participate, consonant with the comments of several pastors, "I need a nonparish outlet for some community social action and participation." These local activities compare in frequency with other direct action alternatives such as contacting a government official (see table 2.6). They also stand out as the most common form of clergy action for which social contact with other participants, important in the formation of social capital (Putnam 2000), is necessary.

Clergy Councils

Historically, local clergy councils have been significant forces for reform. The clergy council in St. Louis has been given credit for ending desegregation practices in that city's hotels and restaurants. Clergy councils in the South coordinated organized resistance to local oppression from whites and to desegregation efforts by the federal government (Campbell and Pettigrew 1959; Morris 1984). Today, clergy councils are involved in a host of issues (recall also the discussion of the Alabama gambling referendum in chapter 6). For instance, a clergy council in Ohio has called on political leaders to address climate change (Edwards 1998) and stop a move to legalize video gambling (Leonard 2001). Orange County, California, clergy councils have worked to abate prejudice and fill the gaps in welfare coverage following federal reforms (Larsen 1998). Another council in Maryland supported a tax increase on tobacco in 1998 in order to curb teen smoking (Rivera 1998). Clergy councils typically do not lead coalitions, but they can add considerable moral weight to existing campaigns. They may also exist purely as social and ecumenical organizations, with little or no inclination toward political activism.

One limiting factor for clergy participation in local clergy councils or councils of churches is that such groups do not exist everywhere. Fifty-five percent of sample ELCA and Episcopal clergy report that their community has a formal clergy council and 57 percent report clergy informal gatherings. Table 7.1 presents some evidence about where clergy councils exist. Suburbs, western states, and counties with very high or very low poverty rates have fewer clergy councils. Suburbs are more likely to have regular, informal gatherings of clergy, which are one form of "loose connections" that appear to be replacing older types of social organizations in suburban com-

Table 7.1.   Characteristics of Communities with Formal and Informal Clergy Councils (percent)

Variable	No Council	Formal Councils	Informal Meetings
Overall	9.9	55.0	57.0
ELCA clergy	9.1	55.2	60.6
Episcopal clergy	11.3	56.5	53.8
Community Type			
Rural	11.6	69.6	54.5
Suburban	12.0	47.1	61.8
Urban	12.6	58.1	59.1
High 1995 county poverty rate	12.8	48.2	58.8
Low 1995 county poverty rate	9.3	51.3	59.6
Region			
Midwest	8.9	57.1	56.9
Northeast	8.9	59.8	57.0
South	10.6	54.2	59.1
West	12.9	50.0	58.6
Religious Context			
High evangelical adherence	10.0	57.4	52.7
Low evangelical adherence	12.7	55.2	54.5
High mainline adherence	6.3	61.8	53.9
Low mainline adherence	20.3	43.8	60.8

Source: 1998 ELCA/Episcopal Church Clergy Study.

munities (Wuthnow 1998). Clergy councils are most common in rural areas (nearly 70 percent), and more common in the northeast, urban centers, and places where mainline Protestants reside in greater numbers; with most U.S. ecumenical efforts spearheaded by mainline bodies, we would expect mainline clergy to have the most interest in organizing regular meetings with colleagues. ELCA clergy were more likely to report informal clergy meetings, mainly because they are more likely to live in towns with more than one Lutheran church. Clergy councils thus are more likely to exist in small towns and areas of dense mainline Protestant populations, high levels of resources, and strongly favorable orientations toward having a council, which favor the development and sustainability of such bodies.

Local Government Boards

Local governing boards are charged with making numerous decisions on contentious as well as more mundane matters, all of which help shape the community where clergy and church members live. Basic decisions about zoning, utilities, and traffic make the community more or less attractive to residents. School textbook adoptions or county social service policies may strike closer to strongly held beliefs of clergy and congregation members. Not surprisingly, individual clergy and organizations with which they are affiliated have been very active in the last two decades, targeting local governments on issues relating to sexual orientation, homelessness, school prayer, policing, and social service delivery, to name a few (Matovina 2002; Wald 1997). Clergy sitting on local councils and boards or testifying before them may help sustain a viable presence for a religious group in a particular community, as well as witness to the church's beliefs in public venues.

Clergy can play a significant role influencing several types of local boards, such as boards of pardon, welfare boards, and zoning/planning commissions. But the most visible unit of local government tends to be the school board. School boards are responsible for curriculum, hiring, and library purchases in over 15,000 school districts nationwide. Not surprisingly, school boards have been targeted heavily by the Christian Coalition and other Christian Right organizations as important offices to seek in order to control policy decisions (Deckman 1999a,b; Reed 1994).

Community Political Groups

The United States has an endless variety of community civic and political groups centered on specific issues and concerns. Some are affiliates of national organizations; most are generated by local interests. These groups are significant in the very fact of their organization and because they exist to address community needs. Community political groups monitor the actions of local officials, keep members and the wider community informed about community needs, take action themselves, and mobilize members and the public to achieve their goals.

One good example is VOICE, located in Buffalo, New York. In the late 1990s, VOICE persuaded city officials to demolish twelve known drug houses near a Catholic church. The group has moved on to interventions in a diverse range of issues—rat control, housing, economic development, and recreational opportunities (Hart 2001, 20–21). Over 130 such congregation-based organizations presently exist throughout the United States, with estimated membership of 3,500 congregations and 1.5 to 3 million people (Hart 2001, 21; Matovina 2002, 13). These efforts constitute what sociologist Richard Wood describes as "arguably . . . the most widespread movement for social justice in America" (Matovina 2002, 13).

THE FOUNDATIONS OF POLITICAL PARTICIPATION

Since so many substantive policies with religious and moral dimensions are shaped and implemented at the local level, it is somewhat surprising that community-oriented clergy political activity has received almost no attention from researchers. We attempt to fill this gap by applying standard secular participation and clergy participation findings to this topic, while adding several possible explanations not thoroughly investigated previously but appropriate for the consideration of local clergy political activity. Throughout, our concern is with the prophetic, representative nature of clergy activism, and particularly the influence of congregational and community factors on types and levels of local clergy activism.

Political participation research has concentrated on three general factors that influence citizen participation most strongly: *personal resources*, such as political interest, efficacy, and tangible assets represented by civic skills, education, and income; *mobilization* through media coverage or based on individual concern for a particular issue or interest; and *recruitment*, including being asked to participate by an interest group, party, or friend (Rosenstone and Hansen 1993; Verba, Schlozman, and Brady 1995). While previous clergy studies have concentrated on ideological and theological motivations that mobilize clergy for political action, this focus is not entirely applicable to the study of local political activity, which is certainly less partisan and often less ideological than national politics. Moreover, clergy of any theological orientation might be expected to react similarly to local government actions that are contrary to their congregation's convictions.

Therefore we posit a stronger emphasis on the connection between clergy and their communities, an emphasis entirely appropriate to the study of local civic and political participation. Clergy are embedded in a number of different social contexts, all of which may bear on their political involvement (see chapter 4), though the congregation is the most important one. To assess the determinants of local political participation by ELCA and Episcopal clergy, we will employ our five-part typology of explanatory factors outlined in chapter 5. As we observed in chapters 5–6, these factors do not have identical impacts on different forms of ELCA and Episcopal clergy political activity. Thus we turn first to a brief review detailing how each of the five factors should affect local political and civic participation, followed by a multivariate regression analysis explaining whether or not our sample clergy join clergy councils, local government boards, and community political groups.

EXPLAINING LOCAL CLERGY PARTICIPATION

Local participation, whether in civic or political endeavors, depends on the existence of issues that induce clergy to act, whether for personal reasons or as representatives of their congregations. Accordingly, explanations for why clergy do or do not engage in various types of local political and civic groups should center on how the congregation relates to its community, and what community influences compel clergy to form or join groups for civic and political ends.

Personal attributes and political beliefs are less salient predictors of local clergy participation. Clergy serving longer in the ministry are more politically active, as we observed in chapter 2, but it remains to be seen whether this heightened level of activity extends to community-based politicking. Partisan ties are not likely to structure local political participation, which generally tends to exist largely outside of these frameworks. Localities can be quite homogeneous in their partisan alignments and many local issues, such as a school levy or zoning decision about a new strip mall, do not divide communities neatly on a liberal-conservative spectrum. We would expect that clergy holding strong political interest and ideological viewpoints will be more engaged in politics generally, which may extend to local political controversies as well.

In contrast to strong partisan viewpoints, theological orientations should have a significant impact on local clergy participation. Theologically modernist clergy should engage in more local activity due to their strong commitment to ecumenism and social justice issues. This orientation is especially important for local activity since, by definition, clergy councils involve more than one faith tradition and most other community groups are not affiliated with a single faith. When we compared the most ecumenically minded clergy in our sample to the least ecumenical clergy, the most ecumenical clergy were ten percentage points more active in clergy councils and community groups, and fifteen percentage points more active on local boards.

Theological perspectives are formed in part through seminary training. As we noted in chapter 4, clergy receive extensive socialization from their seminary education and professional contacts (Carroll, Aleshire, and Wheeler 1997; Carroll and Marler 1995). Seminaries impart and reinforce particular theological visions and styles of ministry, but it is possible that any distinctive seminary-inspired outlook on the role of ministry weakens over time, and that clergy conform more or less to the needs and opportunities of their particular contexts.

Table 7.2. Local Participation Activities Grouped by Seminary Attended (percents)

	Clergy Council	Local Board	Local Political Group
ELCA Seminary			
Seminex (33)	60.0	15.7	37.1
Gettysburg (116)	53.2	37.3	28.6
Philadelphia (65)	49.4	27.1	30.6
Chicago (95)	47.3	35.5	32.7
ELCA clergy average	46.5	31.1	26.3
Luther (345)	46.4	30.8	27.0
Southern (48)	44.6	26.8	16.1
Trinity (122)	43.7	26.4	20.7
Wartburg (127)	41.4	30.7	20.7
Pacific (54)	36.7	23.3	16.7
Episcopal Seminary			
Berkeley at Yale (53)	64.8	40.7	33.3
Bexley Hall (17)	58.8	58.8	35.3
Nashotah (62)	50.8	41.3	17.5
Seabury-Western (82)	47.0	30.1	20.5
Harvard (16)	43.8	37.5	31.3
Virginia Theological (104)	43.4	32.1	24.5
Episcopal Divinity (28)	43.3	33.3	37.9
Episcopal Clergy Average	41.6	30.6	24.7
General Theological (91)	40.9	25.8	26.9
Sewanee (67)	39.4	35.2	22.5
Pacific (59)	37.1	32.3	29.0
Southwest (25)	36.0	24.0	20.0

Source: 1998 ELCA/Episcopal Church Clergy Study. Numbers of cases are in parentheses.

Table 7.2 presents the breakdown of involvement in local political activities for the largest ELCA and Episcopal Church seminary graduate cohorts in our sample. The differences between the most active seminary graduates and the least are quite significant—for each denomination and each type of local political activity, the most active seminary cohorts have roughly double the activity level of the least active. Geography plays a role in this; less political activity is seen among graduates of western seminaries, who tend to serve in the less religious western United States. Clearly there are differences among seminary graduates that persist after graduation and relate to how much clergy become involved in the politics of their communities. We would expect that clergy who have frequent contact with denominational colleagues will engage in similar local activity levels (higher or lower, depending on what colleagues are doing), a byproduct of the ongoing denominational socialization process.

Congregational resources and community influences should account for a substantial share of the influence on ELCA and Episcopal clergy decisions about local political and civic participation. More so than partisan politicking, community political activism typically involves issues that clergy and congregation members are aware of, and the elite status clergy hold in their communities enhances the likelihood that clergy will get involved or that congregants will urge clergy to do so. The unique character of local civic participation (clergy councils and many local boards) suggests that clergy whose political views differ from the congregation's could safely participate in such groups, avoiding the controversy that often attends partisan politics. Most congregants probably expect their clergyperson to attend local clergy councils, especially in small towns.

Congregational isolation from the community should also spark more clergy activism. Clergy in congregations with differing beliefs might find local board participation or testimony to be an effective outlet for presenting the church's viewpoint to outsiders. Activity isolation may well be sparked by clergy council activity, which would help show our sample clergy how their congregations measure up with others in the community. Clergy councils and local boards represent particularly appropriate and efficacious ways for clergy to fulfill a prophetic function and to represent minority interests in the community.

These assertions stress the salience of *social interaction* inside and outside the congregation as the driving force influencing clergy—and citizens in general—to get involved in local politics and civic life (Gilbert 1993; Huckfeldt and Sprague 1995; La Due Lake and Huckfeldt 1998). We test for the importance of social interaction by introducing two new measures—how often sample clergy talk with denominational and nondenominational colleagues. More frequent discussion with either or both sets of peers should enhance clergy participation in local affairs.

We have also conceived of congregational resources and community influences in ways that do not include social interaction. Characteristics of the community and information gathering activities also structure clergy perspectives on their surroundings, which in turn can lead to local participation. Reading the newspaper informs clergy about their local community. Church publications, newsletters from groups a clergyperson belongs to, and other periodicals identify national, group, and denominational issue agendas that may have local angles or implications. Groups may also directly mobilize clergy to participate on issues of interest to the organization and to participate generally at increased levels.

Finally, social environments with large underprivileged populations should encourage more local participation by clergy (Olson 2000, 52). We incorporate two measures into the model to account for this effect: whether the church is located in an urban area, and the 1995 poverty rate in the church's county (U.S. Bureau of the Census 1996). Sample ELCA and Episcopal clergy living in high poverty areas participate more in community political groups and less in clergy councils. In such situations, clergy have a stronger call to action from their faith and congregation, and they may represent one of the few repositories of social capital in their community. Moreover, the decisions community groups may influence can have a greater direct effect on the "basic survival needs of people in their immediate neighborhoods" (Olson 2000, 54).

MULTIVARIATE ANALYSIS
OF LOCAL CLERGY PARTICIPATION

In table 7.3, we present multivariate logistic regression models explaining ELCA and Episcopal clergy participation on clergy councils, local boards, and community political groups in the past year (appendix B explains this regression method in detail). As with previous regression model tables, the independent variables thought to influence clergy behavior are grouped into the five categories of factors just outlined. One dominant factor in the clergy council participation model, not surprisingly, is the existence of a clergy council in the community. The other model results highlight the diversity of roles clergy can take on and the basic motivational differences between the three activities.

Personal attributes offer only modest motivation for local political action, as anticipated. Clergy with doctoral degrees are more likely to participate in community groups, partly because they tend to have more disposable income from serving large churches and are often better known in the community than are clergy of small churches. We found previously that more experienced clergy were more politically active overall, but more years in the ministry make clergy *less likely* to be active in all three types of local organizations. Clergy with a longer tenure at their present churches are more likely to serve on local boards; the community ties that naturally accumulate through years spent in the same place lead to board participation through growing interest as well as more frequent invitations to serve.

Table 7.3 also shows that strong political partisans appear to eschew service on clergy councils and local boards, most likely because they are already active in party politics and do not find councils or local boards to be as conducive to action. Similarly, strong ideologues are more active only in community groups. Politically interested clergy are more active in all three

Table 7.3. Estimated 1998 Participation on Clergy Councils, Local Boards, and Community Political Groups (logistic regression estimates)

Variable	Clergy Council		Local Board		Community Group	
	Coeff.	(S.E.)	Coeff.	(S.E.)	Coeff.	(S.E.)
Personal Attributes						
Doctoral degree	0.078	(0.138)	0.204	(0.141)	0.348	(0.147)***
Male	0.201	(0.179)	0.088	(0.183)	0.053	(0.192)
Years in the ministry	−0.012	(0.007)*	−0.029	(0.007)***	−0.030	(0.008)***
Tenure length at present church	−0.001	(0.009)	0.023	(0.010)**	0.012	(0.011)
Political and Theological Orientations						
Strong partisan	−0.140	(0.071)**	−0.147	(0.072)**	0.008	(0.078)
Strong political ideology	0.138	(0.102)	0.135	(0.104)	0.236	(0.109)**
Political interest	0.151	(0.109)	0.184	(0.112)*	0.255	(0.119)**
Political efficacy	0.033	(0.042)	0.103	(0.043)**	0.078	(0.045)*
Theological conservatism	−0.099	(0.078)	−0.247	(0.080)***	−0.280	(0.084)***
Ecumenical identification	0.282	(0.112)**	0.260	(0.117)**	0.141	(0.123)
Congregational Resources						
Average congregational approval of clergy political activity	0.009	(0.118)	0.167	(0.121)	0.401	(0.129)***
Clergy ideological difference with congregation	0.158	(0.094)*	0.247	(0.097)**	0.048	(0.102)
Less brand loyalty in congregation	0.052	(0.095)	0.104	(0.096)	0.149	(0.101)
Urban church	−0.748	(0.143)***	−0.320	(0.147)**	0.093	(0.150)

Denominational Cues

Denomination perceived as supportive of clergy politicking	−0.081	(0.083)	0.003	(0.083)	−0.126	(0.088)
Colleagues' political activity	0.354	(0.119)***	0.422	(0.122)***	0.294	(0.129)**
Episcopal clergy	−0.208	(0.145)	−0.285	(0.149)*	−0.493	(0.158)***

Community Influences

Clergy council exists	0.481	(0.120)***	—			
Memberships in public affairs groups	0.041	(0.051)	0.100	(0.051)**	0.100	(0.053)*
Newspaper reading	0.018	(0.030)	0.042	(0.031)	0.093	(0.035)***
Periodical subscriptions	0.122	(0.038)***	0.059	(0.038)	0.099	(0.040)***
Belief isolation	−0.067	(0.234)	0.428	(0.239)*	−0.116	(0.255)
Activity isolation	0.782	(0.280)***	−0.093	(0.283)	−0.105	(0.304)
Discussion with denominational colleagues	0.150	(0.083)*	0.040	(0.085)	−0.018	(0.091)
Discussion with colleagues from other denominations	0.390	(0.084)***	0.218	(0.085)***	0.222	(0.090)**
1995 county poverty rate	−0.004	(0.011)	0.018	(0.011)	0.003	(0.012)
Constant	−4.359	(0.923)	−5.011	(0.950)	−5.069	(0.996)
Number of cases	1,338		1,338		1,338	
Percent of cases correctly predicted	56.2		58.4		62.9	

Source: 1998 ELCA/Episcopal Church Clergy Study.
***$p < 0.01$; **$p < 0.05$; *$p < 0.10$

activities, though the effect is strongest for community political groups—the activity with the clearest ties to issue-based politics. The politically efficacious are more likely to serve on local boards and community groups; efficacy does not relate to clergy council membership because the purpose of most clergy councils is civic rather than political. Along similar lines, the table 7.3 models show that an ecumenical orientation strongly promotes clergy council and local board participation, but not community group participation. It clearly signifies the willingness to act in concert with people of other faiths, especially when considered an end unto itself.

Theologically conservative clergy tend to be less active on local boards and in community groups than theological modernists; both participate on clergy councils at the same rate. We observed in chapter 6 that clergy speaking often on moral reform agenda topics participated more in electoral politics; with numerous national groups stressing this agenda, we see again that just holding theologically conservative viewpoints is not sufficient to compel such clergy to become active at the community level. The gap between modernist and conservative participation levels may also reflect the continued existence of theological barriers to significant involvement with the world by more conservative clergy.

Previous multivariate analyses in chapters 5–6 indicated that ELCA and Episcopal congregations tend to encourage rather than retard clergy political activity in general. We observe this trend again with local participation, and notably *both approval from and policy disagreement with members can spark clergy to participate more frequently in local affairs.* Perceived congregational approval of clergy political activity is strongly associated with community group involvement; perceived congregational disagreement with clergy ideological views serves to increase clergy council and local board participation. Again and again we have observed that our sample clergy are "joiners"—they find ways to become involved and congregational attitudes only seem to affect the choice of groups, not whether clergy will join in the first place. This pattern also tells us once again that clergy decisions about participation forms can be strategic in nature. Clergy who know their personal views are out of step with congregants find safer, but still meaningful outlets for civic engagement; they pursue political activities on their own time. Clergy perceiving assent from the pews are more comfortable with the advocacy advanced by community political groups and may participate in more explicitly political ways. These clergy also see themselves more as representatives of their congregation in public decision making, a calculation that does not affect the more individual decision to promote community dialogue via clergy councils.

Table 7.3 also shows that denominational colleague activity and frequent discussion with nondenominational colleagues positively influence all forms of local clergy participation. Active clergy associate with like-minded colleagues, finding support from peers for becoming a visible presence in the community as a legitimate component of ministry. It stands to reason that cues from denominational colleagues resonate most strongly with activities in which clergy act in a professional capacity as representatives and not as individuals, as in community group involvement. Observing the same positive effect from nondenominational colleague contacts further establishes that peer interaction fosters community involvement, broadly speaking, whether to represent the congregation or simply forge personal ties with other people who understand the stresses and rewards of the profession.

Few other congregational resources or denominational cues affect clergy local activity levels. Brand loyalty has no impact, and service in an urban parish leads to less participation on clergy councils and local boards, with no impact on community group participation. Recall from table 7.1 that clergy council membership in rural locations was quite high (70 percent). We anticipated that urban clergy pursue political ends in other venues, but the county poverty rate measure (listed under community influences) does not affect clergy participation in any of the three local activities. Our models also show that Episcopal clergy are significantly less likely than ELCA clergy to participate on local boards or community groups. Most Episcopal clergy work in East Coast, urban settings, generally meaning somewhat fewer opportunities for Episcopal clergy to participate locally in these ways; ELCA clergy, on the other hand, are located more often in the small-town settings where clergy council membership is a routine activity.

The final category of effects to analyze comes from community influences, which we expected to be quite important in structuring local clergy participation. We have already established that discussion with nondenominational colleagues spurs more local involvement, and that the county poverty rate is insignificant.

Additional community influences arise from sources of information and mobilization, as well as measures of perceived congregational isolation. Membership in national public affairs groups spurs clergy to become involved on local boards and community political groups. Frequent newspaper and periodical reading increases clergy activity in community groups, and periodical access also increases a clergyperson's likelihood of joining a clergy council. It stands to reason that clergy who would be attracted to national groups with religious or moral dimensions would also be willing to serve in local civic or political roles. Similarly, news consumption heightens political awareness in ways that encourage sample clergy to take collective action. Most periodicals our sample clergy subscribe to focus on denominational, religious, and theological issues; hence, receiving more of these publications encourages clergy council activity but not local political involvement.

Sample ELCA and Episcopal clergy also seem to be motivated to serve on clergy councils and local boards in part to represent their congregations in the community. As anticipated, ELCA and Episcopal clergy who perceive their congregations to be isolated in terms of activity levels are more likely to join clergy councils; activity isolation has no effect on joining local boards or community groups. Belief isolation spurs greater local board participation, but not participation in clergy councils or community groups. Here again our sample clergy may be thinking strategically about their situation. Trying to mobilize an inactive congregation directly into community politics would be risky. Thus the clergy council is a safe place for pastors, priests, and deacons to build ties to their neighbors and perhaps find ideas for sparking congregational action. Belief-isolated congregations have distinctive views (relative to their surroundings) about the world that appear to motivate prophetic action from clergy to represent those views in the public sphere. Clergy pragmatically pursue local board work to ensure that their congregation's values and needs are represented in community decision making.

The same essential dynamic is present in the African American community, where the church is a political as well as a spiritual home, and where clergy often play important internal and external political roles (Fowler, Hertzke, and Olson 1999; Harris 1999; Lincoln and Mamiya 1990; Morris 1984; Wald 1997). It is intriguing to see similar effects in two elite mainline Protestant denominations. In many communities, however, ELCA Lutherans and Episcopalians are not part of the local majority, and the congregation and clergy can then be a significant source of organizational resources and political strength (Djupe and Grant 2001). Hence, one reason ELCA and Episcopal churches are not known as centers of political activity may be that, on average, more than two-thirds of their churches are perceived to be well integrated into the community.

CONCLUSION

Taken together, the results in this chapter offer insight into how ELCA and Episcopal clergy integrate themselves and their congregations into the local community. Joining the local clergy council is simply "standard procedure" for many of our sample clergy. One responding clergyperson wrote next to his af-

firmative response, "I have to." In smaller towns, especially, ELCA and Episcopal clergy hold numerous group memberships in order to "meet and greet"
other local leaders and to represent their congregations, which often comprise
a sizable share of the town's population. It would be abnormal for clergy in
these situations not to attend clergy council meetings, along with Kiwanis and
Rotary Club functions. Congregational and colleague pressures here are often
subtle, but we have little doubt our sample clergy understand that clergy council membership is expected of them in many circumstances. Activity isolation
simply adds to this expectation, prodding clergy to want to meet their peers in
order to foster stronger civic and social ties.

Taking a step beyond clergy councils, local board participation requires
an additional impetus to action. Colleague behaviors clearly influence clergy
to participate, and a desire for nonpartisan political engagement also com-
pels local board participation. Most intriguing, clergy on local boards are
more likely to be long-serving, politically efficacious, engaged in political
disagreement with members, and able to perceive belief isolation of their
congregations. Local board work stems directly and logically from each of
these factors: living in the community gives clergy more information and
name recognition, hence greater effectiveness and credibility; these consequences combined with efficacy enhance a clergyperson's ability to represent her members and thus address belief isolation through local board
work. Clergy-congregant political conflict can be transferred from inside to
outside the church, reducing internal tensions but still allowing clergy to express their views.

Community group involvement is the least likely form of the three
types analyzed here and appears to be the form most affected by personal
characteristics in addition to congregational and other external influences.
Clergy who join national groups are stronger ideologues, newer to the ministry and possessing significant political awareness. These traits make them
prime candidates to organize or jump into community activism, especially
if the congregation approves. No isolation measures affect community political group involvement, because we expect such involvement where congregations are not isolated—where clergy and congregants perceive needs
to be met, and where clergy view their participation as a necessary facet of
their ministry. One Episcopal priest confirms the nonrepresentative nature
of community political group participation: "Here, I would not wear clerical garb and would be considered just another member." Judging by published reports, community political activism is also centered on social justice
agenda issues, which would naturally attract many ELCA and Episcopal
clergy.

Local civic and political participation by American clergy remains an understudied participatory mode. The constellation of activities in which clergy can engage locally is quite large and the motivations for pursuing different types of local activities are obviously diverse. Scholars have previously documented the myriad ways in which churches provide opportunities for members to develop civic skills and then mobilize members to use them (Djupe and Grant 2001; Leege 1988; Peterson 1992; Putnam 2000; Verba, Schlozman, and Brady 1995; Wald 1997). Building on these findings, our consistent conclusion is that personal motivations and external influences together affect clergy decisions about when and how to get involved locally, an elite-level complement to existing research. The status of the congregation in the community affects clergy choices, and many clergy take on prophetic, representative roles as an outgrowth of their spiritual leadership.

Though these findings are surely related to the type of activities under study, which tend to be less partisan than other participatory forms, they constitute a markedly different set of influences than those already described in the literature. The significance in our models of previously excluded factors (clergy relationships with colleagues, congregational resources, denominational cues, and especially community influences) suggests that such factors cannot be overlooked as potentially salient predictors of other types of clergy political activity. And there is no reason to suspect that these effects are limited to ELCA and Episcopal ministers. Clergy involvement in local public affairs is a prominent avenue through which religious as well as minority voices are heard in U.S. public decision making.

8

SENDING A MESSAGE TO GOVERNMENT: CLERGY CONVENTIONAL AND UNCONVENTIONAL CONTACTING

Evidence from this and other studies demonstrates conclusively that, contrary to the general belief that U.S. Protestant clergy were most politically active in the 1960s, clergy have actually become more engaged in U.S. politics since that era. Numerous changes in society help explain this trend, including the expansion of the interest group universe (Baumgartner and Leech 1998; Loomis and Cigler 1998; Schlozman and Tierney 1986), greater federal deliberations on public policies with significant moral dimensions (Carmines and Stimson 1989), and the explicit mobilization of religious interests by political parties seeking to win elections and control policy making (Green et al. 2003; Kellstedt et al. 1996; Layman 2000; Martin 1996).

Mobilizing grassroots support for interest group policy advocacy has become an especially crucial strategy for organizations wishing to affect federal and state decisions (Rosenstone and Hansen 1993; West and Loomis 1998). Sophisticated modern fund-raising and communications techniques have reinvigorated interest group attempts to enlist the religious and secular publics in lobbying bureaucrats and elected officials (Loomis and Cigler 1998; West and Loomis 1998). Due to these efforts, the frequency with which citizens contact government officials, while lower than in the mid-1960s, has not declined as precipitously as other forms of political participation such as voting (Putnam 2000).

Many clergy are members of public affairs groups and hence are subject to the same appeals for political action as other citizen-members; these appeals also come from denominational lobbying offices seeking to mobilize clergy and congregants (Adams 1970; Ebersole 1951; Hertzke 1988; Hofrenning 1995; Olson 2001; Reichley 1985). However, because of their potential to influence millions of regular churchgoers, the moral weight that their opinions carry, and their tendency to be highly active citizens, clergy have become special targets of interest group mobilization. Religiously oriented interest groups are notorious for inspiring clergy and churchgoers to deluge Congress with letters and calls over such issues as abortion (Fowler, Hertzke, and Olson 1999). Even previously secular interests such as environmental groups are reaching out to ally themselves with religious leaders (Fowler 1995; Johnson 1998).

Sending a message to government—a First Amendment right as fundamental as freedom of religious expression—is thus an integral part of clergy political activity. Many of the other facets of clergy political activism we have covered so far include congregational, community, and private dimensions, and clergy contacting methods are no different. Many congregationally focused clergy actions can be considered indirect messages to government—giving sermons, taking policy stands, organizing social action groups. But clergy also send messages directly to government in many ways. Two methods for doing so, which we term *conventional contacting methods*, are writing or calling elected representatives and sending letters to the editor or composing longer opinion pieces (op-eds) for local newspapers; many citizens undertake these activities on a regular basis. Two other acts can be termed *unconventional contacting methods*—participating in a protest march or demonstration and committing acts of civil disobedience. These latter two activities aim to highlight injustices and may involve breaking the law deliberately as a means of garnering attention and support; consequently, they are less commonly utilized and may carry more weight in attempts to sway the public and elected officials.

In this chapter, we explore the nature and frequency of messages that ELCA and Episcopal clergy send directly to government. Three broad questions frame our analysis: How and why do clergy send messages to government? Why do clergy choose conventional versus unconventional methods of contacting? Do clergy make a choice between contacting government and mobilizing congregation members for political action, or do they pursue both strategies?

Answers to these questions are rooted in the personal motivations that prompt clergy to participate in politics, tempered or augmented by congregational support and denominational norms in unique community contexts. Our analysis will explore conventional and unconventional contacting activities by ELCA and Episcopal clergy, using our fivefold typology of explanatory factors thought to motivate clergy political activity: personal attributes, political and theological orientations, congregational resources, denominational cues, and community influences

HOW DO CLERGY CONTACT AND HOW MUCH?

There are numerous paths by which clergy can send messages to government. Table 8.1 and figure 8.1 show the frequency of sample ELCA and Episcopal clergy past year (1998) and career participation, respectively, in the four methods our survey inquired about: contacting government officials, writing an op-ed column or letter to the editor, protesting or marching, and civil disobedience. The most frequent activity is direct contacting—two in five sample clergy contacted a government official in 1998, and over 80 percent have done so during their careers. Nearly 20 percent of sample clergy say they contact public officials "often." Writing letters to the editor or op-ed pieces is the second most common activity—one in six clergy did so in 1998 and about 60 percent report doing so at least once in their careers. Unconventional activities are far less frequently utilized. Only 22 percent have protested publicly more than rarely and 7 percent have engaged in civil disobedience sometimes or more during their careers; even fewer did either activity in 1998. Sample Episcopal clergy are somewhat more likely than ELCA clergy to have ever protested throughout their careers (60 percent to 53 percent); otherwise there are no significant differences in contacting behavior between ELCA and Episcopal clergy.

How do these contacting activities fit together? Do clergy choose one method to the exclusion of others, or do they pick and choose according to the circumstances motivating them to contact in the first place? Table 8.2 describes in more detail the relationships between the four contacting methods used by sample clergy in 1998. We suspect that clergy do not choose to act in either conventional or unconventional ways; rather, most clergy probably move from conventional methods that are not controversial in most cases to more controversial, unconventional contacting activities

Table 8.1.   1998 and Career Clergy Contacting Methods

Variable	Percent Using Method in Past Year (1998)	Career Average Frequency of Activity	Percent Using Sometimes or More in Career
Contacted public officials	39.8	2.7	62.3
Wrote a letter to the editor or op-ed	16.6	1.9	30.4
Participated in a protest march	7.9	1.8	25.4
Engaged in civil disobedience	1.7	1.3	11.9

Source: 1998 ELCA/Episcopal Church Clergy Study. Number of cases = 2,239 (past year) = 2,058 (career)
Note: For the four contacting variables, Cronbach's α = 0.701 (n = 1885). Average frequency based on 1–4 scale for each contacting method: 1 = never used, 2 = rarely, 3 = sometimes, 4 = often.

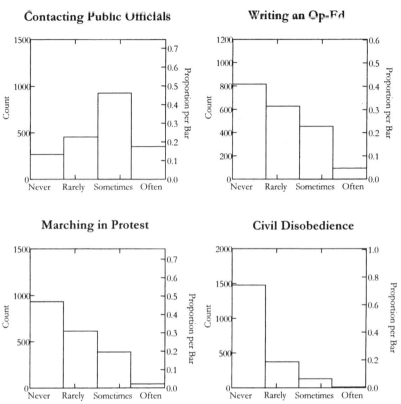

Figure 8.1.   Career Frequencies of Sending a Message to Government
Source: 1998 ELCA/Episcopal Church Clergy Study. Number of cases = 2,058

based on the depth of their grievances or commitment to addressing a specific issue.

The results in table 8.2 confirm this assertion. Very few 1998 conventional contactors engaged in unconventional contacting, but *most clergy who were unconventional contactors also employed conventional contacting methods.* Of the 2 percent in our sample who committed acts of civil disobedience in 1998, 70 percent wrote a letter to the editor or an op-ed, 80 percent contacted an elected representative, and 80 percent participated in a protest march or demonstration. Clergy who had protested were also quite likely to have contacted or written letters to the editor. But letter/op-ed writers and contactors rarely moved on to unconventional contacting methods, and even protesting clergy appear reluctant to engage in civil disobedience. The patterns in table 8.2 suggest that ELCA and Episcopal clergy have a stair-step approach to contacting: conventional methods constitute the first and

Table 8.2.   Interrelationships between Contacting Methods Used in 1998 (row percents)

Contacting in 1998	Contacted a Public Official in 1998	Wrote Op-ed or Letter to to Editor	Participated in Protest March	Committed Civil Disobedience
Contacted public officials	—	34.8	16.3	3.5
Wrote letter/op-ed	83.1	—	24.5	7.0
Protested	82.9	52.0	—	18.3
Civil disobedience	81.6	68.4	84.2	—

Source: 1998 ELCA/Episcopal Church Clergy Study. Number of cases = 2,239.
Note: To read row percents, using the first row as an example, of those clergy who contacted a public official, 35 percent wrote an op-ed, 16 percent marched, and 3 percent committed acts of civil disobedience in 1998.

often the only steps, occasionally leading to unconventional contacting when necessary and desirable from the clergyperson's perspective.

DETERMINANTS OF CLERGY CONTACTING

As in the previous three chapters, our detailed analysis of when and how ELCA and Episcopal clergy send messages to government incorporates several facets of clergy attitudes, behaviors, and environmental pressures. We have seen repeatedly that clergy behavior stems from a complex web of personal qualities, political preferences, theological beliefs, congregational characteristics, denominational signals, and community ties. Generally speaking, with each activity examined we have observed support for the idea that clergy sometimes act as prophetic representatives of their congregations. Shifting the focus to conventional and unconventional contacting methods, we ask what factors might lead to prophetic clergy roles when sending messages to government?

As we have noted in earlier chapters, seminary training cannot help but shape how clergy interact with the social settings in which they are called to preach and serve. In table 4.8 we sorted sample clergy by seminary attended and found modest variations in political and theological conservatism across seminary cohorts. Using this same strategy, we can discern whether some seminary cohorts engage in more or less contacting.

Table 8.3 gives evidence of wide variations across seminary cohorts, both in general contacting frequency and in specific methods utilized. For instance, ELCA Seminex graduates are the most likely to engage in con-

**Table 8.3.   1998 Clergy Contacting Methods, Grouped by
Seminary Attended (percents)**

	Contacted a Public Official in 1998	Wrote Op-ed or Letter to Editor	Marched in Protest	Committed Civil Disobedience
ECLA Seminaries				
Gettysburg (116)	46.8	19.8	4.0	2.4
Seminex (33)	45.7	25.7	0.0	0.0
Chicago (95)	41.8	20.9	13.6	2.7
Philadelphia (65)	38.8	18.8	4.7	2.4
Wartburg (127)	38.6	12.9	5.0	1.4
Luther (345)	37.8	14.3	6.1	1.2
Southern (48)	32.1	14.3	5.4	5.4
Pacific (54)	31.7	13.3	13.3	0.0
Trinity (122)	27.6	8.6	2.9	0.6
Episcopal Seminaries				
Berkeley at Yale (53)	61.1	25.9	14.8	0.0
Harvard (16)	50.0	12.5	12.5	0.0
Nashotah (62)	47.6	22.2	11.1	3.2
Virginia Theological (104)	47.2	17.0	14.2	4.7
General Theological (91)	41.9	21.5	14.0	3.2
Seabury-Western (82)	41.0	10.8	7.2	1.2
Episcopal Divinity (28)	40.0	20.0	13.3	0.0
Pacific (59)	38.7	22.6	9.7	3.2
Bexley Hall (17)	35.3	11.8	5.9	0.0
Sewanee (67)	33.8	14.1	2.8	0.0
Southwest (25)	32.0	20.0	12.5	4.0

Source: 1998 ELCA/Episcopal Church Clergy Study. Numbers of cases in parentheses.

ventional contacting in 1998, but none protested or committed acts of civil disobedience during 1998. ELCA Chicago and Pacific Lutheran graduates are far more likely to have protested in 1998, while Lutheran Theological Southern Seminary graduates are the most likely to have engaged in civil disobedience. ELCA Trinity graduates, found to be the most religiously and politically conservative of any ELCA seminary cohort, contacted the least. Clearly, among ELCA seminary cohorts there are significant differences in form and frequency of contacting methods utilized.

Episcopal seminary cohorts have similarly wide variations in types and levels of 1998 contacting behavior, but a clear linkage between contacting strategies and theological and political ideologies is not present. Berkeley (Yale) graduates are some of the most liberal Episcopal priests and deacons, and they contacted more frequently than any other cohort in 1998. Nashotah House graduates are among the most conservative Episcopal clergy, and they also appear high up on nearly every contacting measure.

No simple pattern appears in table 8.3 to support the claim that some seminary cohorts are more apt to utilize specific methods for contacting government. The table does show that some seminary cohorts are far more or far less likely than average to utilize a specific contacting type, with diverse levels across all four contacting categories. Surely other factors contribute to the patterns observed in table 8.3, especially the political context of the region in which graduates tend to serve. Political context encompasses more than just region and urban versus suburban or rural residence; we must also consider the issues in play, groups at work, and the needs of constituencies of interest to clergy, among other factors.

It should be obvious that congregational approval of clergy sending messages to government will factor strongly in whether clergy actually engage in contacting. Our sample clergy report that a majority of their members approve of clergy directly contacting government officials (67 percent approve), and congregational approval is higher when the congregation constitutes a minority locally. There is far less perceived congregational approval of unconventional contacting, however. About 40 percent of clergy perceive their congregations to disapprove of clergy protesting, and 60 percent perceive disapproval of clergy engaging in civil disobedience. Thus the impact of congregational attitudes on clergy contacting activity varies according to the public exposure of the activity, an issue we take up in detail below.

The potential effects of the community, broadly considered, are complex. Clergy should be motivated to act because of mobilization pressures from community groups, the incidence of social problems surrounding them, and the relationship of the congregation to the community. We might also consider what resources it takes in particular communities to bring a concern to the government's attention (Olson 2000; Crawford and Olson 2001b).

The orientation of the congregation toward clergy contacting practices is also shaped by the congregation's place in the community. Clergy can come to identify strongly with the plight faced by members, especially if their church constitutes a minority locally in numerical or political terms. As a consequence, clergy may kneel in protest outside abortion clinics, march with strikers, or testify to local governments. Clergy should be more active when perceiving that church members' beliefs are not well represented in the community, whether in schools, zoning, welfare, or housing. In such cases members tend to rely on whatever resources are accessible, including the clergyperson, to help push their interests. We will examine this proposition through our belief and activity isolation measures. It is possible that neither isolation measure will in fact affect clergy contacting behavior; there is no reason to believe that most or all clergy contacting takes place on the congregation's behalf.

The effort required to make known one's concerns depends on the nature of the local community, especially its population. Newspapers in small towns can print nearly every letter on public affairs that they receive (Pride 2001). This is obviously not true in large or even medium-sized cities. Not only is it easier to gain access to the newspaper in a small community, access will also gain the attention of more people through this principal news outlet. Having the same effect in an urban area would require more drastic and resourceful steps by clergy and the groups they represent. Hence contacting patterns of clergy in rural versus urban areas will be qualitatively different but probably also quantitatively different.

A final source of influences on clergy contacting comes from the denomination. Our examination of seminary cohorts suggests that neither the ELCA nor the Episcopal Church actively discourages clergy political activity; clergy who feel denominational norms encourage them to act should be more likely to contact government, and perhaps to protest as well. Denominations occasionally appeal directly to clergy on specific issues. In 1964, mainline Protestant churches engaged in a "Midwest strategy," encouraging a letter-writing campaign to Congress in support of the Civil Rights Act. Some analysts considered this effort crucial for the act's eventual passage in the Senate (Findlay 1993).

We suspect that personal engagement with politics will play a significant role in motivating clergy contacting, if only because the most common activity—communicating with a government official—is normally a private act. At the same time, because clergy are representatives of their congregations in religious matters, if not always in political ones, we expect to see some effects from the congregation and community. While personal resources give clergy the skills and interest to contact government, inspiration from community and congregational circumstances also trigger more or less contacting.

PREDICTING CLERGY CONTACTING

We approach the multivariate analysis of clergy contacting government in three ways, estimating models that predict *how many different methods of contacting our sample clergy utilized in 1998; the average frequency of clergy contacting over the career* and *the career frequency of clergy contacting divided into conventional and unconventional acts.* The first two models are presented in table 8.4, and models comparing determinants of conventional and unconventional contacting are presented in table 8.5. As in previous chapters, the independent variables in each table are organized into our five sets of possible explanatory factors.

With four possible methods of sending messages to government available to sample ELCA and Episcopal clergy in 1998, the dependent variable in the table 8.4 past year model ranges from zero (no acts performed in 1998) to four (clergy used every method). The dependent variable in the career frequency model averages clergy reports about how frequently they have performed each act over their career; the resulting measure ranges from one ("never" contacting at all) to four (using all four methods "often"). This modeling strategy allows us to observe short-term forces affecting 1998 clergy contacting strategies, as well as long-term effects on clergy contacting.

Several factors affect past year contacting but not career frequency of contacting, according to table 8.4. Clergy with doctorates and more periodical subscriptions contacted government more in 1998, showing that education and awareness of current events are associated with active citizenship by clergy (as well as other highly educated and aware citizens). Politically efficacious clergy contacted more in 1998 as well, as did clergy in congregations with more new members, who tend to be less partisan and lack strong expectations about clergy political activism (Djupe 1999). None of these factors affects career contacting levels.

On the flip side, clergy who speak frequently about moral concerns have heightened career levels of contacting, but discussing the moral reform agenda has no impact on 1998 contacting activities; clergy focused on social justice issues used more contacting methods in 1998 and contact more frequently over their careers. In chapter 6 we found an identical pattern— moral reform speech was directly related to all forms of electoral activity over the career, but it only affected direct electoral activities undertaken in 1998 (campaigning and contributing money). The table 8.4 models reinforce the argument that moral reform-minded ELCA and Episcopal clergy see electoral politics, rather than writing letters and protesting, as a more effective outlet for advocating their political preferences. Clergy focused on social justice issues embraced more types of contacting methods during the 1998 election cycle and perceive contacting government as a necessary tool for social change over the long term.

Some additional differences between the past year and career contacting models include the fact that Episcopal priests and deacons, clergy with more years in the ministry, and male clergy have higher levels of

Table 8.4. Estimated Clergy Contacting Methods in the Past Year (1998) and Career Average Contacting Frequency (CLS regression estimates)

Variable	Past Year Methods		Career Frequency	
	Coeff.	(S.E.)	Coeff.	(S.E.)
Personal Attributes				
Doctoral degree	0.083	(0.035)**	0.023	(0.020)
Male	0.064	(0.063)	0.071	(0.037)*
Years in the ministry	−0.001	(0.002)	0.006	(0.001)***
Tenure length at present church	−0.000	(0.003)	−0.000	(0.002)
Political and Theological Orientations				
Strong partisan	−0.030	(0.025)	0.021	(0.015)
Strong political ideology	0.119	(0.036)***	0.041	(0.021)*
Political interest	0.14	7(0.041)***	0.095	(0.024)***
Political efficacy	0.049	(0.016)***	0.012	(0.010)
Theological conservatism	−0.058	(0.031)*	−0.043	(0.018)**
Social justice agenda speech frequency	0.137	(0.040)***	0.160	(0.023)***
Moral reform agenda speech frequency	0.059	(0.042)	0.128	(0.025)***

Congregational Resources		
Congregational approval of clergy contacting	0.136 (0.029)***	0.144 (0.017)***
Clergy ideological difference with church	0.083 (0.034)**	0.108 (0.020)***
Less brand loyalty in congregation	0.072 (0.033)**	0.020 (0.019)
Urban church	−0.062 (0.048)	0.017 (0.029)
Denominational Cues		
Denomination perceived as supportive of clergy politicking	0.047 (0.029)	0.022 (0.018)
Episcopal clergy	−0.034 (0.052)	0.068 (0.031)**
Community Influences		
Memberships in public affairs groups	0.057 (0.018)***	0.050 (0.011)***
Periodical subscriptions	0.027 (0.013)**	0.009 (0.008)
Belief isolation	0.082 (0.084)	0.047 (0.049)
Activity isolation	0.125 (0.096)	0.055 (0.057)
Constant	−2.100 (0.304)	−0.380 (0.177)
Number of cases	1,602	1,795
Adjusted R^2	0.141	0.283

Source: 1998 ELCA/Episcopal Church Clergy Study.
***$p < 0.01$ ** $p < 0.05$ * $p < 0.10$

career contacting; these factors do not affect 1998 contacting activity. The first two effects are anticipated, but previous research has identified few gender gaps in the behavior patterns of male and female clergy. Our data show that male clergy are more likely to write letters or op-ed columns, while women protest more often throughout their careers; there are no significant gender differences in levels of contacting or civil disobedience. The relatively greater social justice interests of women clergy probably explain why women and men favor different contacting forms. More career contacting by male clergy implies a greater comfort with contacting in general, while female Protestant clergy perceive more restraints on their political activities due to their gender (Crawford, Deckman, and Braun 2001, 55–59).

Beyond these results, the two models in table 8.4 have very similar sets of significant factors affecting past year and career contacting levels. These results also conform to initial expectations about the determinants of clergy contacting. *Contacting levels and career contacting frequencies are higher among strong ideologues, politically interested clergy, theological modernists, clergy who speak frequently about social justice issues, and clergy who belong to more public affairs groups.* Sending a message to government is a key form of grassroots lobbying; interest groups, politicians, and political parties often mobilize citizens to contact elected and other government officials. Clergy are members of a wide variety of interest groups, both secular and religiously based; 45 percent of our sample clergy belong to at least one public affairs group. Because religiously based interest groups continue to make their views known to government on many levels, so will constituent clergy.

Congregational approval also has a positive influence on past year and career contacting. Clergy who have opinions that differ sharply from their congregations, whether more liberal or more conservative, also used more contacting methods in 1998 and have contacted more frequently over time. We observed these two factors together influencing more clergy activity only once—table 5.3, where ideological differences and congregational approval sparked more clergy public speech in 1998. The table 8.4 results again confirm the prophetic role of ELCA and Episcopal clergy. Just as they speak more on issues on which they perceive political disagreement with congregants and approval to speak out generally, clergy also pursue their agendas with government despite—or perhaps because of—opposing congregational viewpoints, when they perceive approval to contact generally.

Table 8.4 demonstrates that sample ELCA and Episcopal clergy contact government primarily because their high levels of political engagement, information, and external mobilization encourage them to do so. Patterns of clergy contacting reflect more the pathways to activity inherent in the political process, rather than the needs and concerns of the congregation, denomination, and community; denominational cues and isolation measures have little impact on contacting. But congregational approval of clergy contacting, along with clergy–congregation differences, can enhance clergy political activity in the short and long term.

DETERMINANTS OF CONVENTIONAL VERSUS UNCONVENTIONAL CONTACTING

As evidenced in table 8.2, for ELCA and Episcopal clergy the contacting forms exist on a continuum, ranging from relatively safe and common conventional acts that many clergy undertake, to unconventional and often controversial ones that few clergy or citizens dare to pursue. Now we focus our attention on "who does what" to determine what factors lead clergy to go beyond conventional forms and to engage in unconventional contacting. While they are the most uncommon activities, unconventional acts such as protesting and committing civil disobedience are some of the most visible actions clergy can take. Boycotts, rallies, marches, and sit-ins often become celebrated historical events, and clergy have been prominent actors in using unconventional political tactics throughout U.S. political history.

To a large extent, the predictive factors in the table 8.4 career frequency model should also predict levels of career conventional activity in table 8.5 because conventional acts are overwhelmingly the most common ones clergy utilize. But the choice to use unconventional methods of sending messages to government should depend specifically on personal inspiration, and motivations to act unconventionally will be intensified or attenuated by congregational and community influences. Unconventional contactors are likely to be more ideological, have more extreme agendas, and have greater resources with which to engage the political process. As the activities seem to lie further out on the contacting continuum, so will the opinions and values of those clergy pursuing them.

The determinants of career average frequencies of conventional and unconventional contacting are presented in table 8.5. The pattern of results fits with the stereotypical notion of the new breed of Protestant clergy activists who emerged in the late 1960s and early 1970s (Garrett 1973; Winter 1973). Both conventional and unconventional contactors are likely to have served longer in the ministry, to have a strong social justice agenda, to belong to public affairs groups, and to hold different opinions (mostly more

Table 8.5. Estimated Career Average Contacting Frequency for Conventional and Unconventional Contacting (OLS regression estimates)

Variable	Conventional		Unconventional	
	Coeff.	*(S.E.)*	*Coeff.*	*(S.E.)*
Personal Attributes				
Doctoral degree	0.018	(0.027)	0.036	(0.022)
Male	0.078	(0.047)	0.040	(0.041)
Years in the ministry	0.006	(0.002)***	0.007	(0.002)***
Tenure length at present church	0.004	(0.003)	−0.004	(0.002)**
Political and Theological Orientations				
Strong partisan	0.010	(0.020)	0.018	(0.016)
Strong political ideology	0.040	(0.028)	0.069	(0.023)***
Political interest	0.213	(0.032)***	−0.017	(0.027)
Political efficacy	0.027	(0.013)**	0.003	(0.010)
Theological conservatism	−0.046	(0.024)*	−0.030	(0.020)
Social justice agenda speech frequency	0.154	(0.031)***	0.170	(0.025)***
Moral reform agenda speech frequency	0.215	(0.033)***	0.039	(0.027)

	Model 1	Model 2
Congregational Resources		
Congregational approval of clergy Contacting	0.095 (0.020)***	0.169 (0.015)***
Clergy ideological difference with church	0.074 (0.026)***	0.141 (0.022)***
Less brand loyalty in congregation	−0.004 (0.026)	0.030 (0.021)
Urban church	−0.013 (0.038)	0.071 (0.032)**
Denominational Cues		
Denomination perceived as supportive of clergy politicking	0.040 (0.023)*	0.008 (0.019)
Episcopal clergy	0.056 (0.041)	0.095 (0.034)***
Community Influences		
Memberships in public affairs groups	0.059 (0.014)***	0.032 (0.012)***
Periodical subscriptions	0.016 (0.010)	−0.000 (0.008)
Belief isolation	0.117 (0.065)*	−0.031 (0.054)
Activity isolation	0.058 (0.076)	0.061 (0.063)
Constant	−0.464 (0.24)	−0.320 (0.193)
Number of cases	1,758	1,728
Adjusted R^2	0.236	0.236

Source: 1998 ELCA/Episcopal Church Clergy Study.
***$p < 0.01$ **$p < 0.05$ *$p < 0.10$

liberal) than their congregants. *Both types of contactors also have congregational support for their methods,* just as we observed in table 8.4.

The differences between the two types of contactors are more illuminating, however. *Conventional contactors are politically interested and efficacious, while unconventional contactors are driven by strong political ideologies rather than interest or efficacy.* To be effective, a conventional contactor must follow the policy process closely, and politically interested and efficacious clergy are clearly more attuned to that process. Marching and protesting, by contrast, are used to raise public awareness as well as gain the attention of government. These actions could take place at almost any time and are more likely to focus on specific issue grievances, which have a salience for clergy that goes well beyond general political interest. Protestors have no more political efficacy than other contactors due to the same forces that lead them to protest in the first place—the issue in question is not on any governmental agenda, which stalls or precludes policy change through regular channels.

Theology and issue agenda preferences also distinguish conventional and unconventional contactors. Conventional contacting is a common tactic whether clergy have a more liberal (social justice) or more conservative (moral reform) agenda; the frequency of speech, not the content, leads clergy to contact government in conventional ways. But *only frequent social justice speech leads to unconventional contacting.* At the same time, theological conservatives are less likely to contact conventionally, but theology does not affect unconventional contacting. As in chapter 6, clergy speech frequency and content are more salient determinants of political activity than theological perspectives alone.

The table 8.5 model results also indicate that the choice between contacting types depends on the political climate and context. Clergy with social justice concerns, including poverty, discrimination, and housing, believe they must make their voices heard at all levels of government. Social justice clergy also tend to be found in urban churches. Urban areas have more obvious social problems, more constituencies in need of support, and more competition for scarce resources at all levels of government. While urban centers have more groups that can mobilize clergy and others to unconventional action, these groups also perceive a need to resort to more extreme measures, such as protesting, to gain recognition for their cause. Clergy focused on moral reform orient themselves more toward electoral politics and hence are less likely to utilize unconventional methods to pursue their political goals. *Social justice-minded clergy in urban areas choose unconventional contacting methods as one form of representing their congregations in the public square.*

The complex representative roles that ELCA and Episcopal clergy play in their congregations and communities are also reflected in table 8.5 through the effects of congregational isolation. Belief isolation predicts greater conventional contacting only, and activity isolation predicts neither form of contacting. Several possibilities might explain this pattern of results. First, if the community does not reflect the values of the group, then protesting locally would not be a particularly effective strategy; clergy would perceive more potential benefits from directly contacting government officials or in explaining their views first through a newspaper letter or column. Second, groups in the minority may fear a backlash from performing unpopular acts locally.[1] Third, it is possible clergy do not represent the congregation per se when they protest. Engaging in unconventional activity is not necessarily done to highlight the needs or desires of congregation members; wearing the collar during a protest march or sit-in effectively broadcasts a clergyperson's commitment, as a representative of her denomination and faith tradition, in support of underrepresented values and constituencies. Congregations are surely one important audience for the message protesting clergy wish to send, but prophetic witnessing is often viewed by clergy as imperative for reasons running far deeper than congregational needs.

Finally, clergy choices about contacting methods also depend on denominational socialization. Denominational support for clergy political activity in general is a predictor of more conventional contacting but not unconventional contacting, which carries some risks for clergy and by extension for the denominations they represent. Table 8.5 also shows that Episcopal clergy, whom we have asserted throughout to be more politically active than ELCA clergy, are far more likely to engage in unconventional acts over their careers. There is a clear socialization difference between ELCA and Episcopal clergy: both denominations support conventional methods, but only one set of clergy engages in more unconventional behavior. With the effects of location and other factors controlled for in the models, it appears that Episcopal clergy perceive few congregational or denominational barriers to unconventional politicking, while ELCA clergy in general are more reluctant to move beyond routine forms of contacting.

The table 8.5 models demonstrate that conventional activity is well integrated within normal political channels and denominational practices, whereas unconventional activity seems to be sparked by more drastic needs of expression and attention. Moreover, clergy contacting is shaped by community concerns. Unconventional avenues of political expression appear to be precluded when congregational support, denominational culture, and community norms argue against protesting or civil disobedience. Providing representation for their congregations is not a central focus of either conventional or unconventional contacting, although we have modest evidence to suggest that some contacting methods can serve that function.

CONTACTING VERSUS MOBILIZING IN CHURCH

Thus far we have observed that the congregation factors strongly in clergy decisions to send messages to government, though somewhat less so than for other political activities. Conventional modes of contacting, especially communicating with government officials, are not directly observed by anyone and thus incur little personal risk for the contactor. Writing to the newspaper and taking concerns to the streets, however, are highly visible and often controversial activities—that is, after all, the point of engaging in controversial actions. When deciding whether and how to contact government, we suspect that clergy give weight to congregational attitudes in proportion to the visibility of the act. If the congregation will never know a clergyperson called her state representative, the clergyperson has little reason to hesitate in doing so. But highly disagreeable church environments may compel clergy to exercise their political voice outside of congregational earshot, rather than engage in public acts that threaten the clergyperson's stature and perhaps even her job.

While it is reasonable to posit that clergy either work through their congregations *or* move outside of them, there is little empirical support for this conclusion. Table 8.6 investigates this link for 1998 contacting and finds that *contacting activity is strongly related to clergy political activity within the congregation.* Clergy who contact are many times more active in their congregations than are noncontactors, which firmly rebuts the idea that contacting and church political work are mutually exclusive strategies. Moreover, the proportion of contacting clergy who work for political ends through the church *climbs* as the professional risk of the contacting activity increases. Thus, while three-fourths of clergy who contacted a public official took a stand on a political issue while preaching, protest marchers were ten percentage points more likely to take a stand, and nearly all clergy who practiced civil disobedience in 1998 took a stand while preaching. The same relationship holds for organizing within the church; unconventional contactors organized church political discussion and social actions groups far more than conventional contactors.

While it is important to note that less than half of our sample clergy engaged in a contacting activity in 1998, those who did were more likely to

Table 8.6.   Percent of Clergy Contactors Who Also Engaged in Congregational Political Activities (row percents)

Type of Clergy Contacting in 1998	Measures of In-Church Political Action		
	Took a Political Stand While Preaching	Organized a Church Political Discussion Group	Organized a Church Social Action Group
Did not contact	29.8	4.3	9.7
Contacted public officials	74.1	26.4	43.8
Wrote a letter/op-ed	76.1	35.9	46.1
Protested	86.6	43.9	64.9
Civil disobedience	91.9	67.6	73.0

Source: 1998 ELCA/Episcopal Church Clergy Study. Number of cases = 1,814.

engage their congregations in political activity. This may simply reflect a supportive congregation. However, more is probably at work here, especially when we recall that clergy are also more likely to take action when their political views differ from their congregation's and when they are members of public affairs groups. If clergy believe an issue is important enough to generate a letter to a public official or newspaper, then they probably conclude it is also worth bringing the issue to the attention of the congregation. This pattern of results indicates to us that clergy wish to fulfill prophetic roles, serving when they are motivated to do so as links between government and citizens, as well as encouraging public discourse on matters of importance to the congregation and community (Page 1996).

CONCLUSION

In this chapter, we have analyzed how and why ELCA and Episcopal clergy send messages to government. The means by which clergy can do so differ dramatically. Conventional contacting methods constitute some of the most common clergy activities, unconventional some of the least; contacting a government official is one of the most private political acts clergy can engage in, while marching is one of the most public. Yet conventional and unconventional contacting belong together; for clergy, they both constitute ways to send a message directly to government.

What have we learned about the contacting behavior of our sample clergy? For the most part, clergy do not start engaging in direct contacting when they are turned away from politicking in church due to congregational opposition. There is not a separate, or "deviant," breed of clergy who protest and march. Rather, clergy respond to many of the same stimuli that motivate ordinary citizens to send messages to government. strong personal views, re-sources and a willingness to expend them, and interest group mobilization.

Moreover, patterns of clergy contacting respond to pressures and op-portunities beyond the clergyperson's ideology and personal motivation. Protestors are more likely to minister in urban areas, where unconventional action is required to gain attention, and clergy tend to contact convention-ally more often when their congregation has differing beliefs from the sur-rounding community, when more public attention to their concerns would not necessarily be beneficial. These results do not give a strong impression of clergy as representatives of their congregations when it comes to sending messages to government, especially since the most typical contacting method takes place out of the spotlight of public scrutiny.

While the motivations of clergy contacting may resemble those of the mass public, the impact of clergy political activity is much greater. This is due in part to the moral authority of the clergyperson's presence and voice, but also because clergy political activism does not end with a phone call. In-stead, contacting—whether through a letter to the local newspaper or a mass protest—is one part of a broader pattern of political activity that may change the hearts, minds, and actions of a large number of citizens in the congregation. This link furthers our understanding of why churches have formed the base of significant and insignificant, local and national, large and small social movements throughout U.S. history.

NOTE

1. A story from Chicago's past provides support for this argument. In 1966, Martin Luther King Jr. brought the civil rights movement to Chicago to integrate the schools and public housing, eliminate slums, and open private housing—to end de facto seg-regation. While King faced other obstacles to achieving these objectives, most notably Mayor Daley and King's rival, Reverend Joseph Jackson of the National Baptist Con-vention, he also had difficulty mobilizing his natural allies—supportive black clergy. Public support of the movement, whether in the streets or even from the pulpit, could endanger their ministries. One pro-movement reverend commented, "Many ministers who supported us had to back off because they didn't want their buildings to be con-demned or given citations for electrical work, faulty plumbing, or fire code violations" by Daley's Democratic machine (Cohen and Taylor 2000, 359).

9

DENOMINATIONAL POLITICS: CLERGY OPINIONS AND ACTIONS REGARDING FULL COMMUNION

Our analysis so far has centered on how and why ELCA and Episcopal clergy engage in political action, motivated by personal beliefs and salient signals from their congregations and communities. Although our focus has been on political activity, it stands to reason that the forces affecting levels and types of clergy political activity might also motivate clergy behavior on other issues that require public speech or action. A thorough test of clergy responsiveness to congregational and community influences should include consideration of how these same influences affect clergy activity in realms other than politics.

One good place to find such an issue is within the denomination, which regularly considers, through a political process, subjects that hold considerable interest for clergy and parishioners. Questions about how clergy interpret and act on denominational issues shed light on how clergy perceive their social and religious surroundings, and what difference these contextual factors make in determining clergy behaviors and attitudes. We chose the ELCA and Episcopal Church for analysis in part because at the time of our study, they were debating an issue that has caused celebration and strife within both denominations—full communion. We asked our sample clergy about their attitudes and actions regarding this issue, and we will use full communion as a test of the extent to which congregational and community factors influence clergy speech and actions beyond the political domain.

In this chapter we explain what full communion entails for the ELCA and Episcopal Church, and we analyze clergy attitudes and activities related to full communion. By extending our empirical analysis to this denominational issue, we intend to confirm our core argument that in and out of politics, clergy attitudes and actions are affected by more than just personal and theological beliefs; the beliefs of their congregations and the status of their churches within the local community and the denomination also influence clergy perceptions of important denominational issues and actions regarding them.

A BRIEF OVERVIEW OF FULL COMMUNION

In 1997, at the culmination of decades of dialogue, leaders of the Episcopal Church and the ELCA reached agreement on establishing full communion between the two denominations, through a document called the Concordat of Agreement. At its 1997 General Convention, the Episcopal Church overwhelmingly ratified the Concordat. But at the 1997 ELCA General Assembly, the Concordat fell six votes shy of the two-thirds required for passage (out of 1,000 votes cast). Leaders of the two churches then developed a revised document, known as *Called to Common Mission* (CCM), which the ELCA narrowly approved in 1999 and the Episcopal Church overwhelmingly approved in 2000. Debates over the merits of the Concordat and CCM continue in both denominations, especially the ELCA, where serious doubts have been raised about theological and practical effects resulting from their new full communion relationship with the Episcopal Church.

Full communion does not mean that the Episcopal Church and the ELCA have merged in an official, institutional way. As the revised CCM document states, "in this new relationship the churches become interdependent while remaining autonomous" (ELCA *Outline of CCM* 2000, 1). Extensive negotiations leading to the Concordat and CCM produced agreements about matters of doctrine and faith, recognition of the differing ministries of each church (insofar as ordained ministries are concerned, this means that the ELCA accepts the three-level Episcopalian conception—bishop, priest, deacon—and the Episcopal Church accepts the single ELCA office of pastor), and mutual goals in evangelizing and pursuing mission activities. With full communion, the two denominations can share clergy where needed, celebrate the Eucharist together, and collaborate on social service and community projects.

One of the most contentious issues involved in developing the documents that have brought these denominations into full communion is the question of the historic episcopate—the tradition of an unbroken line of succession of bishops dating to the early Christian church, to which the Episcopal Church and the worldwide Anglican Communion adhere

("ELCA's Hanson Sees" 2001, 13). Some Lutheran churches around the world also adhere to the historic episcopate. But the ELCA has sharp internal discord over this issue, centered on theological and ethnic divisions that we will explore later in this chapter. The 1997 ELCA General Assembly debate raised strong concerns about ordaining future pastors into the historic episcopate, and many believe this was the critical reason why full communion (the Concordat) failed narrowly at that time.[1]

The revised document frames the historic episcopate in ways amenable to both sides, although its language reveals something less than full agreement:

> While our two churches will share the historic institution of the episcopate, . . . each remains free to explore interpretations of this ministry. The Episcopal Church is free to maintain that sharing in the historic catholic episcopate is necessary when Anglicans enter full communion. . . . [The] ELCA is free to maintain that sharing in this same episcopate is not necessary for the relationship of full communion. (ELCA *Outline of CCM* 2000, 13)

The question of the historic episcopate is by no means the only theological point of contention in considering full communion, but it became one of the most publicly discussed points, sparking considerable dialogue and strong reactions within both denominations (Marty 1998).

Interestingly, while the heated rhetoric surrounding full communion may suggest otherwise, there are some interesting examples of cooperative arrangements between U.S. Lutherans and Episcopalians dating back to colonial times. For example, in the mid-eighteenth century Pennsylvania and Delaware Anglicans

> maintained cordial relations with and supplied clergy for the Swedish Lutherans who remained from the seventeenth-century colony of New Sweden along the banks of the Delaware River. This relationship prepared the way for the seven "Old Swedes" churches of Pennsylvania, Delaware, and New Jersey to become Episcopalian in time. (Holmes 1993, 32)

Historically Swedish Lutheran synods in the United States have remained closer to the Episcopal Church through the present day.

Full communion brings the ELCA and the Episcopal Church, the offspring of very different sixteenth-century protest movements, into a relationship that critics argue has the potential of subsuming their individual liturgical and theological identities over the long run. Although such an outcome seems highly unlikely to occur, at least because of this relationship, such proposals are almost certain to stir up strong passions, and debates over the merits of full communion can only be described as highly political, not to mention highly charged. Hence an understanding of how clergy in both denominations perceive the issue and its implications can shed more light on how clergy react to external influences on contentious political issues. At the very least, analyzing clergy attitudes and public speech on full communion offers an interesting case study of contemporary intra- and interdenominational church politics.

CLERGY ATTITUDES TOWARD FULL COMMUNION: AN OVERVIEW

At the time of our survey (the summer and fall of 1998) the ELCA and Episcopal Church were working on revisions to the Concordat of Agreement, which had been voted down by the ELCA in 1997. The revised Called to Common Mission document was released while second waves of our survey were still in the field, but we did not revise the question wording because first wave responses had already been received. Our survey questions on full communion thus used "Concordat" as a specific reference in questions about the frequency of clergy speech, and "full communion" as the reference in the key question inquiring about clergy opinions: "The ELCA/Episcopal Church should enter into full communion with the Episcopal Church/ELCA." Clergy opinions on this statement are displayed in table 9.1, which also gives clergy perceptions of how a majority of their congregations feel about full communion.

Table 9.1 reveals that Episcopal clergy are more supportive than ELCA clergy (65 percent agree or strongly agree, versus 58 percent of ELCA pas-

Table 9.1.   Clergy and Perceived Congregational Majority Support for Full Communion (percent)

	Strongly Agree	Agree	Not Sure/Neutral	Disagree	Strongly Disagree
ELCA clergy	29.3	29.3	12.8	16.6	11.9
ELCA congregations as perceived by clergy	7.5	28.4	38.6	17.4	8.1
Episcopal clergy	34.0	31.0	17.8	9.6	7.5
Episcopal congregations as perceived by clergy	13.0	35.0	41.3	6.6	4.2

Source: 1998 ELCA/Episcopal Church Clergy Study. Number of cases varies

tors), and Episcopal clergy perceive more congregational support than do their ELCA counterparts; 48 percent of Episcopal clergy feel that a majority of their congregation supports full communion, while only 35 percent of ELCA clergy report this sentiment. Setting aside the large number of clergy (about 40 percent) who perceived their congregations as neutral or who could not estimate, Episcopal clergy were about five times more likely to perceive support for rather than opposition to full communion, while ELCA clergy found support moderately more often than opposition (35 percent to 26 percent). The results in table 9.1 suggest a strong relationship between clergy attitudes and perceptions of congregational support for full communion.

PREDICTING CLERGY OPINIONS ON DENOMINATIONAL ISSUES

Conventional wisdom about patterns of support and opposition to full communion has held that clergy and parishioners are more supportive if they live in communities where the ELCA and Episcopal Church have few members, compared to other denominations and faith traditions. Such places already offer many examples of cooperation in mission and pulpit sharing (Emery 2000). Opposition within the ELCA is always said to be concentrated in upper midwestern states, where Lutherans represent a visible and often dominant cultural and numerical population and hence see little advantage to joining forces with relatively small Episcopal parishes. Faculty at Luther Seminary (St. Paul, Minnesota) and ELCA Lutherans with Norwegian roots have arguably been the most visible in opposing full communion, raising the most serious theological objections —specifically acceptance of the historic episcopate and the Episcopal threefold ministry.[2]

With these thoughts in mind, we need to reevaluate how our fivefold typology of explanatory factors will influence clergy attitudes and speech patterns regarding full communion. The factors that have predicted different types and frequencies of clergy political activities in the preceding four chapters have not been identical, and we expect a unique set of factors to be significantly related to full communion attitudes. In this section we review our theoretical expectations, focusing especially on explanatory factors (e.g., seminary training) that have previously received less attention, as well as some new independent variables appropriate for investigating full communion opinions and speech patterns.

Common Indicators

We expect many factors to affect clergy speech and opinions on full communion in the same ways that they have affected clergy political beliefs and actions. These factors include numerous congregational resources and community influences. Congregational views of full communion should relate directly to clergy attitudes and speech frequency—clergy who support full communion are in position to shape their members' views of it, and clergy with less strong feelings might be more apt to agree with the majority view (particularly on the negative side of the issue) or might discuss the issue less often. Larger congregations might see less need to join in full communion to carry out missions or to staff pulpits, and high levels of brand loyalty might provoke a more parochial view driven by a commitment to tradition that hampers ecumenical initiatives.

Measures of regional location and community type should also reveal sources of clergy opinions on full communion. Small-town churches in many areas are already sharing a clergyperson within the denomination and hence might see full communion as a way of addressing clergy shortages. Competition among churches is stronger in suburban areas, hence clergy serving suburban congregations might support ties with the other denomination as a way of building or maintaining membership versus faster-growing denominations (Finke and Stark 1992). Regional measures will be included in our multivariate regression models to determine the extent of regional clergy blocs in both denominations for or against full communion; the salience of clergy seminary training and congregational ethnic roots, which we discuss in detail below, are also incorporated into the models in part through these regional variables.

Community influences test the salience of attributes of the clergyperson and her congregation relative to their surroundings. Once again we utilize clergy perceptions of belief and activity isolation from the local community, and we also incorporate clergy perceptions of whether their church differs from others in the denomination (termed *denominational isolation*). As we have shown previously, clergy whose congregations differ from others in the local community tend to take on prophetic roles in representing their congregations—both in presenting minority status and its implications to the congregation, and in representing the congregation's unique voice to the larger, dominant surrounding community. Generally speaking, most Episcopal priests and deacons find themselves as minority voices; beyond some northeastern, high-status communities, there are few sizable concentrations of Episcopalians in the United States today. Hence full communion with the larger ELCA might be seen by these Episcopal clergy as a good thing—with a similarly strong emphasis on scripture and sacrament, feelings of isolation from community might be reduced with the full communion relationship. Many ELCA congregations are in similar situations, but others represent the largest (or a subset of the largest) denominations in their towns and regions; hence this factor should be less salient for ELCA clergy.

We can also test the isolation hypothesis using two objective measures: county concentrations of ELCA and Episcopal adherents. The relative strength of each denomination is expected to affect support generally. The ELCA in particular has strong concentrations in upper midwestern states, and from this position of strength in numbers it would be less likely to perceive full communion as necessary. Clergy located in areas where ELCA and/or Episcopal membership is low, relative to other denominations and faith traditions, are probably more likely to see full communion as necessary and appropriate to carry out the common missions of the denominations.

Finally, contacts with colleagues from the other denomination should be an important community influence on full communion attitudes and speech frequencies. Having a personal relationship with a clergyperson from the other denomination might well influence sample clergy to be more supportive, especially ELCA clergy who have more reservations about full communion, according to table 9.1.

In one important way, our models estimating clergy attitudes and speech patterns regarding full communion will look quite different than previous models. Preliminary analysis revealed that *personal attributes of clergy play no role in determining speech or opinions about full communion*. No significant relationships were found between opinions on full communion and gender, years in the ministry, or education. Accordingly these variables are not included in the models we present later in the chapter. The models also contain no explicitly political orientation; we would not expect strong partisanship or political ideology to relate to this denominational issue in any way.

Theological Self-Identification and Denominational Evaluations

It stands to reason that the theological perspectives our sample clergy hold will be very influential in determining how they perceive full communion and whether they speak out on the issue. As we noted earlier in the chapter, significant theological disputes have been and remain part of the debate about full communion in both denominations (Lyles 2001). We test for theological determinants of full communion perspectives by using our measure of theological conservatism and three indicators of theological self identification. The theological terms utilized have direct relevance to the content and implications of full communion—*ecumenical, high church,* and (to a lesser extent) *liberal.* Support for ecumenism in particular should relate strongly and directly to support for full communion; similarly, ELCA clergy who identify with the "high church" label may feel more comfortable with Episcopal practices, while high-church Episcopal priests may be more skeptical of Lutheran liturgical practices.

Important signals about the implications of full communion also come from within the denomination. Clergy in both denominations are quite aware that while they direct *their churches,* other individuals have a great deal of authority over *the church.* The ELCA and the Episcopal Church are hierarchically organized into synods (ELCA) or dioceses (Episcopal) headed by elected bishops (albeit with somewhat different roles in each denomination), and subdivisions exist within these groupings. The process that led to national votes on full communion included both ordained and lay leaders in both denominations. As with national and local politics, clergy hold elite status in denominational debates but are not the sole actors charged with decision making.

The national denominational offices also play a role in shaping church policies. Clergy "in the trenches" appear to orient themselves toward their national leadership in ways similar to regional offices of large national corporations—perceiving central management as "the other," located in some far-off place and making important decisions without full awareness of what is really taking place on the front lines. Within the ELCA, this kind of tension is exacerbated by the relative youth of the denomination (see chapter 2). Our ELCA survey respondents frequently referenced "Chicago" as a (not often complimentary) shorthand reference to the national ELCA offices located there.

We did not ask sample clergy about the effectiveness of their national headquarters. We did inquire how clergy felt about their local synods or dioceses, presenting an opportunity to see how internal denominational tensions might affect attitudes toward this contentious proposal, particularly within the ELCA. There is growing evidence that clergy opinions of church bodies with which they are more familiar (like local synods) should lead to corresponding views of the national church—good evaluations locally beget good evaluations nationally, and negative experiences close to home mean negative perceptions of denominational activities (Djupe, Olson, and Gilbert 2002).

Seminary Education and Full Communion

To this point we have found only modest differences in ELCA and Episcopal clergy behavior patterns when examining seminary cohorts. Full communion, however, provides a more salient test of how seminaries differ from one another, and how seminary education shapes the views and actions of graduates in the field. We expect to find clear differences in attitudes toward full communion across ELCA and Episcopal seminary cohort groups. As with previous analyses of the effects of seminary education, we expect more immediate factors to shape personal and public clergy responses to full communion, but in this case seminary education serves as an important formative influence on the theological beliefs of our sample clergy.

Table 9.2 displays full communion attitudes of our sample clergy, grouped by seminary attended. Among ELCA clergy, Luther graduates (by far the largest group in the ELCA clergy sample, about one-fourth of all ELCA respondents) are closest to a split opinion, with only 46 percent in

Table 9.2.   Full Communion Attitudes, Grouped by Seminary Attended (percents)

ELCA Seminary	Agree	Disagree
Southern (48)	72.9	20.8
Chicago (95)	70.5	18.9
Seminex (33)	69.7	12.1
Gettysburg (116)	67.2	22.4
Trinity (122)	61.5	25.4
Pacific (54)	61.1	24.1
Philadelphia (65)	58.5	23.1
Wartburg (127)	51.2	30.7
Luther (345)	45.8	41.4

Episcopal Seminary	Agree	Disagree
Episcopal Divinity (28)	89.3	3.6
Sewanee (67)	76.1	6.0
Pacific (59)	72.9	11.9
Berkeley at Yale (53)	71.7	13.2
Harvard (16)	68.8	6.6
Seabury-Western (82)	68.3	15.9
Bexley Hall (17)	64.7	11.8
Southwest (25)	64.0	20.0
Virginia Theological (104)	62.5	21.2
General Theological (91)	61.5	23.1
Nashotah (62)	51.6	35.5

Source: 1998 ELCA/Episcopal Church Clergy Study. Number of cases in parentheses.

favor and 41 percent opposed. Wartburg (Iowa) graduates are the only other ELCA seminary cohort close to 50 percent agreement and over 30 percent disagreement. Levels of agreement and disagreement for the other ELCA seminary cohorts cluster around 60–70 percent agreement and 20 percent disagreement; Seminex graduates are least likely to disagree. Seminary training and formation clearly affect the full communion opinions of ELCA clergy.

Episcopal clergy show stronger agreement and, with few exceptions, quite low disagreement with full communion, according to table 9.2. Graduates of Episcopal Divinity School (Cambridge, Massachusetts) are overwhelmingly in favor (almost 90 percent); recall that EDS graduates ranked among the most theologically liberal of all Episcopal seminary cohorts (table 4.8). At the other end, Nashotah House (Wisconsin) has the lowest agreement rate and by far the highest disagreement rate (over one-third). Nashotah has remained staunchly conservative on several denominational issues, for example, opposing the ordination of women as priests. Except for Nashotah graduates, Episcopal clergy strongly support ecumenism regardless of the seminary attended.

The Salience of Ethnic Ties for ELCA Clergy

We noted previously that ELCA opposition to full communion is thought to be rooted in upper midwestern states for two main reasons: the denomination's high membership numbers there, which argue against the need for full communion, and the influence of Norwegian Lutherans, opposed on theological grounds to this ecumenical venture. To test for the effects of ethnic ties and old Lutheran fault lines, table 9.3 presents ELCA clergy and perceived congregational support for full communion, sorted by the dominant ethnic group (as reported by clergy) and prior denominational affiliation of the churches where our sample ELCA clergy work.

The ethnic roots of disputes about full communion become obvious here. Clergy working in churches composed mainly of Norwegian Americans are the least supportive (44 percent) and most opposed (41 percent), compared with clergy in predominantly Swedish, German, or Danish congregations. Moreover, clergy working in mainly Norwegian-descent congregations are more likely to report that a majority of their members are opposed to full communion (38 percent opposed, versus 21 percent in favor). Swedish-descent and Danish-descent congregations are fairly evenly split on full communion, while German-descent congregations, like their clergy, are most supportive.

Table 9.3.   ELCA Clergy and Perceived Congregational Majority Support for Full Communion by Congregation's Ethnicity and Pre-ELCA Affiliation (percents)

Predominant Ethnicity of Congregation	*Norwegian*	*Swedish*	*German*	*Danish*
Clergy attitude on full communion				
Agree	43.6	55.4	64.9	60.7
Neutral	15.7	18.9	11.1	7.1
Disagree	40.7	25.7	24.0	32.1
Number of churches	280	148	558	28
Congregation attitude on full communion, as perceived by clergy				
Agree	21.0	31.8	37.5	32.1
Neutral	40.9	39.9	41.1	35.7
Disagree	38.0	28.4	21.4	32.1
Number of churches	276	148	552	28
Prior Affiliation of Congregation	*LCA*	*AELC*	*ALC*	
Clergy attitude on full communion				
Agree	65.1	68.5	49.6	
Neutral	11.9	8.7	14.2	
Disagree	22.9	22.8	36.3	
Number of churches	637	92	571	
Congregation attitude on full communion, as perceived by clergy				
Agree	43.4	50.0	26.0	
Neutral	36.3	38.0	40.6	
Disagree	20.3	12.0	33.4	
Number of churches	625	92	566	

Source: 1998 ELCA/Episcopal Church Clergy Study.

Table 9.3 also shows differences in full communion attitudes between the three church bodies that came together to form the ELCA in 1988. Clergy in former Lutheran Church in America (LCA) and former Association of Evangelical Lutheran Churches (AELC) congregations are about equally supportive (around two-thirds each) and opposed (23 percent each) to full communion, while clergy in former American Lutheran Church (ALC) congregations are far less supportive (50 percent) and far more opposed (36 percent). The former ALC churches are much more likely to be predominantly Norwegian, accounting for the fact that former ALC congregations on the whole oppose full communion, while former AELC and LCA congregations tend to support full communion (former AELC congregations especially so).

The roots of Norwegian Lutheran opposition to full communion, especially ELCA acceptance of the historic episcopate, run deep. From its founding in the late 1840s, the U.S. branch of Norwegian Lutheranism (named after Norwegian religious reformer Hans Nielsen Hauge) kept its distance from the state–church traditions that marked other Lutheran U.S. synods dominated by Swedes, Germans, Finns, and some Danes (Ahlstrom 1972, 756–62). In the last century numerous mergers have combined and recombined the original synod organizations, and some old divisions have been subsumed for the sake of unity (Mead and Hill 1992, 139–45); nonetheless, the ethnic bases of the old ALC, AELC, and LCA show through in the table 9.3 patterns of clergy and congregational support and opposition to full communion. While Lutheran bodies in the United States have always remained on speaking terms with one another, ethnic heritage continues to be a potent force affecting ecumenical efforts and ongoing discussions toward further intra-Lutheran unification. We incorporate these ethnic distinctions into our multivariate models with a variable indicating previous American Lutheran Church affiliation.

DETERMINANTS OF FULL COMMUNION ATTITUDES

Table 9.2 and table 9.3 expose the salience of divisions within the ELCA based on seminary socialization, old ethnic ties, and previous denominational affiliations. We now turn to a multivariate analysis incorporating these and other factors to explain ELCA and Episcopal clergy attitudes toward full communion. We will use regression analysis to discern the extent to which our modified sets of explanatory factors relate to clergy opinions on full communion. The table 9.4 models demonstrate that clergy opinions on full communion are influenced by a broad set of factors. We will review these factors for the two denominations separately.

ELCA clergy who self-identify as ecumenical are more supportive of full communion, as are ELCA clergy who have professional contact with an Episcopal priest or deacon; both of these findings fit with our expectations. Theological conservatism translates to less full communion support, likely due to the theological aspects of full communion that have made many ELCA clergy and lay members uneasy. Model results for self-identification as theological liberals and high church supporters are somewhat misleading; liberal theology and high-church identification are positively related to full communion support.[3] Finally, contrary to our expectations, attitudes toward full communion are inversely related to views on the local ELCA synod, ac-

Table 9.4. Estimated ELCA and Episcopal Clergy Support for Full Communion (OLS regression estimates)

Variable	ELCA		Episcopal Church	
	Coeff.	(S.E.)	Coeff.	(S.E.)
Political and Theological Orientations				
Theological conservatism	−0.106	(0.041)***	−0.177	(0.064)***
Ecumenical identification	0.327	(0.058)***	0.143	(0.086)*
High church identification	−0.161	(0.046)***	0.178	(0.068)***
Liberal theological identification	−0.257	(0.047)***	−0.217	(0.081)***
Congregational Resources				
Perceived congregational support for full communion	0.764	(0.032)***	0.816	(0.057)***
Church size	−0.000	(0.000)	0.000	(0.000)
Less brand loyalty in congregation	−0.041	(0.051)	−0.018	(0.071)
Rural church	0.079	(0.082)	−0.059	(0.124)
Urban church	0.052	(0.070)	−0.245	(0.117)**
Southern church	0.078	(0.092)	0.243	(0.132)*
Northeastern church	−0.081	(0.081)	0.345	(0.136)***
Upper midwestern church	−0.247	(0.099)**	0.170	(0.286)
Former ALC church	−0.146	(0.079)*	—	
Denominational Cues				
Synod/diocese evaluation	−0.075	(0.034)**	−0.117	(0.050)**

(continued)

Table 9.4. Estimated ELCA and Episcopal Clergy Support for Full Communion (OLS regression estimates) *(continued)*

Variable	ELCA		Episcopal Church	
	Coeff.	(S.E.)	Coeff.	(S.E.)
Community Influences				
Belief isolation	−0.186	(0.120)	−0.046	(0.184)
Activity isolation	0.028	(0.138)	0.634	(0.231)***
Denominational isolation	0.130	(0.155)	0.014	(0.249)
Episcopal clergy contact	0.186	(0.069)***		
ELCA clergy contact	—		0.119	(0.104)
Percent ELCA in county	0.890	(0.450)**	−2.081	(1.844)
Percent Episcopalians in county	−2.225	(3.872)	−10.662	(6.993)
Constant	1.819	(0.328)	1.576	(0.458)
Number of cases	1,014		716	
Adjusted R^2	0.549		0.354	

Source: 1998 ELCA/Episcopal Church Clergy Study.
***$p < 0.01$; **$p < 0.05$; *$p < 0.10$

cording to the table 9.4 model. This finding reflects the regional roots of dissatisfaction among full communion opponents, who are now in the process of fighting the implementation of several provisions of CCM at the synod level. Clergy whose synods disliked full communion put the blame for it elsewhere. Moreover, clergy who believe their synod is already an effective body likely do not see a great need for full communion.

Relatively few congregational resources affect ELCA clergy views on full communion, but the ones that are significant fit precisely with the arguments and evidence presented earlier. Perceptions of the congregation's attitude have a direct relationship to attitudes on full communion—whether clergy are projecting their views onto the congregation or reflecting member opinion, a strong connection is clearly present. Furthermore, *the model confirms that ELCA clergy serving in upper midwestern and former ALC churches are more likely to oppose full communion.* No other regional factor, community type indicator, or measure of church characteristics is a significant predictor among ELCA clergy. No isolation measures predict full communion views, either.

The only other significant factor affecting ELCA clergy views on full communion is the county concentration of ELCA adherents. Residing in a county with more ELCA adherents actually leads to greater support for full communion, not less as anticipated. ELCA clergy do not appear to equate high membership totals with a belief that ecumenical efforts are unnecessary; instead, this finding suggests that high concentrations of ELCA members in a county offer a good starting point for alliances that can implement or increase existing mission and service activities.

The table 9.4 model predicting indicators of Episcopal clergy full communion attitudes reveals some intriguing differences between the sources of Episcopal and ELCA clergy full communion opinions. Ecumenical self-identification predicts greater support, and theological conservatism translates to less support; high church and theological liberal self-identification are also related, though as in the ELCA model the signs mislead—high-church Episcopal clergy are actually less supportive of full communion, while self-identified theological liberals are more supportive. Interestingly, having an ELCA clergy contact does not affect Episcopal clergy views on full communion, while support for the local diocese again leads to less enthusiasm for this ecumenical agreement.

Like their ELCA counterparts, Episcopal clergy view full communion clearly in tandem with perceived congregational views. Episcopal clergy in southern and northeastern parishes also have more positive views of full communion. In these two areas ecumenical efforts already exist with the

ELCA and other partners, and seminary graduates (particularly EDS and Sewanee, located in Tennessee) are most supportive of full communion (table 9.2). Priests and deacons serving urban congregations are less supportive; most likely these congregations already engage in community activities. Recall from chapter 1 the numerous ways that one Episcopal congregation was involved in its urban context. Couple this with the fact that greater activity isolation leads to *more* support for full communion. Simply residing in a place with pressing social needs may not be enough; rather, perceiving that one's church is doing less than one's neighbors seems to prod Episcopal clergy to embrace the potential that full communion offers to redress Episcopal activity isolation and to meet local community needs more effectively.

Overall the models in table 9.4 show that *clergy theological orientations, congregational views on full communion, and regional-ethnic ties are the key predictors of attitudes toward full communion.* The models explain over half the variance in full communion attitudes among ELCA clergy, and over one-third of the variance for Episcopal clergy—both are impressive for regression analyses of this type. While relatively few contextual effects are present, the contextual findings support the contention that clergy read and react to their surroundings—inside and beyond their own congregations—and what they find helps structure their attitudes, in conjunction with theological and denominational orientations.

PREDICTING PUBLIC COMMENT ON FULL COMMUNION

An additional way to understand how contexts affect clergy comes from the frequency of clergy public commentary on the Concordat of Agreement. We asked ministers how often they discussed the 1997 Concordat in the past year (1998). These discussions could occur in any forum, not just in the context of a sermon or church setting. As shown in table 9.5, 40 percent of Episcopal clergy addressed the Concordat often or very often in 1998, compared to just 30 percent of ELCA clergy; Episcopal priests and deacons were twice as likely to discuss the Concordat "very often." These are intriguing differences, considering that most of the disagreements over full communion took place within the ELCA, while Episcopalians twice approved the idea with nearly unanimous consent.

The models in table 9.6 explain how often our sample clergy spoke about the Concordat in 1998. We again estimate separate models for ELCA and Episcopal clergy, using the same factors tested in the table 9.4 models predicting full communion views, plus the clergyperson's own opinion on

Table 9.5.   Frequency of Publicly Addressing the Concordat in the Past Year (1998) (percents)

	Very Often	Often	Seldom	Rarely	Never
ELCA clergy	10.0	20.1	30.6	29.3	10.0
Episcopal clergy	20.9	19.0	27.8	24.4	7.7

Source: 1998 ELCA/Episcopal Church Clergy Study. Number of cases varies.
Note: Clergy were asked, "How often have you addressed the 1997 Concordat with the [Episcopal Church/ELCA] in the last year?"

full communion; once again, other personal attributes and political indicators were found to be insignificant and hence are not included in the final analysis. With the large differences between the two sets of clergy in their frequency of addressing this issue, we expect significant factors to differ considerably in the two models. This is in fact what we find in table 9.6.

ELCA clergy generally represent congregations perceived as less supportive of full communion than their clergy (recall table 9.1 and table 9.3). We might expect that ELCA clergy would talk more about the Concordat if they wish to lead their congregations toward their own viewpoint. But table 9.6 shows that in fact *neither the ELCA clergyperson's personal view of the Concordat nor the congregation's perceived opinion is a significant predictor of the frequency with which the Concordat was addressed publicly in 1998.* Here we are observing a "canceling out" effect: roughly equal numbers of the strongest proponents and the strongest opponents felt more compelled or more restrained when it came to discussing full communion. Factoring in congregational views produces the same situation, with proponents and opponents about equally likely to talk more or less when the congregation does not agree.

With no significant effects emanating from pastoral or perceived congregational opinions, we find an intriguing set of influences on ELCA clergy, most of which are theological orientations of the pastor. Self-identification as ecumenical and greater theological conservatism led to more frequent mention of the Concordat in 1998, with ecumenically minded pastors tending to express support and conservative pastors verbalizing stronger opposition. ELCA pastors with an Episcopal clergy contact also spoke more often, perhaps prompted by their interactions to share their viewpoints with congregants. Along the same lines, urban pastors and pastors in counties with more Episcopalians also spoke more often—once again demonstrating that proximity sparks discussion.

Finally, ELCA pastors who describe themselves as high church spoke out *less often*—a reaction, perhaps, to social surroundings. If the congregation uses the *Lutheran Book of Worship* each Sunday, it might also feel comfortable with Episcopalian liturgies; hence, there is little to discuss publicly

Table 9.6.   Estimated ELCA and Episcopal Clergy Frequency of Publicly Addressing the Concordat in the Past Year (1998) (OLS regression estimates)

Variable	ELCA		Episcopal Church	
	Coeff.	(S.E.)	Coeff.	(S.E.)
Political and Theological Orientations				
Theological conservatism	0.205	(0.050)***	0.043	(0.056)
Ecumenical identification	0.212	(0.071)***	0.108	(0.074)
High church identification	−0.203	(0.057)***	−0.221	(0.060)***
Liberal theological identification	0.032	(0.058)	−0.053	(0.071)
Support for full communion	0.007	(0.038)	0.127	(0.033)***
Congregational Resources				
Perceived congregational support for full communion	−0.004	(0.048)	0.164	(0.056)***
Church size	−0.000	(0.000)	−0.000	(0.000)
Less brand loyalty in congregation	−0.041	(0.061)	0.013	(0.062)
Rural church	−0.109	(0.100)	0.184	(0.108)*
Urban church	0.163	(0.085)*	−0.035	(0.102)
Southern church	−0.173	(0.113)	−0.107	(0.116)
Northeastern church	−0.051	(0.098)	−0.382	(0.119)***
Upper midwestern church	0.188	(0.120)	0.386	(0.253)
Former ALC church	−0.018	(0.096)	—	
Denominational Cues				
Synod/diocese evaluation	0.011	(0.041)	−0.026	(0.044)
Community Influences				
Belief isolation	0.227	(0.146)	0.147	(0.161)
Activity isolation	0.239	(0.167)	−0.047	(0.201)
Denominational isolation	−0.270	(0.188)	−0.177	(0.217)
Episcopal clergy contact	0.261	(0.084)***	—	
ELCA clergy contact	—		0.399	(0.090)***
Percent ELCA in county	−0.329	(0.544)	−0.431	(1.606)
Percent Episcopalians in county	11.167	(4.681)**	−3.068	(6.070)
Constant	2.049	(0.403)	1.936	(0.406)
Number of cases	1,002		701	
Adjusted R^2	0.059		0.176	

Source: 1998 ELCA/Episcopal Church Clergy Study.
***$p < 0.01$; **$p < 0.05$; *$p < 0.10$

since the liturgies are not at all incompatible. On the flip side, a high-church ELCA pastor whose congregation has embraced more contemporary worship forms might be reluctant to press for full communion with the high-church Episcopalians.

Residing in an upper midwestern parish had no statistically significant effect on the frequency of ELCA clergy speaking about the Concordat in

1998, although the conventional wisdom suggests that more Concordat discussions took place in upper midwestern congregations. No other factors explain ELCA clergy speech frequency, and we note especially that none of the isolation measures predicts the frequency of 1998 Concordat public speech.

In contrast to their ELCA counterparts, Episcopal clergy were motivated to greater public discussion of the Concordat in 1998 by their own support and the congregation's perceived support. Serving in a rural parish and having an ELCA clergy contact also led to more public discussion of the Concordat. With little internal opposition to full communion efforts, as well as ongoing efforts at establishing similar relationships with other denominations, Episcopal priests and deacons appear to be reflecting their denomination's concern for its future by more frequently calling members' attention to the significance and implications of ecumenical endeavors.

Only two factors relate to less Episcopal clergy discussion of the Concordat in 1998—service in a northeastern parish and high church self-identification. Despite their overall support for full communion, northeastern Episcopal clergy and congregations are less likely to have large numbers of ELCA Lutherans nearby; the reverse situation helps explain why rural Episcopal clergy spoke more often about the Concordat. High-church self-identification again may lead Episcopal clergy to be somewhat skeptical of the contemporary worship forms gaining popularity within the ELCA.

The models in table 9.6 are generally weak predictors of the 1998 frequency of public discussion of the Concordat, especially when compared to the models in table 9.4. But the models do show that regardless of their point of view on full communion, ELCA and Episcopal clergy are prompted simply by knowing one another to talk more about this issue with their congregations. The congregation's location also affects frequency of discussion, and high-church identification breeds some reluctance for clergy in both denominations. Table 9.6 demonstrates again that personal and contextual factors play a role in affecting the frequency of clergy public discussion of contentious issues.

CONCLUSION

One of our primary goals in developing and conducting this clergy study was to understand better how social environments influence clergy attitudes and decisions about what to say and do. We have generally explored these questions in political terms—electoral activity, participation in myriad ways, partisanship and other political attitudes, and general orientations toward politics and the interplay of religion and politics. This chapter illustrates a simple, related point—if the congregational and community context do affect clergy political actions and beliefs, they should also matter for issues facing clergy beyond the realm of politics and public affairs. As opinion leaders within their own churches and in their communities, clergy have incentives and opportunities to discern public attitudes and help shape them.

Full communion, and its implications for the religious and public activities of these two denominations, is a weighty issue with intra- and interdenominational dimensions that can only be described as political in nature. Our analysis in this chapter demonstrates that our sample clergy—especially ELCA pastors—grapple with profound cross pressures in developing viewpoints about these issues and determining when and where to disseminate such viewpoints. In sorting through these issues, it is not surprising that theological beliefs, derived in part from seminary training but also from personal experience, are critical sources of cues on how to think and act. The congregation's location also influences clergy responses in complex ways, sometimes restricting and sometimes encouraging clergy comments on the issue.

The results of investigations of contextual effects on citizen attitudes and behavior do not always yield to a straightforward interpretation. Still, the results presented here support our contention that clergy care about how their congregations fit within the social and political structures of their community and their denominations, and they act accordingly, sometimes to reflect the congregation's point of view and sometimes to transform it into action.

NOTES

1. In the summer of 2001, the ELCA altered its bylaws, granting local synod bishops the option (following a lengthy synodical process) to permit the ordination of new ELCA pastors without requiring bishops to be present. This alternative approach (bypassing the historic episcopate for ELCA pastors so ordained) can only be utilized "for pastoral reasons in unusual circumstances" ("ELCA's Hanson Sees" 2001, 13). The Episcopal response has been cautious, both criticizing the move and affirming the fact that full communion will require both denominations to have patience with the implementation of new practices mandated by the Called to Common Mission agreement ("Episcopal Church Nods" 2001, 11–12). The first ELCA pastor to be ordained under the new bylaw—a Luther Seminary graduate—was ordained in July 2002 ("Luther Seminary Graduate Ordained" 2002).

2. Passage of CCM by the 1999 ELCA General Assembly led to the formation of a group called Word Alone, which is concentrated primarily in Minnesota and surrounding states and devoted to resisting "Chicago" (ELCA headquarters) efforts to "impose" the historic episcopate on ELCA pastors. Word Alone emerged after our survey was conducted, although some of our empirical results hint at the types of pastors who would be receptive to Word Alone's stance on the theological issues involved.

3. For technical reasons, the coefficients on these variables are reversed in the table 9.4 models. The interrelationships between high-church and liberal self-identification and other independent variables (especially in the ELCA model) cause a shift in sign on high-church and liberal self-identification, from positive to negative. In fact both measures are strongly *positively* correlated with support for full communion.

10

CLERGY ROLES
IN AMERICAN POLITICS

Our analysis of the political activities and opinions of ELCA and Episcopal clergy has ranged over a broad variety of topics and explanatory factors to offer a comprehensive portrait of what our sample clergy do and from whence the impetus to political action arises. In this concluding chapter we first highlight the major findings of the book, leading to a consideration of how to place these findings in their appropriate context. Some of the major questions to address involve the status of the ELCA and Episcopal Church in American public life. For example, to what extent did ELCA and Episcopal clergy participate in the "culture wars" of the 1990s (Hunter 1991, 1994)? Can our results shed light on the perceived decline in the public presence of mainline Protestant churches (e.g., Reeves 1996; Wuthnow 1997)? Finally, we will describe the ways in which our analysis of two mainline Protestant denominations can be generalized to the study of clergy political behavior in general, and in doing so we offer a critical review of the state of this field of scholarly inquiry.

THE DETERMINANTS OF CLERGY POLITICAL ACTIVITY

Throughout this volume, we have asserted that clergy perform meaningful political activities, with choices shaped by the environment in which they live and work. Clergy are called to serve God and a community of believers. They therefore engage several reference systems that reflect the contextual application of their profession: personal attributes, political and theological orientations, congregational resources, denominational cues, and community influences. These sets of factors interact to shape the contours of clergy political activity, operating with differential relative strengths for each kind of political activity.

Clergy involvement in political activity clearly results from the interplay between internal and external sources of influence. At times clergy are driven to participate by their own predilections and a sense of their role. In other situations clergy can be mobilized to political action through awareness and response to local or national issues and events, or direct recruitment from organized groups and church members. Internal and external influences can conflict when the congregation disagrees with the clergy's political views; these forces can also intersect, as when the needs and mission of the church enlarge in scope and consequence because of local conditions. Local conditions might take the form of mission opportunities (e.g., to the poor) or because the clergy must represent congregational needs and perspectives to the broader community. Most clergy feel comfortable involving themselves and portions of their congregations in their civic and political endeavors—such activity is a natural product of who they are as clergy—though most of our sample clergy would feel uncomfortable wearing a partisan political label, instead preferring to think of their endeavors in terms of social or civic activism.

Reviewing the key findings from each of the political activity chapters (chapters 5–9) will further delineate the conditions through which ELCA and Episcopal clergy become engaged in political and civic life. We also reiterate these findings to demonstrate the ways in which they may apply to clergy political behavior beyond the two denominations under close study here.

Political Speech

The church venue dictates that political information is most commonly conveyed to the congregation by public speech. Previous research has largely focused on whether clergy bring politics into their weekly sermons. We expand this literature by not only asking how much they talk politics in public but also asking about what ELCA and Episcopal clergy are discussing. Incorporating precise measures of *content* allows us to make more specific connections to the political environment and to assess more concretely the possibilities for clergy political influence.

We conclude that sample ELCA and Episcopal clergy are responsive to the political environment, thus enhancing their potential influence. They are highly networked and are well informed through media usage, interaction with colleagues, and messages from the denomination. Hence clergy can respond relatively quickly to calls for action at times when policy windows are open. In this way, clergy help knit together the public sphere, acting as links between government and citizens. Clergy may not call out for all congregation members to write their representative (though it has been done), but they can lay the groundwork for such appeals by an interest group or social action campaign to bear fruit.

Furthermore, we find that ELCA and Episcopal clergy take up political topics more often when their churches constitute a minority in the community. In part, this pattern reflects circumstances in which the clergy's own voice is underrepresented in the community. It also suggests that clergy are attuned to how their congregations fit into community power structures, and that clergy adapt their degree and methods of public action accordingly. In this way, the voiceless are given at least some representation in the public sphere by clergy.

Electoral Activism

Clergy activism in elections is the most individualistic of the political activities studied in this volume, and, interestingly, the only activity type in which clergy do not appear responsive to the congregation's place in the community (except for the civic activity of encouraging the congregation to vote). As we showed in chapter 2, ELCA and Episcopal clergy tend to identify overwhelmingly as Democrats, but they feel uneasy with partisan politics and do not organize their own political activism around their party affiliation.

These clergy are also profoundly influenced by their understanding of the First Amendment Establishment Clause, which in their minds delegitimates clergy politicking for candidates within the congregation. This is not to say that ELCA and Episcopal clergy are not involved in electoral politics; they are. Instead, these clergy act as resourceful and active citizens: they rarely lead partisan efforts, they place importance on encouraging civic virtues in their congregations, and they are at times swept up on partisan bandwagons in communities that have political sympathies consonant with their own. Although most ELCA and Episcopal congregations tend to support the Republican Party, the clergy are overwhelmingly Democratic: American electoral politics is not oriented neatly around the concerns of mainline Protestants.

Local Activity

It is surprising that most scholars of clergy activity have not investigated local political activities, which we find to be one of the most common activities in which clergy engage. This finding is not unexpected considering the importance clergy attach to their communities and the unique voice their congregation brings to local civic and social life. Because of their strong and direct ties to the community, we find that personal and partisan orientations exert the weakest effects on local clergy political and civic activity. Clergy respond less to their own motivations for local action and respond more positively to recruitment efforts by various community sources, as well as the perception of a representational vacuum around their congregations.

James Madison (in *Federalist* 10) feared most the mischief of factions operating against minority populations in homogeneous locales. While churches and clergy cannot rectify this imbalance and eliminate the potential for abuse, they can and do represent interests to government that would otherwise go unheard. The status of the congregation in the local community thus can propel ELCA and Episcopal clergy to take on prophetic, representative roles when necessary and appropriate. In this regard our sample clergy are not likely to differ from ministers in other denominations and faith traditions. Local civic involvement is the norm for clergy from nearly all U.S. faith traditions, and representational deficits appear to enhance that involvement for our sample clergy.

Contacting Government

While some scholars have labeled clergy who engage in civil disobedience as deviant (Winter 1973), we find that contacting behavior shows most directly how the reference systems can work together to produce considerable political activity. We suspected that in order to avoid conflict, clergy would pursue sending a message directly to government if their political opinions clashed with their congregation's views. Rather than confront a disagreeable congregation, clergy would take their concerns directly to government, whether contacting the media, marching, or writing letters.

Instead, we find that contacting government in its various forms is undertaken *at the same time* that clergy bring their concerns to the congregation. Moreover, clergy contacting is shaped by their communities and how the congregation fits into them. Clergy engage in more extreme measures where such measures are needed to draw attention (e.g., in urban areas). They pursue conventional contacting strategies when their churches constitute minorities locally, most likely out of a sense that extreme measures would backfire in the court of public opinion. We believed that contacting would be driven by individualistic concerns, but instead found the opposite: sending a message to government is properly construed as yet another extension of the professional duties of clergy to their faith and their faith community.

Denominational Politics

In our analysis of the debate over full communion between the ELCA and Episcopal Church, we find that clergy attitudes toward denominational issues are driven by many of the same factors that affect choices about conventional political actions. The same reference systems (personal, denominational, congregational, and community) influence the opinions and activities of clergy on this denominational issue, especially the institutional traditions and theological beliefs of the denominations. In the ELCA, opinions are fractured along the fault lines of the denomination: the ethnic identification of congregations and clergy as well as the pre-ELCA denominational affiliation of the churches our sample clergy serve. Seminaries still fuel this identification and outlook, highlighting at least one reason why such traditions are slow to change and how important seminaries are to the direction and unity of a denomination (Ammerman 1990).

In summary, we find strong evidence that the political activity of sample ELCA and Episcopal clergy revolves around the interplay between personal beliefs and their duties to a faith and faith community. As a consequence of living and working in this complex web of interrelated factors, clergy often take their political concerns to the secular community and government. However, clergy do not use the electoral process very often as a means to press their concerns as institutional representatives, although they are highly engaged in partisan politics relative to average citizens. We will return to this point in our discussion of what our results have to say about the recent American "culture wars" below.

THE GENERALIZABILITY OF THE STUDY

How generalizable are the results of this study—to what other parts of American religion do these conclusions apply? The ELCA and Episcopal Church stand solidly in the U.S. Protestant mainline; both denominations are hierarchically organized, are liturgical, and hold moderate to liberal theologies. The specific relationships found in these chapters and the levels of political activity and particular opinions clergy reported hold only for these denominations. For instance, we could not claim that the proportion of Democratic-identifying sample clergy could be extrapolated to all clergy.

The goal of this project, however, was not to establish definitively the level of the political activity or the amount of support among ELCA and Episcopal Church clergy for abortion rights, school prayer, or some other public policy. Instead, we have sought to lay out a theory applicable to a wide swath of American religion and to test that theory in the specific context of clergy samples drawn from the ELCA and Episcopal Church.

In that theory, clergy reference the views and needs of their congregations and denominations, the opportunities and threats presented by the community, and their own desires. At first glance it appears to fit patterns of clerical activism in the black and Jewish communities better than among Lutherans and Episcopalians. In African American communities, it is still far more common to see clergy acting as representatives of their congregations and communities in highly visible, even elected roles. There is no doubt this is the result of the important place of the church in the community and the historic discrimination that has slowed the emergence of secular leaders in many black communities.

For our sample clergy, the tie between church and community is less frequent and less salient, and a typical Lutheran or Episcopalian congregation's need for a representative in the public sphere is often minimal. Nevertheless, we still find evidence of clergy referencing a variety of systems before choosing to act, including the place of the congregation in the community.

Therefore, we have chosen to test a general theory of clergy political activity using less than ideal sample denominations. We have looked for a representative role for clergy as a natural extension of their professional duties and we have found it where it was *least* expected. Combined with the largely anecdotal evidence about the role of churches and clergy in the development of many communities (McGreevy 1996; Moore 1986; Morris 1984), we can suggest with some confidence that our theory is generalizable, even if the specific results reported are not.

PARTICIPANTS IN THE CULTURE WAR?

In the late 1980s and 1990s, many scholars and social commentators speculated whether American democracy would be torn apart by value conflicts over issues not amenable to the compromises encouraged by the U.S. constitutional system. The "culture wars" thesis asserts that America is divided into two opposing camps that logically cannot reconcile their belief systems (Hunter 1991; for a comprehensive review, see Williams 1997a). Escalating tension between these camps—which Hunter (1991) termed progressive and orthodox—was said to be driven by such hot-button issues as abortion, gay rights, school prayer, and welfare. Hunter (1994) went on to suggest that the metaphorical culture war would eventually become a literal one. One of the most visible manifestations of this growing conflict was Pat Buchanan's 1992 prime-time call for Republican convention delegates to prepare for a "religious war going on in our country for the soul of America" (Buchanan 1992).

There is some evidence for culture-based conflict among activists on the extreme right and left of U.S. politics, though the appearance of a broader war is largely confined to the most common arena for such conflict—elections. As Williams notes, "Elections are structured so that they lend themselves to Manichean rhetoric. Political activism, however, is not so reducible—there are many ways of getting involved, many issues around which to become active, and a variety of rationales for such participation" (Williams 1997b, 288).

Are ELCA and Episcopal clergy preparing for such a battle? Our evidence shows that the answer is unquestionably no. As Williams suggests, however, staying out of partisan elections does not mean quiescence. Confirming this conclusion, we have shown that clergy in two mainline denominations are politically involved in significant and extensive ways. The types and content of their activity do not fit neatly within the typical conception of U.S. politics as two-sided, where one is either liberal or conservative, Democratic or Republican. While our sample clergy overwhelmingly identify as Democrats and hold liberal stances on public policy issues, their political activities are largely civic in nature, locally oriented, and centered on the congregation. One Episcopal priest summarizes this pattern of evidence neatly: "My involvement in local community affairs is not so overtly political or focused on elections. Rather, I work extensively with community agencies and groups." ELCA and Episcopal clergy tend to eschew involving their congregations (and often themselves) in partisan, electoral politics as well as most confrontational political actions. Instead, clergy look to make a difference for the underrepresented and the voiceless, reflecting the theological roots of their ministry and intending to manifest their own visions of how the world should work.

Guth et al. (1997) conclude their study of clergy in eight other Protestant denominations with the suggestion that American clergy are arrayed in a two-party religious system, paralleling the two-party political system. They arrive at this unsatisfying conclusion by grouping clergy according to overall political activity levels—heavily skewed toward electoral activity—and theological perspectives. As they note, however, the explanation works well for only about 18 percent of their sample, whom they label Christian Right clergy and the New Breed (on the left). The vast middle is squeezed uncomfortably between these two camps.

As we have shown throughout this book, a political explanation, especially a partisan and electorally oriented one, is less than adequate to interpret the bulk of the political activity of our sample clergy. Furthermore, theological explanations alone are not particularly applicable to our sample clergy. This is not to say that theology does not matter to ELCA and Episcopal clergy. Rather, our sample clergy find that their theologies, applied to the specific contexts in which they work and live, lead to particular activist roles, including a potential nonactivist role. Contextual explanations that incorporate the diverse systems clergy reference begin to explain the patterns of activity, but even this dodges the real question—whom and what do clergy represent when they act? Considered alone as with any other citizen, clergy political activity means little, but as a representative of a faith tradition and faith community, clergy activity takes on a new importance. Therefore, we have focused our efforts on not only explaining the patterns of clergy political activity but also answering this larger question of significance—the question of representation.

The political activities of our sample ELCA and Episcopal clergy are undertaken in pursuit of objectives and policies that lie outside the contours of Hunter's culture wars, and it is unlikely that ELCA and Episcopal clergy were involved much more during the early 1990s. Likewise, because much of ELCA and Episcopal political activity cannot be packaged under the label of organized interests, they have wrongly been assumed to sit increasingly on the sidelines of American politics. Obviously, both the culture wars and the quiescence arguments are wrong, at least when applied to these clergy.

WHITHER THE MAINLINE?

The decline of mainline Protestantism as a religious and political force in U.S. society has been well documented and thoroughly analyzed in the last three decades (Finke and Stark 1992; Kelley 1977; Wuthnow 1996). Building on previous research, Finke and Stark argue that because conservative Protestant churches offer a firm set of precepts to members, while mainline churches promote a less strict adherence to a particular worldview, mainline bodies will inevitably decline as evangelical churches gain in market share (Finke and Stark 1992). Moreover, as we have noted throughout our analysis, theological liberalism and its attendant political activism, especially among clergy, are also often cited as evidence for the departure of large numbers of mainline Protestants from their former church homes since the late 1960s.

Whether there is a cause and effect relationship between mainline clergy activism, weakened or muddled belief structures, and mainline membership decline is certainly debatable. That debate will not be settled with evidence from our study. But our results do cast light on the political implications that the "mainline to sideline" trend has for the denominations involved. Echoing other recent studies (Wuthnow and Evans 2002), we find conclusively that ELCA and Episcopal clergy have in fact become more engaged in politics and civic affairs, instead of moving to the sidelines as the size of their flock dwindles.

The nature of ELCA and Episcopal clergy political engagement is qualitatively and quantitatively different than it was in the 1960s, when mainline Protestantism was a dominant cultural force across the United States. A representative and prophetic role in pursuit of affordable housing, safer streets, better social service delivery, and environmental awareness may not at first glance possess the historic import that we associate with lunch counter sit-ins or anti-Vietnam marches. But the impulses motivating today's ELCA and Episcopal clergy to pursue these ends inside and beyond their congregations are identical to the forces motivating clergy in the turbulent 1960s. Furthermore, today's clergy have come to their ministries with an expectation that political activism is acceptable and at times necessary—an expectation taught and reinforced by seminary education and denominational engagement with politics at the national, state, and local levels.

If the need to engage congregations in social action is imbued in ELCA and Episcopal clergy as one facet of congregational leadership and development, it follows that levels of clergy political activism (especially in local communities) will expand over time, rather than contract. Faced with congregation members who increasingly have not grown up in their denomination, clergy may have more freedom to pursue political ends. Ironically, the politicization of clergy in other denominations has helped legitimate the unique, civic-oriented, and agenda-setting political activity of ELCA and Episcopal clergy. As Wuthnow and colleagues contend, mainline Protestants are hardly silent or irrelevant as a cultural and political force in contemporary U.S. civic life (Wuthnow and Evans 2002). Our findings here bolster that contention and demonstrate the basis for lasting and significant engagement of mainline clergy and congregations with their communities of concern.

REFLECTIONS ON THE STUDY OF CLERGY ACTIVITY

One of the major limitations of research into the nexus of religion and politics is that current theories work best with evangelical Protestants and do not apply equally well to all denominations and faith traditions, notably treating African American clergy and church members as special cases. The primary distinction in many of these works appears to be that in much of the black community religion has not been separated from politics, but is considered an integral part of the black church's mission. Why is this not the case for white clergy serving substantially white congregations? Our evidence suggests that the theoretical structure of the subfield is unnecessarily narrow, and that a unified and coherent theory of clergy political behavior can indeed be derived from existing evidence. To achieve this unity, we argue that *the primary focus of students of clergy political activity should be on what clergy do politically and who or what they represent when they engage in political action.*

Clergy are important political actors to the extent that they attempt to influence the political process, with their relevance growing when they attempt to engage congregants to share and communicate their concerns to government. The interesting variations in what clergy believe only become important when they are expressed. Of course, the type of political activity matters too, with more importance placed on activities clergy undertake in their leadership roles. Therefore, the prophetic, representative nature of clergy political activity is essential to consider because it bears on the workings of civil society to ensure that a wider selection of views are brought to the public sphere, and because it helps explain clergy political influence. Elected and appointed public officials have considerable respect for views that have the backing of significant numbers of people; at times clergy speak for such constituencies. When clergy speak for themselves directly to government, their views and influence tend to count the same as average citizens.

It has been most common for students of clergy activism to envisage a two-party system reflecting H. Richard Niebuhr's discussion of Christ and culture: clergy either do or do not engage in politics, and the choice is driven primarily by theological imperatives (Niebuhr 1951; Marty 1970). Pope (1942) found clergy to be focused on personal salvation, supportive of the social status quo, and wholly ineffective in dealing with economic problems facing communities, though clergy were willing to take a stand on prohibition and other moral issues. To reflect an acknowledgment of some political involvement by clergy, Blizzard (1956), among many others, asserted that clergy have a separate political role distinct from their congregational, pastoral roles. Political engagement was seen as something apart, a choice made to do something beyond the congregation. The clear indication was that politics and religion are distinct entities. Garrett (1973) went so far as to suggest that politically active clergy were a "new breed," entirely different from other clergy.

Tellingly, the authors of *The Bully Pulpit* adopt this language, suggesting that the professional ideology of clergy—their social theology—structures political activism (Guth et al. 1997). The outcome of such an argument, constructed from data on clergy representing a broad variety of Protestant denominations, is that "the evidence points clearly to the existence of a 'two-party' system in American Protestantism, one that extends beyond the theological meaning Martin Marty intended with this coinage, into the real 'two-party' world of politics and government" (Guth et al. 1997, 191).

Though these studies suggest politics is largely something apart from religion, at the same time as the early studies of clergy were written, mainline Protestants *were* mobilized through their churches. In one famous instance, the strategy to mobilize Midwestern mainline Protestants worked and pushed just enough moderate Midwestern senators to overcome procedural delays to allow passage of the Civil Rights Act in 1964 (Findlay 1993).Of course black churches formed the organizational and leadership base of the civil rights movement (Morris 1984).

Since the clergy studies conducted in the aftermath of the civil rights and antiwar movements, the understanding of clergy engagement in politics shifted to a discussion of their involvement in the rise of the Christian conservative movement (among them Guth 1996; Hadden 1981; Hadden and Swann 1987; Liebman 1983). Here, as in studies of secular political participation, researchers came to emphasize the importance of organizational mobilization. This academic focus followed such political shifts as the Republican Party's southern strategy to realign white, southern religious conservatives, which encouraged Richard Viguerie to prod Jerry Falwell to found the Moral Majority (Martin 1996). A whole host of supportive organizations attempted to work through clergy to bring religious conservatives into national politics through the 1980s and 1990s. Guth's analysis of Southern Baptist clergy in 1996 melds the organizational and theological approaches to understand these events. Guth argues that theological beliefs shape the political ideology and partisanship of clergy, which then directly affects their political activity (Guth 2001b). At the same time, these dominant forces are related to issue mobilization and organizational mobilization from national and denominational groups pushing issues important to the Christian Right.

Similarly, Guth et al. conclude *The Bully Pulpit* with this synopsis: "Whenever national issues engage the theological sensitivities of the clergy, left or right, some will resort to the 'bully pulpit,' as they have done repeatedly throughout American history" (1997, 192). However, these instances are relatively rare and miss a great portion of the social and political concerns clergy typically occupy themselves with, which tend to focus on local rather than national issues. Further, from the perspective of standard survey questions, many clergy take on only the appearance of being party activists. It is true that clergy are often strong partisans, have structured ideologies, and tend not to consider themselves moderate (which has more to do with having enough information to choose a side). Yet most clergy are uncomfortable with partisan politics, especially in mainline churches. This discomfort also exists among many evangelicals, both white (Martin 1996; Thomas and Dobson 1999) and black (Lincoln and Mamiya 1990). Reluctance to engage in partisan politics stems somewhat from clergy disappointment with the compromises necessary in political deliberation, but also because the major political parties ignore many of the issues these clergy care about. Researchers tend to miss this point because the questions we ask do not often tap these concerns. Moreover, researchers continue to define the political activity of clergy in ways that are consonant with partisan politics and political organizations, instead of locating clergy political activity within the experiences, contexts, needs, and professional obligations of clergy.

Almost nowhere in the literature on clergy politicking is the political activism of clergy seen as a natural extension of pastoral duties, undertaken for the benefit of the congregation or the faith tradition both clergy and congregants share. This is quite surprising, considering that most politics in the United States is local and that satisfaction of congregational and clergy desires will depend on the social and political predispositions of the particular community in which they live.

Indeed, we show that local political and civic activity is one of the most common forms of clergy activism. ELCA and Episcopal clergy involve themselves locally to represent the interests of their congregation and church; they tend to become more active locally when the congregation does not have other representatives to plead its case. The congregation cannot be conceived solely as the target of activism or a barrier that must be circumvented. Instead, we should envision clergy working to represent their congregations in public venues and, at times, involving their congregations in their civic and political projects.

Because clergy live and work in distinctive environments and often consider themselves servants of their congregations and communities, it should not be surprising that the political activity of clergy has local roots. Numerous other researchers have begun making the case that an understanding of clergy political activity must begin by considering the context in which the activity occurs (Crawford and Olson 2001b; Olson 2000). We concur and add that we need to build in an understanding of *for whom* the activity is done. Clergy are leaders and their political activity should be understood in many cases as representational. Clergy may represent themselves, their theology, their congregations, and sometimes all of these at once through their political action.

And this is the most important question. The ultimate concern of the study of American political behavior and political organizations is the amount and quality of the expression of the public interest in the republic. Churches are one significant avenue through which citizens are trained, mobilized, and recruited to add their voices to the public sphere (Djupe and Grant 2001; Leege 1987; Peterson 1992; Rosenstone and Hansen 1993; Verba et al. 1995; Wald 1997). Clergy certainly may play a role in this process, though perhaps a lesser one than common sense and anecdotal evidence suggests. However, the mere finding that clergy are active in politics does not indicate for whose benefit the action is performed. Are clergy just one more vendor hawking ideological wares to a marketplace of citizens? Are they pursuing their own goals? Or are clergy acting in the interests of their congregations and communities? The answer matters and the truth is elusive, but asking the question is most important.

Appendix A

VARIABLE CODING

A BRIEF GUIDE TO USAGE

This appendix presents coding information for variables organized by chapter and table of *first appearance*.

Variable labels are presented exactly as used in the table of first appearance and in the same order as in the table.

Variables referring to the "county" refer to the county in which the church is located, not necessarily the county in which the clergy reside.

If the coding for a variable is evident from the table or is described in the text, it is not listed in this appendix.

CHAPTER 2: AN OVERVIEW OF ELCA AND EPISCOPAL CLERGY

Figure 2.2

Self-identification of theological terms: "Admittedly, no one likes labels, but here are some terms that are sometimes applied to ministers. How well does [ecumenical/evangelical/liberal/high church/fundamentalist] fit your views?" 1 = not at all, 2 = somewhat, 3 = very well.

Table 2.5

1998 mean number of political activities: Ranges from 0 to 19, gaining one point for doing each of the following political activities in 1998:

Publicly (not preaching) taken a stand on a political/social issue; Publicly (not preaching) endorsed a candidate; While preaching, taken a stand on a political/social issue; While preaching, endorsed a candidate; Urged your congregation to register and vote; Publicly (including preaching) offered prayer on a political/social issue; Publicly (including preaching) offered prayer for candidates; Organized a political discussion group in church; Organized a social action group in church; Active in a national political group; Active in a local political or community group; Active on a local board or council; Served on a local clergy council; Contributed to a candidate, party, or PAC; Contacted public officials on a political/social issue; Written a letter to a newspaper editor about a political or social issue; Actively campaigned for a party or candidate; Participated in a protest march or demonstration; and Engaged in some form of civil disobedience.

Mean clergy political ideology: "Many people use the terms liberal, moderate, and conservative to recognize different political viewpoints. On a scale from 1 to 5, where 1 is the most liberal position and 5 the most conservative, where would you rank yourself when you think of your general political views?" 1 = Most liberal, 2, 3 = Moderate, 4, 5 = Most conservative.

Table 2.6

Political activity index, average frequency: An average measure ranging from 1 to 4 of the frequency of performing all included political activities: 1 = never, 2 = rarely, 3 = sometimes, or 4 = often. See *1998 mean number of political activities* above for the complete list of activities.

Clergy approval of political activity: For each activity, approval is coded 1 = strongly disapprove, 2 = disapprove, 3 = neutral, 4 = approve, 5 = strongly approve.

Table 2.7

Clergy frequency of addressing public policy issues: "How often have you addressed the following issues publicly in any way in the last year?" 1 = never, 2 = rarely, 3 = seldom, 4 = often, 5 = very often. The "Percentage Addressing Issue" column sums the responses to all categories except never; the "Frequency of Addressing Issue" column reports the mean score.

CHAPTER 3: CONGREGATIONAL RESOURCES
FOR CLERGY POLITICAL ACTION

Table 3.5

Congregational approval of clergy political activity: For each activity, approval is coded 1 = strongly disapprove, 2 = disapprove, 3 = neutral, 4 = approve, 5 = strongly approve.

Table 3.9

Clergy capacity to influence church: "Ministers have great capacity to influence the political and social views of their congregation." 1 = strongly disagree, 2 = disagree, 3 = neutral, 4 = agree, 5 = strongly agree.

Clergy average frequency of congregation-based political acts: An average measure ranging from 1 to 4 of the frequency of performing the following activities: While preaching, taken a stand on a political/social issue; While preaching, endorsed a candidate; Urged your congregation to register and vote; Organized a political discussion group in church; Organized a social action group in church. Each activity is coded 1 = never, 2 = rarely, 3 = sometimes, or 4 = often.

Church–clergy ideological differences: "How would you compare your own political views with those of members of your congregation?" 1 = about the same, 2 = more conservative/liberal, and 3 = much more conservative/liberal.

Congregation is theologically divided: "Would you say that your church is theologically united (members agree on theological issues)?" 1 = no, my church is theologically divided, 2 = mostly united, 3 = yes, my church is theologically united.

Congregation is politically divided: "Would you say that your church is politically united (members agree on political issues)?" 1 = no, my church is politically divided, 2 = mostly united, 3 = yes, my church is politically united.

Percentage of church involved in groups, activities: Clergy were asked to report the percentage of members "who are active in church beyond attending weekly services (in activities, governing boards, or small groups)."

Church size: Numbers of total members, children included (self-report).

Belief isolation: An index measure; the index gains one point if the clergyperson's church had different theological beliefs, political beliefs, worship and music styles, levels of church activity, and more racial/ethnic minorities, as judged by the clergy. The index is averaged to take account of the fact that not all clergy answered all questions; thus the final index ranges in value from 0 to 1. Higher scores suggest more isolation from the community.

Activity isolation: An index measure; the index gains one point if the clergyperson's church was less involved in the community, had a lower social status, and was less active in politics than other community churches. We then averaged the index to take account of the fact that not all clergy answered all questions; thus the final index ranges in value from 0 to 1. Higher scores suggest more isolation from the community.

CHAPTER 4: COMMUNITIES OF CONCERN: THE CONTEXT OF CLERGY POLITICAL ACTIVITY

Table 4.1

Religious adherence: The percentage of the total county population that affiliated with a church in 1990 according to the 1990 NCCC church census. For denominational measures, see specific religious tradition and denominational adherence measures.

Evangelical Protestant adherence (1990): The percentage of a county's residents in 1990 who are estimated to be affiliates of an evangelical Protestant body as reported by the 1990 NCCC church census. Of those listed in the church census, we included the following denominations (principal denominations only): Advent Christian Church, Assemblies of God, Baptist, Christian Reformed, Church of the Brethren, Churches of Christ, Churches of God, Evangelical Lutheran Synod, Evangelical Free Church, Independent Charismatic Churches, Lutheran Church Missouri Synod, Nazarene, Independent Noncharismatic Churches, Pentecostal Church of God, Pentecostal Holiness, Presbyterian Church in America, Reformed Church in the United States, Salvation Army, Seventh-Day Adventists, Southern Baptist Convention, Wisconsin Evangelical Lutheran Synod.

Mainline Protestant adherence (1990): The percentage of a county's residents in 1990 who are estimated to be affiliates of a mainline Protestant body as reported by the 1990 NCCC church census. Of those listed in the church census, we included the following (principal denominations only): Congregationalist/United Church of Christ, Disciples of Christ, Episcopal Church, Evangelical Lutheran Church in America, Presbyterian Church (USA), Reformed Church in America, United Methodist Church.

Table 4.3

Poverty rate, 1995: The percentage of households in the county that live at or below the poverty line as estimated by the Census Bureau for 1995.

Local political activity: A summary index ranging from 0 to 3, giving a point if the clergy served on a local clergy council, on a local board or council, or in a local community/ political group in the past year (1998).

Spoke out on hunger, poverty: "How often have you addressed [hunger and poverty] publicly in any way in the last year?" 1 = never, 2 = rarely, 3 = seldom, 4 = often, 5 = very often.

Held adult education on poverty, hunger: "Has your church held adult education sessions about any of the following topics? Circle all that apply." 1 = held a session, 0 = did not.

Government should do more to solve social problems: 1 = strongly disagree, 2 = disagree, 3 = neutral, 4 = agree, 5 = strongly agree.

Table 4.4

Congruent voting counties: 1 = clergy voted for the same presidential candidate as the plurality of county voters; 0 = otherwise.

Competitive counties: 1 = when the difference in the vote percentage for Bob Dole and Bill Clinton in 1996 in a county was less than 10 percent; 0 = otherwise.

Table 4.5

Democratic dominance: A continuous measure equaling Clinton's 1996 vote percentage in the county minus Dole's vote share.

Electoral activity: Ranges from 0 to 7, giving a point for endorsing candidates publicly, while preaching, or while praying, contributing to a campaign, party, or PAC, actively campaigning for a party or candidate, urging voting and registration in church, and/or personally participating in a voter registration drive in the past year (1998).

Candidate support: Ranges from 0 to 3, giving a point for "publicly (including preaching) offered prayer for candidates," "publicly (not preaching) endorsed a candidate," or "while preaching, endorsed a candidate" in the past year (1998).

Church organizing: Ranges from 0 to 2, giving a point if the clergy had "organized a political discussion group in church" and "organized a social action group in church" in the past year (1998).

Public speech: Ranges from 0 to 3, giving one point if the clergy had "publicly (not preaching) taken a stand on a political/social issue," "while preaching taken a stand on a political/social issue," and "publicly (including preaching) offered prayer on a political/social issue" during the past year (1998).

Marching/Protesting: Ranges from 0 to 2, giving one point if clergy had "participated in a protest march or demonstration" and "engaged in some form of civil disobedience" in the past year (1998).

Local activity: Ranges from 0 to 3, giving one point if the clergy served on a local clergy council, on a local board or council, or in a local community/ political group in the past year (1998).

Table 4.7

Community isolation: Clergy were asked to compare their church with others in the community on eight items: theological beliefs, political beliefs, income and social status, ethnicity/race, church activity, community involvement, worship and music styles, and political activity. The separation into the two dimensions, belief and involvement isolation, were confirmed by a factor analysis. See *activity isolation* and *belief isolation* entries for more.

CHAPTER 5: THE POLITICAL VOICE OF CLERGY

Table 5.3

Doctoral degree: 1 = doctoral degree, 0 = some other degree (primarily a master's).

Male: 0 = female, 1 = male.

Strong partisan: 1 = independent, 2 = independent leaner, 3 = weak partisan, 4 = strong partisan.

Strong political ideology: 1 = moderate, 2 = weak liberal/conservative, 3 = strong liberal/conservative.

Political interest: 1 = not interested, 2 = somewhat interested, 3 = very interested in the 1998 political campaigns.

Political efficacy: Ranges in value from 2 to 10, adding responses from strongly agree (1) to strongly disagree (5) to the following questions: "Ministers have great capacity to influence the political and social views of their congregation." and "It is difficult for ministers to know the proper political channel to use to accomplish some goal." Those strongly agreeing with the first question and strongly disagreeing with the second constitute the high end of the scale (10).

Less brand loyalty in congregation: Clergy's perception of whether the congregation is composed of members: 1 = almost all raised Lutheran/ Episcopalian, 2 = most, but not all members raised Lutheran/Episcopalian, 3 = less than a majority raised Lutheran/Episcopalian, or 4 = most are newcomers to the ELCA/Episcopal Church.

Rural church: 1 = clergy reported that their church is located in "rural or farm" community; 0 = otherwise.

Southern church: 1 = if the church is in a southern state (Alabama, Arkansas, Florida, Georgia, Kentucky, Louisiana, Mississippi, North Carolina, South Carolina, Tennessee, Texas); 0 = the church is not in a southern state.

Denomination perceived as supportive of clergy politicking: "Some ministers are more politically involved than others for a variety of reasons. Do the following factors generally encourage or discourage your political involvement? [the attitudes of denominational leaders]" Coded 1 = strongly discourage, 2 = discourage, 3 = neutral, 4 = encourage, 5 = strongly encourage.

Colleagues' political activity: To generate a network of same denomination colleagues we asked respondents: "Thinking of your closest ELCA/ Episcopal colleagues in the ministry (under 5 people), how similar or different are their political and religious views from yours?" If the respondent indicates that the colleague network has on average a similar level of political activity they receive the respondent's average frequency of political activity score. The average frequency of the respondent's political activity is constructed by averaging the responses to questions about the nineteen political activities listed in Table 2.6: "How often [do] you undertake such an activity: 1 = never, 2 = rarely, 3 = sometimes, 4 = often." We use this measure because it stands to reason that respondents would not compare their network's average activity to their personal political activity in a *particular* year, which may fluctuate, but to their *average* activity level. Further, using the frequency rather than the annual incidence measure avoids the unpleasant situation of having to use 1998 activity (with some error) to predict 1998 activity. If the respondent replied that their network was more active we added the denomination specific standard deviation to the respondent's score. If the respondent replied that the network was less active we subtracted the denomination specific standard deviation. The standard deviation was used as an average, since "more active" could mean much more or a little more active.

Episcopal clergy: 0 — ELCA clergy, 1 — Episcopal clergy

Memberships in public affairs groups: We provided a list of religious or moral concerns groups to which clergy might belong (Christian Coalition, Focus on the Family, American Family Association, Traditional Values Coalition, Americans United for Separation of Church and State, National Association of Evangelicals, Bread for the World, Habitat for Humanity, Operation Rescue, and The Interfaith Alliance). We also provided space to list groups which we had not enumerated. For this additive index ranging from 0 to 8, clergy receive one point for each group membership listed.

Newspaper reading: The number of days per week (0–7) that the clergy report they read a newspaper.

Periodical subscriptions: We gave space to list periodicals related to theology, denominational issues, or religion and public affairs. For this index, respondents receive one for each periodical listed. Clergy listed anywhere from 0 to 10 periodicals.

Table 5.4

Democrat: 0 = all other partisan affiliations, 1 = independent, leaning Democratic, 2 = weak Democrat, 3 = strong Democrat.

Republican: 0 = all other partisan affiliations, 1 = independent, leaning Republican, 2 = weak Republican, 3 = strong Republican.

Liberal: 0 = all other ideological identifications, 1 = weak liberal, 2 = strong liberal.

Conservative: 0 = all other ideological identifications, 1 = weak conservative, 2 = strong conservative.

Average congregational approval of clergy speech: Ranges in value from 1 to 5, including approval of praying about an issue in public, taking a stand on a social or political issue while preaching, and taking a stand on a social or political issue in public (not preaching). Each approval question has the same wording as the corresponding dependent variable and is coded: 1 = strongly disapprove, 2 = disapprove, 3 = neutral, 4 = approve, 5 = strongly approve.

Clergy issue stance differs from congregation's issue stance: Clergy were asked their own agreement and their perceptions of their congregations' agreement (1 = strongly disagree, 2 = disagree, 3 = neutral/not sure, 4 = agree, 5 = strongly agree) with a list of statements on public policy issues. We then calculated the difference between the two positions, providing a range from −4 (clergy are much more liberal) to 4 (clergy are much more conservative).

CHAPTER 6: LEADERS OF THE FLOCK OR
LONE RANGERS? CLERGY IN ELECTORAL POLITICS

Table 6.2

Candidate support over the career. Average of an additive index ranging from 1 to 4, including "publicly (including preaching) offered prayer for candidates," "publicly (not preaching) endorsed a candidate," or "while preaching, endorsed a candidate," where each variable is coded 1 = never, 2 = rarely, 3 = sometimes, or 4 = often.

Mobilizing over the career. "Urging the congregation to register and vote." 1 = never, 2 = rarely, 3 = sometimes, or 4 = often.

Social justice agenda speech frequency: An additive index ranging from 1 to 5 (once averaged), indicating the frequency of clergy addressing the following issues: hunger and poverty, women's issues, civil rights, gay rights, homosexuality, the environment, unemployment, and education. The frequency of each is measured: 1 = never, 2 = rarely, 3 = seldom, 4 = often, 5 = very often.

Moral reform agenda speech frequency: An additive index ranging from 1 to 5 (once averaged), indicating the frequency of clergy addressing the following issues: national defense, budget deficits, abortion, gambling laws, current political scandals, prayer in public schools, and capital punishment. The frequency of each is measured: 1 = never, 2 = rarely, 3 = seldom, 4 = often, 5 = very often.

Average congregational approval of electoral activity: These variables range in value from 1 to 5. Each approval question has the same wording as the corresponding dependent variable and is coded 1 = strongly disapprove, 2 = disapprove, 3 = neutral, 4 = approve, 5 = strongly approve.

Urban church: 1 = if clergy reported that their church is located in a "small city (20,000 to 50,000)," "medium sized city (50–100,000 people)," a "large city (100–250,000 people)," or in a "very large city (over 250,000 people)"; 0 = otherwise.

Partisan contact sources in career. An additive index, ranging from 0 to 8, of contacts received during 1996 and 1998 from "a political party or candidate committee," "a religious or moral concerns organization," "an Episcopal/ELCA agency or ministerial group," or "a group of laity from your congregation."

CHAPTER 7. THE LOCAL PARTICIPATION OF ELCA
AND EPISCOPAL CLERGY

Table 7.1

High/low county poverty rate: A county is considered to have high poverty rate (equal to or above 17.3 percent) if the poverty rate is one standard deviation higher than the mean and has a low incidence of poverty (equal to or below 6.6 percent) if the rate is one standard deviation lower than the mean.

Suburban church: 1 = the church is a suburb of a large or very large city (clergy self-report); 0 = otherwise.

Midwestern church: 1 = the church is located in a midwestern state (Iowa, Illinois, Indiana, Kansas, Michigan, Minnesota, Missouri, North Dakota, Nebraska, Ohio, South Dakota, Wisconsin); 0 = the church is not in a midwestern state.

Northeastern church: 1 = the church is located in a northeastern state (Connecticut, Washington D.C., Delaware, Massachusetts, Maryland, Maine, New Hampshire, New Jersey, New York, Pennsylvania, Rhode Island, Vermont); 0 = the church is not in a northeastern state.

Western church: 1 = the church is located in a western state (Alaska, Arizona, California, Colorado, Hawaii, Idaho, Montana, New Mexico, Nevada, Oregon, Utah, Washington, Wyoming); 0 = the church is not in a western state.

High/low evangelical adherence: 1 = a county is considered to have high evangelical adherence (equal to or above 25.4 percent) if the rate is one standard deviation higher than the mean; 0 = a county has a low percentage of evangelicals (equal to or below 3.0 percent) if the rate is one standard deviation lower than the mean.

High/low mainline adherence: 1 = a county is considered to have high mainline adherence (equal to or above 28.2 percent) if the rate is one standard deviation higher than the mean; 0 = a county has a low incidence of mainline Protestants (equal to or below 3.8 percent) if the rate is one standard deviation lower than the mean.

Table 7.3

Average congregational approval of clergy political activity: The index ranges in value from 1 to 5, averaging an additive index of fifteen different political activities. Each approval question has the same wording as the corresponding dependent variable and is coded: 1 = strongly disapprove, 2 = disapprove, 3 = neutral, 4 = approve, 5 = strongly approve.

Clergy council exists: 1 = clergy report a formal or informal clergy council exists in the community; 0 = if the clergy report neither exists in the community.

Discussion with denominational colleagues / colleagues from other denominations: "On average, how often do you talk with these (denominational/non-denominational) colleagues?" 1 = never, 2 = rarely, 3 = sometimes, 4 = often, 5 = very often.

CHAPTER 8: SENDING A MESSAGE TO GOVERNMENT: CLERGY CONVENTIONAL AND UNCONVENTIONAL CONTACTING

Table 8.4

Contacting in the past year: The index ranges from 0 to 4, giving one point if the clergy contacted public officials on a political/social issue, wrote a letter to the editor, participated in a protest march, or engaged in some form of civil disobedience in the past year (1998).

Contacting over the career: An index ranging from 1 to 4, averaging how often the respondent clergy had contacted public officials on a political/social issue, writen a letter to the editor, participated in a protest march, and engaged in some form of civil disobedience. Each variable is coded 1 = never, 2 = rarely, 3 = sometimes, 4 = often.

Congregational approval of clergy contacting: Ranges in value from 1 to 5, averaging the clergy's perception of congregational approval of clergy contacting public officials on a political/social issue, writing a letter to the editor, participating in a protest march, or engaging in some form of civil disobedience. Each approval question is coded 1 = strongly disapprove, 2 = disapprove, 3 = neutral, 4 = approve, 5 = strongly approve.

Table 8.5

Conventional contacting over the career: An index ranging from 1 to 4, averaging how often clergy contact a public official and write a letter to the editor. Each activity is coded 1 = never, 2 = rarely, 3 = sometimes, 4 = often.

Unconventional contacting over the career. An index ranging from 1 to 4, averaging how often clergy protest and engage in civil disobedience. Each activity is coded 1 = never, 2 = rarely, 3 = sometimes, 4 = often.

CHAPTER 9: DENOMINATIONAL POLITICS: CLERGY OPINIONS AND ACTIONS REGARDING FULL COMMUNION

Table 9.4

Upper Midwestern church: 1 = the church is in the upper Midwest (Minnesota, North Dakota, South Dakota, Iowa, Wisconsin); 0 = the church is not in the upper Midwest.

Former ALC church: 1 = the clergy report the ELCA church had a premerger affiliation with the American Lutheran Church; 0 = it did not have an ALC affiliation.

Synod/diocese evaluation: "How well are these (ELCA/Episcopal Church) institutions doing their jobs?" 1 = poor, 2 = fair, 3 = don't know, 4 = good, 5 = excellent.

Denominational isolation: Clergy were asked to compare their church with others in their denominations on eight items: theological beliefs, political beliefs, income and social status, ethnicity/race, church activity, community involvement, worship and music styles, and political activity. The index gains one point if the clergy indicate their church differs from other denominations in the church and is then averaged, so that the final index ranges in value from 0 to 1.

Episcopal/ELCA clergy contact: If the clergy indicates regular association with non-denominational clergy, they were asked the denomination of those clergy. 1 = an Episcopal priest listed the ELCA or an ELCA pastor listed the Episcopal Church; 0 = otherwise.

Appendix B

METHODOLOGICAL NOTES

In this appendix, we explain briefly the statistical methods used in this book. Our goal is to provide enough information for readers to have a functional knowledge of what the results produced by the various statistical procedures mean. It will be useful to keep in mind that clergy attitudes and actions—the attributes of clergy that we wish to explain—are called *dependent variables*. As this term implies, the particular attributes captured in a specific dependent variable are hypothesized to depend on—be explained by—other factors. These other factors are called *independent variables*, and in most of our tables more than one independent variable is incorporated into the analysis.

We have employed a powerful set of statistical methods to analyze the data generated by our study. The goal of this form of quantitative, empirical analysis is to determine whether the actual political behavior of ELCA and Episcopal clergy is consistent with our theoretical expectations about that behavior. While it is tempting to state that statistical results consistent with theory constitute *proof* that our hypotheses are correct, such language overstates the implications and ignores the limitations of statistical analysis. As a leading text on social scientific methodology explains, "Consistency between data and the predictions of a given theory does not rule out the possibility that the same observations are also consistent with alternative explanations" (Hanushek and Jackson 1977, 3). What we can claim, and in fact what our empirical analysis demonstrates throughout the book, is that the consistent marriage of expected findings with actual statistical results lends very strong credence to the theoretical assertions we have made. We hope this brief appendix gives readers confidence that we have constructed and interpreted our statistical results with appropriate methods and proper modesty regarding their interpretation.

STATISTICAL SIGNIFICANCE

The empirical analysis of the relationship between an independent and dependent variable generally begins with the assumption that no such relationship actually exists. We call this a *null hypothesis*, and the conservative nature of assuming the null hypothesis to be true constitutes an important check on the tendency to believe that statistical results are a perfect representation of the real characteristics of any population. Social scientists working with survey data always keep in mind that survey respondents are one subset of the larger population from which they are drawn, and that no two subsets of a population will have identical characteristics. With a modest amount of error thus inherent in any sample, even a very large one such as ours, it is essential to establish standards for determining when two variables are truly related, as opposed to having no relationship or some spurious connection.

These standards constitute levels of *statistical significance*—the likelihood that an observed relationship between an independent and dependent variable differs from random chance to a very high degree, such that we can reject the null hypothesis and describe the nature of this relationship. All of the statistical methods described below have associated tests of statistical significance. Social scientific research establishes a very high standard to be exceeded in order to reject a null hypothesis and hence to assert that a statistically significant relationship is present. This standard is called a *confidence level*. In our tables we report the confidence level of the estimated relationship between independent and dependent variables. Confidence levels of 90 percent or 95 percent are standard in social science research; these levels correspond to a statistical likelihood of 10 percent or 5 percent (reported as 0.1 or 0.05) that the observed relationship does not in fact exist. In other words, we must be at least 90 percent certain, in statistical terms, that a given independent variable is related to a dependent variable, before we can reject the null hypothesis, declare two variables to be statistically significantly related, and talk more specifically about the relationship between the variables.

Our tables using statistical significance tests report three levels of statistical significance, corresponding to three confidence levels. Asterisks are utilized to represent these three levels, with more asterisks indicating more statistical significance, hence greater confidence that hypothesized relationships actually exist:

- $*$ = $p < 0.10$, usually termed *statistically significant at the 0.10 level*; this means that we have *90 percent confidence* that a relationship exists between the independent and dependent variables; the null hypothesis is thus rejected

- ** = $p < 0.05$, *statistically significant at the 0.05 level*; we have *95 percent confidence* that a relationship exists
- *** = $p < 0.01$, *statistically significant at the 0.01 level*, with *99 percent confidence* that a relationship exists
- *No asterisks* (in effect a blank space where asterisks usually appear) indicates that statistical significance at the 0.10 level has not been reached, hence a confidence level below 90 percent exists; in this case we must accept that *the null hypothesis is true*—no relationship exists between the independent and dependent variables under investigation. In situations where the significance level is close to 0.10, we often report this in the text, although the corresponding table entry would still have zero asterisks.

For the sake of convenience and simplicity, when our statistical procedures indicate significance at the 0.10 level (90 percent confidence or better), we simply declare that the relationship being investigated is statistically significant; readers can identify the specific significance/confidence level by examining the table with the statistical results.

Significance tests are all associated with statistical procedures. While the procedures calculate significance levels in slightly different ways, the reporting of significance levels is always done in the same manner, using the asterisk system. We thus turn now to details about the commonly employed statistical procedures used in the book.

T-TEST

The T-test is also often called a *difference of means* test. Specifically, it compares the difference in mean scores on a variable of interest for two different groups. For instance, we might compare gender differences in abortion opinions—the T-test would compare the mean abortion opinion scores for men and women. The test will return a statistically significant result if the difference in the means is judged to be statistically different from zero. The greater the difference in the means, the more likely the t-test procedure will report statistical significance. As with all procedures employing significance tests, a significance level of 0.10 or better (90 percent confidence or more) is the standard used. Our tables do not report actual t-test scores, but they do report the interpretation of statistical significance based on the t test values.

CORRELATION

There are several types of correlation coefficients, which are standardized measures of association between two variables. Our analysis uses the Pearson's *r*, perhaps the most commonly employed form of correlation coefficients. Correlations allow us to assess the direction, strength, and statistical significance of the relationship between two variables. The statistical procedure used to calculate correlations does not specify independent and dependent variables, but it is possible (and usually desirable) for researchers to identify which variables are which.

Correlations range in value from -1.0 to $+1.0$. A correlation of $r = -1.0$ indicates a perfect inverse (or negative) relationship between the two variables—as one goes up the other goes down by equal amounts, and vice versa. All inverse correlations thus indicate that values of two variables are moving in opposite directions, with correlations closer to -1.0 indicating stronger inverse relationships than correlations close to 0. A correlation of $r = +1.0$ (reported without the $+$ sign) indicates that values for both variables move together (both up or both down) in direct (or positive) lockstep. As with inverse correlations, direct correlations are stronger as they move farther from 0 and closer to 1. A correlation of $r = 0.0$ means that there is no relationship between the two variables.

Most correlations using survey data are considerably lower than $+/-1.0$. Generally a correlation of $+/-0.20$ is considered evidence of a reasonably strong relationship between two variables, although correlations below $+/-0.20$ can still be statistically significant (these are often termed weak correlations). Correlations of $+/-0.50$ or greater are rare but not exceptionally so. Statistical significance depends to some extent on the strength of the correlation; with sample sizes as large as ours, a correlation greater than $+/-0.10$ is always statistically significant.

It is important to remember that correlations are not used to assess a causal relationship between two variables. We use correlations to determine whether two variables are significantly related in any way, which would justify their use in further analyses. Thus all correlation tables include the asterisk system to assess the statistical significance of each *r* value.

FACTOR ANALYSIS

Factor analysis is generally used with several variables to find groupings within the data. That is, factor analysis looks for closely related sets of variables and reports how strongly they are interrelated. In the parlance of factor analysis, the procedure assesses how strongly variables "load" on a common underlying factor, which the variables are trying to measure. This is particularly useful to justify the separation of a group of variables into different categories, which can then be employed as index variables and used in further analysis. Our grouping of clergy speech topics into moral reform and social justice indexes is a good example of how factor analysis can assist in clarifying how different variables relate to one another. With this procedure we can then show the degree of harmony between theory and observation.

ORDINARY LEAST SQUARES (OLS) REGRESSION

Ordinary least squares (OLS) regression is a tremendously useful technique for predicting the values of a dependent variable based on the values of one or more independent variables. The OLS regression procedure estimates the linear relationship between the dependent and independent variables, filling in values for the standard formula describing a line: $Y = bX + C$. This formula is termed a model, with the following components:

- Y = the dependent variable, the values of which are being explained by the model
- X = the independent variable, the change in which is hypothesized to affect resulting values of Y
- b = the *coefficient* (also termed the *slope*)—the change in Y for each unit change in X, that is the effect of each independent variable on the dependent variable
- C = the constant, technically the Y intercept, which is the value of the dependent variable when $X = 0$; this constant can be thought of as a baseline measure, the value of the dependent variable in the absence of any independent variables

The technique employs calculus to produce the estimated direction and strength of the relationship between X and Y, an estimate captured by the coefficient. These coefficients have associated statistical significance tests, and once again we employ the asterisk system to report significance, looking for at least 0.10 significance (90 percent confidence) to conclude that the null hypothesis should be rejected. Once we have the equation for a line, we can predict values of Y by using the estimated slope and values of X that are of interest.

As noted in chapter 5, the power of OLS regression lies in its ability to estimate the effects of *more than one independent variable* on the dependent variable. The OLS procedure is a complex sorting device, calculating the separate, distinct impact that each X variable has on Y. The ability to sort among different potential explanatory factors allows us to test models that approximate "the real world"—to understand how a complex set of attributes and characteristics come together to affect the beliefs and actions of individual clergy. When estimating the impact of one X variable, OLS regression holds all of the other independent variables constant at their means (also referred to as "controlling for the effects" of another variable). This is useful since social science variables (such as education and income) are often interrelated.

The coefficient and its standard error (S.E.) are the components reported in regression tables. The coefficient allows a reader to state substantively what effect the independent variable would have on the dependent variable given a one-unit change in the independent variable. If the coefficient is 0.5, for instance, then for every one unit shift in the independent variable, the dependent variable will increase by 0.5. This may be a large or small effect, depending on how the two variables are coded; there is no good way to compare coefficient values to one another.

The standard error measures the error inherent in determining a single coefficient from a data set of disparate people. Standard errors are generally reported because they help to determine statistical significance—the coefficient divided by its standard error gives a t-test value that indicates the significance level for that particular independent variable. If the absolute value of a coefficient divided by its standard error equals 2 or greater, then the estimate is statistically significant.

OLS regression also provides an overall measure of how well the estimated model explains the change in the dependent variable. This measure is known as the *adjusted R^2*, and takes on values between 0 and 1.0. An adjusted R^2 of 0.0 indicates that the model explains none of the variance in the dependent variable. Values greater than 0.0 can be expressed as percentages; thus an adjusted R^2 of 0.20 means that 20 percent of the variance in the dependent variable is explained by the model. Adjusted R^2 values of 0.1 or higher are considered reasonable when estimating individual behavior.

LOGISTIC REGRESSION

Logistic regression results take on the same appearance as OLS regression results but they are calculated using a different method. Logistic regression—

commonly called *logit*—is used only when the dependent variable is dichotomous (meaning it has two and only two values, generally coded 0 and 1). In such situations, OLS regression estimates lose many desirable qualities. Logit is one of a class of maximum likelihood estimators (MLE); MLE estimation attempts to fit a distribution that best fits the data (as opposed to OLS, with which we assess how well the data fit a line). This technique also allows other independent variables to vary while estimating the impact of each independent variable, in contrast to OLS (in which other variables are held constant). Further, the logit coefficients reported are not identical to OLS coefficients; some computation is required to produce the estimated effects of each independent variable, meaning that OLS and logistic coefficients are not directly comparable. Logit coefficients do have one advantage, should one actually compute their substantive impact on the dependent variable being analyzed—the estimated effects can be expressed as percentages (e.g., having a college education produces a 20 percent increase in the likelihood of having a white-collar job). The statistical significance of logit coefficients is reported just as in other procedures.

One final difference between logistic and OLS regression is that logit comes with a different indicator of the overall effectiveness of the regression model. Logit models do not have an adjusted R^2; rather they present the percent of cases correctly predicted. The model should correctly predict a greater percentage of cases than the incidence of the behavior in the population; if 50 percent of citizens voted, a model predicting voting or not voting should do better than predicting 50 percent of the cases (a random choice model would predict 50 percent of the cases correctly).

REFERENCES

Adams, James L. 1970. *The Growing Church Lobby in Washington.* Grand Rapids, Mich.: Eerdmans.

Ahlstrom, Sydney E. 1972. *A Religious History of the American People.* New Haven, Conn.: Yale University Press.

Alwin, Duane F. 1976. "Assessing School Effects: Some Identities." *Sociology of Education* 49: 294–303.

Ammerman, Nancy T. 1990. *Baptist Battles: Social Change and Religious Conflict in the Southern Baptist Convention.* New Brunswick, N.J.: Rutgers University Press.

Baumgartner, Frank R., and Bryan D. Jones. 1993. *Agendas and Instability in American Politics.* Chicago: University of Chicago Press.

Baumgartner, Frank R., and Beth L. Leech. 1998. *Basic Interests: The Importance of Groups in Politics and Political Science.* Princeton: Princeton University Press.

Beatty, Kathleen, and Oliver Walter. 1989. "A Group Theory of Religion and Politics: The Clergy as Group Leaders." *Western Political Quarterly* 42: 129–46.

Bellah, Robert. 1975. *The Broken Covenant: American Civil Religion in a Time of Trial.* New York: Seabury.

Berelson, Bernard, Paul Lazarsfeld, and William McPhee. 1954. *Voting.* Chicago: University of Chicago Press.

Blanton, Thomas. 2002. "Houston Church Responds to Record Layoffs at Enron." Episcopal News Service, January 14. www.episcopalchurch.org/ens/2002-007.html.

Blizzard, Samuel W. 1956. "The Minister's Dilemma." *Christian Century* 73: 508–9.

———. 1958. "The Protestant Parish Minister's Integrating Roles." *Religious Education* 53: 374–80.

Bradley, Martin B., Norman M. Green Jr., Dale E. Jones, Mac Lynn, and Lou McNeil. 1992. *Churches and Church Membership in the United States 1990.* Atlanta: Glenmary Research Center.

Briggs, David. 2001. "Changed Spiritual Scene." *Christian Century*, October 17, 7–8.

Bromley, David G., ed. 1988. *Falling from the Faith: Causes and Consequences of Religious Apostasy*. Newbury Park, Calif.: Sage.

Buchanan, Pat. 1992. "1992 Republican National Convention Speech." *Internet Brigade*. www.buchanan.org/pa-92-0817-rnc.html. Accessed June 15, 2002.

Called to Common Mission: A Lutheran Proposal for a Revision of the Concordat of Agreement. Evangelical Lutheran Church in America. www.dfms.org/ecumenism/concordat. Accessed January 16, 2000.

Campbell, Angus, Phillip E. Converse, Warren E. Miller, and Donald E. Stokes. 1960. *The American Voter*. New York: Wiley.

Campbell, Ernest Q., and Thomas F. Pettigrew. 1959. *Christians in Racial Crisis: A Study of Littlerock's Ministry*. Washington, D.C.: Public Affairs Press.

Carmines, Edward G., and James A. Stimson. 1989. *Issue Evolution: Race and the Transformation of American Politics*. Princeton: Princeton University Press.

Carroll, Jackson W., Daniel O. Aleshire, and Barbara G. Wheeler. 1997. *Being There: Culture and Formation in Two Theological Schools*. New York : Oxford University Press.

Carroll, Jackson W., and Penny Long Marler. 1995. "Culture Wars? Insights from Ethnographies of Two Protestant Seminaries." *Sociology of Religion* 56: 1–20.

Cavendish, James C. 2001. "To March or Not to March: Clergy Mobilization Strategies and Grassroots Antidrug Activism." In Sue E. S. Crawford and Laura R. Olson, eds., *Christian Clergy in American Politics*. Baltimore: Johns Hopkins University Press.

Chaves, Mark. 1999. "Religious Congregations and Welfare Reform: Who Will Take Advantage of 'Charitable Choice'?" *American Sociological Review* 64, no. 6: 836–46.

Chaves, Mark, Mary Ellen Konieczny, Kraig Beyerlein, and Emily Barman. 1999. "The National Congregations Study: Background, Methods, and Selected Results." *Journal for the Scientific Study of Religion* 38: 458–80.

Cheal, David J. 1975. "Political Radicalism and Religion: Competitors for Commitment." *Social Compass* 2: 245–59.

Cohen, Adam, and Elizabeth Taylor. 2000. *American Pharaoh: Mayor Richard J. Daley: His Battle for Chicago and the Nation*. New York: Little, Brown.

Cohen, Cathy J., and Michael C. Dawson. 1993. "Neighborhood Poverty and African-American Politics." *American Political Science Review* 87: 286–302.

Craig, Barbara Hinkson, and David M. O'Brien. 1993. *Abortion and American Politics*. Chatham, N.J.: Chatham House.

Crawford, Sue E. S., Melissa Deckman, and Christi Braun. 2001. "Gender and the Political Choices of Women Clergy." In Sue E. S. Crawford and Laura R. Olson, eds., *Christian Clergy in American Politics*. Baltimore: Johns Hopkins University Press.

Crawford, Sue E. S., and Laura R. Olson, eds. 2001a. *Christian Clergy in American Politics*. Baltimore: Johns Hopkins University Press.

———. 2001b. "Clergy as Political Actors in Urban Contexts." In Sue E. S. Crawford and Laura R. Olson, eds., *Christian Clergy in American Politics*. Baltimore: Johns Hopkins University Press.

Dart, John. 2001. "God Blessing America?" *Christian Century*, October 10, 11–12.

Day, Katie. 2001. "The Construction of Political Strategies among African-American Clergy." In Sue E. S. Crawford and Laura R. Olson, eds., *Christian Clergy in American Politics*. Baltimore: Johns Hopkins University Press.

Deckman, Melissa M. 1999a. "Christian Soldiers on Local Battlefields: Campaigning for Control of America's School Boards." Ph.D. diss., American University.

———. 1999b. "School Board Elections and the Christian Right: Strategies and Tactics at the Grassroots." *American Review of Politics* 20: 123–40.

Djupe, Paul A. 1997. "The Plural Church: Church Involvement and Political Behavior." Ph.D. diss., Washington University, St. Louis.

———. 1999. "Religious Brand Loyalty and Political Loyalties." *Journal for the Scientific Study of Religion* 39, no. 1: 78–89.

———. 2001. "Cardinal O'Connor and His Constituents: Differential Benefit Exchanges and Public Evaluations." In Sue E. S. Crawford and Laura R. Olson, eds., *Christian Clergy in American Politics*. Baltimore: Johns Hopkins University Press.

Djupe, Paul A., and Christopher P. Gilbert. 2000. "Are the Sheep Hearing the Shepherds? An Evaluation of Church Member Perceptions of Clergy Political Speech." Paper presented at the annual meeting of the American Political Science Association, Washington, D.C.

———. 2002. "Politics in Church: Byproduct or Central Mission?" Paper presented at the annual meeting of the American Political Science Association, Boston.

Djupe, Paul A., Christopher P. Gilbert, and Kristina R. Hisey. 1995. "Nature and Consequences of Misperception in Political Discussion." Paper presented at the annual meeting of the Western Political Science Association, Portland.

Djupe, Paul A., Christopher P. Gilbert, David A. M. Peterson, and Timothy R. Johnson. 1997. "American Two Party Systems: Religious Competition and Political Outcomes, 1906–1926." Paper presented at the annual meeting of the American Political Science Association, Washington, D.C.

Djupe, Paul A., and J. Tobin Grant. 2001. "Religious Institutions and Political Participation in America." *Journal for the Scientific Study of Religion* 40, no. 2: 303–14.

Djupe, Paul A., Laura R. Olson, and Christopher P. Gilbert. 2002. "Sources of Clergy Support for Denominational Lobbying in Washington." Unpublished manuscript.

Djupe, Paul A., and Anand Sokhey. 2001. "Political Activity of Rabbis in the 2000 Elections." Paper presented at the annual meeting of the American Political Science Association, San Francisco.

Donovan, Mary. 2001. "St. Paul's Chapel in New York Still Providing 'Radical Hospitality.'" *Episcopal News Service*, December 18. www.episcopalchurch.org/ens/2001-353.html.

Downs, Anthony. 1957. *An Economic Theory of Democracy*. New York: Harper & Row.

Earle, John R., Dean D. Knudsen, and Donald W. Shriver Jr. 1976. *Spindles and Spires: A Re-Study of Religion and Social Change in Gastonia*. Atlanta : John Knox.

Ebersole, Luke. 1951. *Church Lobbying in the Nation's Capital*. New York: Macmillan.

Edwards, Randall. 1998. "Religious Leaders Call for Agreement on Climate Change." *Columbus Dispatch,* October 27, 4C.

"ELCA's Hanson Sees New Ecumenism Agenda." 2001. *Christian Century,* October 24–31, 13.

Emery, Michelle. 2000. "Lutheran-Episcopal Alliance Off to Positive Start in Maine." *Chicago Tribune,* September 22, 2–8.

"Episcopal Church Nods to ELCA Bylaw Change." 2001. *Christian Century,* November 14, 11–12.

Episcopal Public Policy Network. 1994. "Access to Abortion" [General Convention resolution]. www.episcopalchurch.org/eppn/display.asp?DocID=422.

———. 1995. "Church Partnership with Government" [Executive Council resolution]. www.episcopalchurch.org/eppn/display.asp?DocID=302>.

Evangelical Lutheran Church in America. 1991a. "Abortion" [Social statement adopted by churchwide assembly]. www.elca.org/dcs/abortion.pf. Accessed July 14, 2002.

———. 1991b. "The Church in Society: A Lutheran Perspective" [Social statement adopted by churchwide assembly]. www.elca.org/dcs/churchin.pf.html. Accessed July 14, 2002.

———. 2000. "Cooperative Congregational Studies Project, Faith Communities Today Survey." www.elca.org/re/ccsp/ccspfreq.pdf. Accessed June 4, 2001.

———. "Outline [precis] of Called to Common Mission." 1998. www.dfms.org/ecumenism/concordat/cmoutlin.html. Accessed January 16, 2000.

Findlay, James F., Jr. 1993. *Church People in the Struggle: The National Council of Churches and the Black Freedom Movement, 1950–1970.* New York: Oxford University Press.

Finifter, Ada. 1974. "The Friendship Group as a Protective Environment for Political Deviants." *American Political Science Review* 68: 607–25.

Finke, Roger, and Rodney Stark. 1992. *The Churching of America 1776–1990: Winners and Losers in our Religious Economy.* New Brunswick, N.J.: Rutgers University Press.

Fowler, Robert Booth. 1995. *The Greening of Protestant Thought.* Chapel Hill: University of North Carolina Press.

Fowler, Robert Booth, Allen D. Hertzke, and Laura R. Olson. 1999. *Religion and Politics in America.* 2d ed. Boulder: Westview.

Garrett, William R. 1973. "Politicized Clergy: A Sociological Interpretation of the 'New Breed.'" *Journal for the Scientific Study of Religion* 12: 384–99.

Genovese, Michael A. 2001. *The Power of the Presidency, 1789–2000.* New York: Oxford University Press.

Gilbert, Christopher P. 1993. *The Impact of Churches on Political Behavior.* Westport, Conn.: Greenwood.

Gilbert, Christopher P., David A. M. Peterson, Timothy R. Johnson, and Paul A. Djupe. 1999. *Religious Institutions and Minor Parties in the United States.* Westport, Conn.: Praeger.

Graber, Doris. 2002. *Mass Media and American Politics.* 6th ed. Washington, D.C.: CQ Press.

Granovetter, Mark. 1973. "The Strength of Weak Ties." *American Journal of Sociology* 78: 1360–80.

Gray, Virginia, and David Lowery. 1996. *The Population Ecology of Interest Representation: Lobbying Communities in the American States.* Ann Arbor: University of Michigan Press.

Green, John C., James L. Guth, Corwin E. Smidt, and Lyman A. Kellstedt. 1996. *Religion and the Culture Wars: Dispatches from the Front.* Boulder: Rowman & Littlefield.

Green, John C., Mark Rozell, and Clyde Wilcox. 2003. *Marching toward the Millennium: The Christian Right in the States, 1980–2000.* Washington, D.C.: Georgetown University Press.

Greider, William B. 1992. *Who Will Tell the People? The Betrayal of American Democracy.* New York: Simon & Schuster.

Guth, James L. 1996. "The Bully Pulpit: Southern Baptist Clergy and Political Activism, 1980–1992." In John C. Green, James L. Guth, Corwin E. Smidt, and Lyman A. Kellstedt, eds., *Religion and the Culture Wars: Dispatches from the Front.* Lanham, Md.: Rowman & Littlefield.

———. 2001a. "Clergy in Politics: Reflections on the Status of Research in the Field." In Sue E. S. Crawford and Laura R. Olson, eds., *Christian Clergy in American Politics.* Baltimore: Johns Hopkins University Press.

———. 2001b. "The Mobilization of a Religious Elite: Political Activism among Southern Baptist Clergy in 1996." In Sue E. S. Crawford and Laura R. Olson, eds., *Christian Clergy in American Politics.* Baltimore: Johns Hopkins University Press.

Guth, James L., John C. Green, Corwin E. Smidt, Lyman A. Kellstedt, and Margaret Poloma. 1997. *The Bully Pulpit: The Politics of Protestant Clergy.* Lawrence: University of Kansas Press.

"A Habit of Ministry." 2001. *Christian Century*, October 10, 5.

Hadden, Jeffrey K. 1969. *The Gathering Storm in the Churches.* Garden City, N.Y.: Doubleday.

———. 1987. "Religious Broadcasting and the Mobilization of the New Christian Right." *Journal for the Scientific Study of Religion* 26, no. 1: 1–24.

Hadden, Jeffrey K., and Charles E. Swann. 1981. *Prime Time Preachers: The Rising Power of Televangelism.* Reading, Mass.: Addison-Wesley.

Hanushek, Eric A., and John E. Jackson. 1977. *Statistical Methods for Social Scientists.* Orlando, Fla.: Academic.

Harris, Fredrick C. 1999. *Something Within: Religion in African-American Political Activism.* New York: Oxford University Press.

Hart, Stephen. 2001. "Getting Organized: Faith-based Alliances Make a Difference." *Christian Century*, November 7, 20–25.

Hauser, Robert M. 1974. "Contextual Analysis Revisited." *Sociological Methods and Research* 2: 365–75.

Hertzke, Allen D. 1988. *Representing God In Washington: The Role of Religious Lobbies*. Knoxville: University of Tennessee Press.

Hofrenning, Daniel J. B. 1995. *In Washington But Not of It: The Prophetic Politics of Religious Lobbyists*. Philadelphia: Temple University Press.

Holmes, David T. 1993. *A Brief History of the Episcopal Church*. Valley Forge, Pa.: Trinity Press International.

Huckfeldt, Robert, Paul Allen Beck, Russell J. Dalton, and Jeffrey Levine. 1995. "Political Environments, Cohesive Social Groups, and the Communication of Public Opinion." *American Journal of Political Science* 39: 1025–54.

Huckfeldt, Robert, and John Sprague. 1987. "Networks in Context: The Social Flow of Political Information." *American Political Science Review* 81: 1197–1216.

———. 1995. *Citizens, Politics, and Social Communications: Information and Influence in an Election Campaign*. New York: Cambridge University Press.

Hunter, James Davison. 1991. *Culture Wars: The Struggle to Define America*. New York: Basic.

———. 1994. *Before the Shooting Begins: Searching for Democracy in America's Culture War*. New York: Free Press.

Iannaccone, Laurence R. 1994. "Why Strict Churches Are Strong." *American Journal of Sociology* 99: 1180–1211.

———. 1996. "Reassessing Church Growth: Statistical Pitfalls and Their Consequences." *Journal for the Scientific Study of Religion* 35: 197–216.

Ice, Martha Long. 1987. *Clergy Women and Their Worldviews: Calling for a New Age*. New York: Praeger.

Initiative and Referendum Institute. 1999. "Historical Database: 1998." www.iandrinstitute.org. Accessed January 15, 1999.

Interfaith Alliance. 2002. "About Us." www.interfaithalliance.org/AboutUs/aboutus.htm. Accessed January 19, 2002.

Jelen, Ted. 1993. *The Political World of the Clergy*. New York: Praeger.

———. 2001. "Clergy as Political Leaders: Notes for a Theory." In Sue E. S. Crawford and Laura R. Olson, eds., *Christian Clergy in American Politics*. Baltimore: Johns Hopkins University Press.

Johnson, Benton. 1966. "Theology and Party Preference among Protestant Clergymen." *American Sociological Review* 31: 200–208.

———. 1967. "Theology and the Position of Pastors on Public Issues." *American Sociological Review* 32: 433–42.

Johnson, Trebbe. 1998. "The Second Creation Story: Redefining the Bond between Religion and Ecology." *Sierra* 83, no. 6: 50–57.

Joint Religious Legislative Coalition. 2002. www.jrlc.org. Accessed July 14, 2002.

Kellstedt, Lyman A., John C. Green, James L. Guth, and Corwin E. Smidt. 1996. "Has Godot Finally Arrived? Religion and Realignment." In John C. Green, James L. Guth, Corwin E. Smidt, and Lyman A. Kellstedt, eds., *Religion and the Culture Wars: Dispatches from the Front*. Boulder: Rowman & Littlefield.

Kelzer, Garret. 2001. "Faith, Hope, and Ecology: A Christian Environmentalism." *Christian Century*, December 5, 16–21.

Key, V. O. 1949. *Southern Politics in State and Nation*. New York: Knopf.

Kingdon, John W. 1995. *Agendas, Alternatives, and Public Policies*. 2d ed. New York: HarperCollins.

Kleppner, Paul. 1970. *The Cross of Culture: A Social Analysis of Midwestern Politics, 1850–1900*. New York: Free Press.

———. 1979. *The Third Electoral System, 1853–1892: Parties, Voters, and Political Cultures*. Chapel Hill: University of North Carolina Press.

Kohut, Andrew, John C. Green, Scott Keeter, and Robert C. Toth. 2000. *The Diminishing Divide: Religion's Changing Role in American Politics*. Washington, D.C.: Brookings Institution.

Koller, Norman B., and Joseph D. Retzer. 1980. "The Sounds of Silence Revisited." *Sociological Analysis* 41: 155–61.

Kosmin, Barry, and Seymour Lachman. 1993. *One Nation under God: Religion in Contemporary American Society*. New York: Harmony.

La Due Lake, Ronald, and Robert Huckfeldt. 1998. "Social Capital, Social Networks, and Political Participation." *Political Psychology* 19, no. 3: 567–84.

Larsen, Peter. 1998. "Using Faith as a Tool to Unify." *Orange County Register,* July 26, B1.

Layman, Geoffrey. 2000. *The Great Divide: Religious and Cultural Conflict in American Party Politics*. New York: Columbia University Press.

Lazerow, Jama. 1995. *Religion and the Working Class in Antebellum America*. Washington, D.C.: Smithsonian Institution Press.

Leege, David C. 1988. "Catholics and the Civic Order: Parish Participation, Politics, and Civic Participation." *Review of Politics* 50: 704–37.

Lenski, Gerhard. 1961. *The Religious Factor*. Garden City, N.Y.: Doubleday Anchor.

Leonard, Lee. 2001. "Critics of Lottery Commission's Lobbying Play a Bad Hand." *Columbus Dispatch,* November 26, 11A.

Liebman, Robert C. 1983. "Mobilizing the Moral Majority." In Robert Liebman and Robert Wuthnow, eds., *The New Christian Right: Mobilization and Legitimation*. New York: Aldine.

Lincoln, C. Eric, and Lawrence H. Mamiya. 1990. *The Black Church in African-American Experience*. Durham: Duke University Press.

Loomis, Burdett A., and Allan J. Cigler. 1998. "Introduction: The Changing Nature of Interest Group Politics." In Allan J. Cigler and Burdett A. Loomis, eds., *Interest Group Politics*. 5th ed. Washington, D.C.: CQ Press.

Lopatto, Paul. 1985. *Religion and the Presidential Election*. New York: Praeger.

"Luther Seminary Graduate Ordained without His Bishop's Participation." 2001. *Metro Lutheran,* August, 3.

Lyles, Jean Caffee. 2001. "Jeopardizing a Pact: ELCA Tinkers with Ecumenism." *Christian Century,* September 12–19, 6–8.

Manuel, Marlon. 1998. "Election '98: Governors, Alabama." *Atlanta Journal Constitution*, November 5, 3K.

Manuel, Marlon, and Peter Mantius. 1999. "Alabama Governor Vows to Try Again after Crushing Lottery Defeat." *Atlanta Journal Constitution*, October 13, 1A.

Martin, William. 1996. *With God on Our Side*. New York: Broadway.

Marty, Martin. 1970. *Righteous Empire: The Protestant Experience in America*. New York: Dial Press.

———. 1998. "Called to Common Mission: A Lutheran Proposal for a Revision of the Concordat of Agreement." Evangelical Lutheran Church in America document. www.dfms.org/ecumenism/concordat/letter2.html. Accessed January 26, 2000.

Matovina, Timothy. 2002. "Family, Church, and Neighborhood: Latinos of Faith Exercising Collective Power to Improve Daily Life." *Witness* 85, no. 5: 12–17.

Mayhew, David. 1986. *Placing Parties in American Politics*. Princeton: Princeton University Press.

McCormick, Kathryn. 2000. "Episcopalians among 900 to Endorse Religious Declaration on Sexual Morality." Episcopal News Service, January 31. www.episcopalchurch.org/ens/workshop/2000-021D.html. Accessed July 13, 2002.

McFarland, Andrew S. 1976. *Public Interest Lobbies: Decision Making on Energy*. Washington, D.C.: American Enterprise Institute.

McGreevy, John T. 1996. *Parish Boundaries: The Catholic Encounter with Race in the Twentieth-Century Urban North*. Chicago: University of Chicago Press.

McPhee, William. 1963. "A Theory of Informal Social Influence." In William McPhee, ed., *Formal Theories of Mass Behavior*. New York: Free Press.

Mead, Frank S. Revised by Samuel S. Hill. 1992. *Handbook of Denominations in the United States*. 9th ed. Nashville: Abingdon.

Miller, Warren E., and J. Merrill Shanks. 1996. *The New American Voter*. Cambridge: Harvard University Press.

Moore, R. Laurence. 1986. *Religious Outsiders and the Making of Americans*. New York: Oxford University Press.

Morris, Aldon D. 1984. *The Origins of the Civil Rights Movement: Black Communities Organizing for Change*. New York: Free Press.

University of Michigan. National Election Studies, Center for Political Studies. 2001. *The NES Guide to Public Opinion and Electoral Behavior*. www.umich.edu/~nes/nesguide/nesguide.htm. Ann Arbor, Mich.: University of Michigan, Center for Political Studies.

Nelsen, Hart M., Ratha L. Yokely, and Thomas W. Madron. 1973. "Ministerial Roles and Social Actionist Stance: Protestant Clergy and Protest in the Sixties." *American Sociological Review* 38, no. 3: 375–86.

Newman, William. 1993. "The Meanings of a Merger: Denominational Identity in the United Church of Christ." In Jackson Carroll and Wade Clark Roof, eds., *Beyond Establishment: Protestant Identity in a Post-Protestant Age*. Louisville: Westminster/John Knox.

Niebuhr, H. Richard. 1951. *Christ and Culture*. New York: Harper.

Noll, Mark A. 1990. *Religion and American Politics: From the Colonial Period to the 1980s*. New York: Oxford University Press.

Olson, Laura R. 2000. *Filled with Spirit and Power: Protestant Clergy in Politics*. New York: State University of New York Press.

———. 2001. "Mainline Protestant Washington Offices and the Political Lives of Clergy." In Robert Wuthnow and John H. Evans, eds., *The Quiet Hand of God: Faith-Based Activism and the Public Role of Mainline Protestantism*. Berkeley: University of California Press.

Olson, Laura R., Sue E. S. Crawford, and James L. Guth. 2000. "Changing Issue Agendas of Women Clergy." *Journal for the Scientific Study of Religion* 39, no. 2: 140–53.

Olson, Mancur, Jr. 1965. *The Logic of Collective Action*. Cambridge: Harvard University Press.

"Ordained against the Rules." 2001. *Christian Century,* May 16, 7–8.

Page, Benjamin I. 1996. *Who Deliberates? Mass Media in Modern Democracy*. Chicago: University of Chicago Press.

Peltason, Jack W. 1961. *Fifty-Eight Lonely Men: Southern Federal Judges and School Desegregation*. Urbana: University of Illinois Press.

Peterson, Steven A. 1992. "Church Participation and Political Participation: The Spillover Effect." *American Politics Quarterly* 20: 123–39.

Phillips, Kevin P. 1969. *The Emerging Republican Majority*. Garden City, N.Y.: Doubleday Anchor.

Pope, Liston. 1942. *Millhands and Preachers: A Study of Gastonia*. New Haven, Conn.: Yale University Press.

"Prelates and Provocations." 2001. *Christian Century,* July 4–11, 9–10.

Pride, Mike. "The Mail Call." *Brill's Content* 3, no. 10: 87–88.

Putnam, Robert D. 1966. "Political Attitudes and the Local Community." *American Political Science Review* 60: 640–54.

———. 2000. *Bowling Alone: The Collapse and Revival of American Community*. New York: Simon & Schuster.

Quinley, Harold E. 1974. *The Prophetic Clergy: Social Activism among Protestant Ministers.* New York: Wiley.

Reed, Ralph. 1994. *Mainstream Values are No Longer Politically Incorrect: The Emerging Faith Factor in American Politics*. Dallas: Word.

Reeves, Thomas C. 1996. *The Empty Church: The Suicide of Liberal Christianity*. New York: Free Press.

Reichley, A. James. 1985. *Religion in American Public Life*. Washington D.C.: Brookings Institution.

Religious News Service. 2002. "ELCA Names Director of Sexuality Study." *Christian Century,* January 30–February 6, 15.

Rivera, John. 1998. "Clerics Back MD Tobacco Tax Increase." *Baltimore Sun,* July 14, 1B.

Roof, Wade Clark, and William McKinney. 1987. *American Mainline Religion: Its Changing Shape and Future*. New Brunswick, N.J.: Rutgers University Press.

Roozen, David A., William McKinney, and Jackson W. Carroll. 1984. *Varieties of Religious Presence: Mission in Public Life*. New York: Pilgrim.

Rosenstone, Steven J., and John Mark Hansen. 1993. *Mobilization, Participation, and Democracy in America*. New York: Macmillan.

Sabato, Larry J., Howard R. Ernst, and Bruce A. Larson, eds. 2000. *Dangerous Democracy? The Battle over Ballot Initiatives in America*. Boulder: Rowman & Littlefield.

Salisbury, Robert H. 1975. "Research on Political Participation." *American Journal of Political Science* 19: 323–41.

Schlozman, Kay Lehman, and John T. Tierney. 1986. *Organized Interests and American Democracy*. New York: Harper & Row.

Schmidt, Frederick W., Jr. 1996. *A Still Small Voice: Women, Ordination, and the Church*. Syracuse, N.Y.: Syracuse University Press.

Schneier, Edward V., and Bertram Gross. 1993. *Congress Today*. New York: St. Martin's.

Shupe, Anson D., Jr., and James R. Wood. 1973. "Sources of Leadership Ideology in Dissident Clergy." *Sociological Analysis* 34: 185–201.

Solheim, James. 1998. "Lambeth Conference Marks 'Defining Moment' for Anglican Communion." Episcopal News Service, August 28. www.episcopalchurch .org/ens/workshop/Lambeth. Accessed July 12, 2002.

Stark, Rodney. 1964. "Class, Radicalism, and Religious Involvement in Great Britain." *American Sociological Review* 29: 698–706.

Stark, Rodney, Bruce D. Foster, Charles Y. Glock, and Harold Quinley. 1971. *Wayward Shepherds: Prejudice and the Protestant Clergy*. New York: Harper & Row.

Strate, John M., Charles J. Parrish, Charles D. Elder, and Coit Ford III. 1989. "Life Span, Civic Development, and Voting Participation." *American Political Science Review* 83:443–67.

Thomas, Cal, and Ed Dobson. 1999. *Blinded by Might: Can the Religious Right Save America?* Grand Rapids, Mich.: Zondervan.

Thomas, Charles B., Jr. 1985. "Clergy in Racial Controversy: A Replication of the Campbell and Pettigrew Study." *Review of Religious Research* 26 no. 4: 379–90.

Thomas, Norman C., and Joseph A. Pika. 1997. *The Politics of the Presidency*. 4th rev. ed. Washington, D.C.: CQ Press.

Thomas, William I., and Dorothy S. Thomas. 1928. *The Child in America*. New York: Knopf.

U.S. Dept. of Commerce, Bureau of the Census. 1992. *Census of Population and Housing, 1990*. Washington, D.C.: U.S. Dept. of Commerce, Bureau of the Census.

———. 1996. "Small Area Income and Poverty Estimates: 1995 State and County FTP Files and Description." www.census.gov/hhes/www/saipe/stcty/ sc95ftpdoc. Accessed December 8, 1999.

Verba, Sidney, and Norman H. Nie. 1972. *Participation in America: Political Democracy and Social Equality*. New York: Harper & Row.

Verba, Sidney, Kay Lehman Schlozman, and Henry E. Brady. 1995. *Voice and Equality: Civic Voluntarism in American Politics*. Cambridge: Harvard University Press.

Wald, Kenneth D. 1997. *Religion and Politics in the United States*. 3d ed. Washington, D.C.: CQ Press.

Wald, Kenneth D., Dennis Owen, and Samuel Hill. 1988. "Churches as Political Communities." *American Political Science Review* 82: 531–48.

————. 1990. "Political Cohesion in Churches." *Journal of Politics* 52: 197–215.

Welch, Michael R., David C. Leege, Kenneth D. Wald, and Lyman A. Kellstedt. 1993. "Are the Sheep Hearing the Shepherds? Cue Perceptions, Congregational Responses, and Political Communication Processes." In David C. Leege and Lyman A.Kellstedt, eds., *Rediscovering the Religious Factor in American Politics*. Armonk, NY: Sharpe.

West, Darrell M., and Burdett A. Loomis. 1998. *The Sound of Money How Political Interests Get What They Want*. New York: Norton.

Wheeler, Barbara G. 2001. "Fit for Ministry? A New Profile of Seminarians." *Christian Century*, April 11, 16–23.

Wilcox, Clyde, Sharon Linzey, and Ted Jelen. 1991. "Reluctant Warriors: Premillenialism and Politics in the Moral Majority." *Journal for the Scientific Study of Religion* 30: 245–58.

Williams, Rhys H., ed. 1997a. *Cultural Wars in American Politics: Critical Reviews of a Popular Myth*. Hawthorne, N.Y.: Aldine De Gruyter.

Williams, Rhys H. 1997b. "Culture Wars, Social Movements, and Institutional Politics." In Rhys H. Williams, ed., *Cultural Wars in American Politics: Critical Reviews of a Popular Myth*. Hawthorne, N.Y.: Aldine De Gruyter.

Winter, J. Alan. 1973. "Political Activism among the Clergy: Sources of a Deviant Role." *Review of Religious Research* 14, no. 3: 178–86.

Wolcott, Roger T. 1982. "The Church and Social Action: Steelworkers and Bishops in Youngstown." *Journal for the Scientific Study of Religion* 21: 71–79.

Wolfinger, Raymond, and Steven Rosenstone. 1980. *Who Votes?* New Haven, Conn.: Yale University Press.

Wood, David J. 2001. "Where Are the Younger Clergy?" *Christian Century,* April 11, 18–19.

The World Almanac and Book of Facts 1994. 1993. Mahwah, N.J.: World Almanac Books.

The World Almanac and Book of Facts 1996. 1997. Mahwah, N.J.: World Almanac Books.

The World Almanac and Book of Facts 1998. 1999. Mahwah, N.J.: World Almanac Books.

Wortman, Julie A. 2002. "Contextualizing the Church: An Interview with Geoffrey Curtiss." *Witness* 85, no. 5: 6–11.

Wuthnow, Robert. 1988. *The Restructuring of American Religion*. Princeton: Princeton University Press.

————. 1997. *The Crisis in the Churches: Spiritual Malaise, Fiscal Woe*. New York: Oxford University Press.

————. 1998. *Loose Connections: Joining together in America's Fragmented Communities*. Cambridge: Harvard University Press.

Wuthnow, Robert, and John H. Evans. 2002. *The Quiet Hand of God: Faith-Based Activism and the Public Role of Mainline Protestantism*. Berkeley: University of California Press.

INDEX

ABOUT THE AUTHORS

Paul A. Djupe is assistant professor of political science at Denison University and specializes in the effects of religion on American political behavior, interest group politics, and primary elections. He is a coauthor of *Religious Institutions and Minor Parties in the United States* (Praeger, 1999) and coeditor of the *Encyclopedia of American Religion and Politics* (Facts-on-File, 2003).

Christopher P. Gilbert is associate professor and chair of the Political Science Department at Gustavus Adolphus College in St. Peter, Minnesota. He has written extensively on religion and political behavior, third parties in the United States, and Minnesota politics. He has authored or coauthored two other books on religion and politics, including *Religious Institutions and Minor Parties in the United States* (Praeger, 1999).